Assisted

AN AUTOBIOGRAPHY

Assisted

AN AUTOBIOGRAPHY

John
STOCKTON

with **Kerry L. Pickett**

SHADOW
MOUNTAIN

First printing in hardbound 2013
First printing in paperbound 2014

Visit us at ShadowMountain.com

Library of Congress Cataloging-in-Publication Data

Stockton, John, 1962– author.
  Assisted : an autobiography / by John Stockton with Kerry L. Pickett.
    pages cm
  Includes bibliographical references and index.
  ISBN 978-1-60907-570-5 (hardbound : alk. paper)
  ISBN 978-1-60907-925-3 (paperbound)
  1. Stockton, John, 1962– 2. Basketball players—United States—Biography. I. Pickett, Kerry L., author. II. Title.
  GV884.S76A3 2013
  796.323092—dc23
  [B]   2013019430

Printed in the United States of America
Publishers Printing, Salt Lake City, UT

10   9   8   7   6   5   4   3   2   1

To my Mom and Dad, Clemy and Jack Stockton,
with all my love and appreciation.

—John

To those who sustained me and live always in my heart:
Mom and Dad, Grandma Lee, Uncle Jack Pickett,
Aunt Gert, and Clemy. You lighted my path.

To those still looking out for me:
My brother and three sisters, Tim, Cindy, Sally, and Linda;
Mark and Sharon Bowman; Sully; Shakey;
Dr. Muelheims; Jack and John; all of my Sandpipers
—and my wife and guiding star, Gini.
Thank you.

—Kerry

CONTENTS

CONTENTS

FOREWORD

The first time I met John Stockton was on the Indiana University campus playing basketball at the 1984 Olympic Trials. The basketball was easy but the trials were hard. John and I sat at the same lunch table and watched as the daily cuts were posted on Coach Knight's wall-hung yellow board. The three practices per day were no picnic and neither of us was asking for seconds, though we somehow chewed what Coach put on our plates. John was a senior and I was a sophomore then.

The partnership we formed a few years later while playing for the Utah Jazz lasted almost twenty years. It happened just like it was supposed to happen. I believe that. I think our easy, relaxed, and honest friendship grew partly from our family backgrounds. Though I was from a single parent home, raised by my mom, and John had both parents, the way we were brought up wasn't very different. Our parents had to work hard to provide for us, and they gave us strong values along the way. We soon knew we had this in common.

From the very first, I realized that what you see is what you get with John. He lined up without excuses. Stocks never wavered

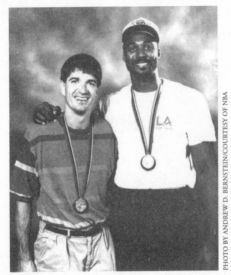

John and Karl Malone, Olympic gold medalists, 1992.

one iota from his beliefs. He never shared them publicly, so people thought he didn't have them. He did, and he stayed true to them.

Inside the lines many people thought he and I worked constantly on the pick-and-roll and outlet passes. It just didn't happen that way. We clicked. We came to believe and trust in each other at a level I never approached with any other teammate. No matter what mistakes Stocks made, I covered for him, and whatever errors I made, he covered for me. Our main concern was always: *how can we make it easier for our teammates?* We knew we were being counted on, but never had to tell each other that.

We did push each other in our preparation for each season. I believed in my heart of hearts that John was training harder than me, and I'm pretty sure he thought I was training harder than him. This turned into an almost two-decade competition, with never a word spoken about a "contest." We both became better players in the process.

FOREWORD

It's neat to be able to say today, long after the smoke of fame and glory has cleared, that if he called at two-thirty in the morning and needed something, I'd say, "Where are you at? I'll be there." Anytime, anyplace. That's how it is with John Stockton.

I never, never, dreamed I could become so close with a teammate. John and I could talk about absolutely anything, from race to religion. I talked to him to get an honest opinion. He always gave it to me straight and never said he wouldn't talk about any issue, if it was important to me.

I have a very private abbreviation I use with only those closest to my heart. "2THEN"—"To the end." Not much lasts that long—our friendship will.

As you turn the pages that follow, I hope you enjoy getting to know my very best friend.

—Karl Malone

PREFACE

When John first approached me with his request to help him write this book, I was flattered but uncertain about my qualifications. He explained that he wanted someone he knew he could work with for an extended time period within and around his unpredictable schedule. He pointed out to me that I had a unique qualification: Our lives had closely intertwined for nearly four decades. In many ways John, my wife, Gini, and I had grown up together under the tutelage of John's parents, Jack and Clemy.

Before surrendering his life's story to the gauntlet of unknown literary agents, ghostwriters, and publishers, John wanted to try to write his own story. He thought a completed manuscript might have a chance of surviving the process in some recognizable form. Knowing this, I agreed to help him—well aware of the magnitude of the challenge he was proposing.

We launched with some invaluable assistance from the nationally renowned Spokane author Jess Walter. Jess is John's friend and a fellow parishioner at St. Al's in Spokane. He pointed us in the right direction on an unmarked path and offered invaluable insights for our journey. He sketched out the process from

A to Z, and John and I worked hard to follow his advice and become serious students of a craft that Jess had mastered.

Our official "staff" consisted only of the tireless Stephanie Hawk Freeman. She is a former Gonzaga All-American basketball player and West Coast Conference Player of the Year, sporting two master's degrees. She has worked with us since we began the project. Steph was added for brains but additionally brought needed beauty and grace.

Teamwork was the key to fruition. John manned the author's first draft pen as well as the command and control post. I grasped the editor's pencil and eraser, while Stephanie focused the technical microscope to examine the product. She also assembled our picture library and organized and completed our research. The reader will have to judge the success of our troika. I've always felt John's story was a remarkable one. I'm glad to have been a small part of it and to have had the opportunity to help in its telling.

The story told in the pages that follow is John's, written the way he wanted to tell it. The views and opinions set forth are his, expressed with the hope that they accurately convey his perspectives and priorities on important issues and values. John has crafted his autobiography as a thoughtful recounting of the people, places, and events that have connected to become an extraordinary story of success. He has tried to "dog-ear" those that serendipitously collided to form the inflection points of his life.

The tale finds its footing backward from an unlikely and unimaginable summit to the rich soils of the Inland Empire and the tiny town of Ferdinand, Idaho. The road winds forward from there to the city of Spokane, Washington, inside a small hospital resting solidly on an impenetrable geologic foundation in a room with an ill-tempered soup salesman and a conscientious country nurse. From that infirmary begins an unlikely ascent to basketball history.

This account could only be told around John's lifelong relationship with basketball. His final reckoning on the question of "How did this wonderful life come to find me?" is the substance of the story that follows. Perhaps there is an appropriate irony in the fact that John's singularly spectacular art form—the assist—is inextricably a part of the answer to that question.

—COACH KERRY L. PICKETT

ACKNOWLEDGMENTS

I want to offer my thanks to Coach Pickett for taking on the project of helping me write this book. With no guarantees other than a lot of work, he spent four years meeting with me, organizing my thoughts, reading, editing, making suggestions, and completing all the details necessary to produce this book. I am particularly grateful for his willingness to share some of his poetry, which has struck a deep and personal connection for me. I have enjoyed his work privately and with groups we have both been involved with, such as the Sandpipers. He never rides alone with his wife, Virginia, his wingman, always present, always reliable at his side, at our side. Working humbly—and beyond capably—in the shadows, she is our MVP. Thanks, Gini!

A special thanks to all the people that have made my story possible, especially those that weren't mentioned in the book, or whose part didn't escape the editor's pen. I am thankful for the kindness and caring of some, and the harshness and bare-boned competitiveness of others that helped shape me and my career.

As usual, with anything regarding my family, I choke up too much to say what I feel. I miss Mom, but feel her presence every day and see her charm and grace occasionally reappear in her grandchildren. I am grateful to Dad for his guidance, wisdom, and availability. I've always been able to count on him. To my brother Steve and sisters Stacey and Leanne, I can only say I owe you so much. I've come to appreciate each of you for the good people and friends that you are, almost as much as I value you as family.

Last but not least, to Nada and the kids, Houston, Michael, David, Lindsay, Laura, and Samuel: Thanks! You are the center of my world. I am so very proud of each of you. Your comments and opinions were invaluable in completing my story. To my wife, Nada, who proved exceedingly capable in helping me proofread the manuscript, my many heartfelt thanks! Far more important, however, she has been an answer to my prayers as a wife and as a mother to each of our kids, helping them grow into solid and productive young men and women.

—JOHN STOCKTON

PART I

Connections

Connections

The skipping stone intones beyond its whispered splash
With perturbations undesigned sets the frogs upon a dash.
An undirected smile touches a broken heart by chance;
A random renovation borne by unintended glance.
A long forgotten mason exacts a cornerstone's compliance;
From the restive prairie wind stands a cottage in defiance.
An athlete, cold beneath the rain, thrusts his soul to shape the fray
Against an outcome long determined, though a child watched that day.
A mouse scurries across a dim-lit road, nearly unobserved;
An elephant roars in fear as a slumbering driver swerves.
The fabric holds or frays with anonymous stitches sown.
Each, a portent undetermined, to piece a pattern unbeknown,
Such that all things undertaken—offhanded or attended well—
Are seldom incidental to the larger stories we tell.

—Kerry L. Pickett

CHAPTER 1

Thoughts from behind a Podium

"If you have built castles in the air, your work need not be lost; that is where they should be. Now put foundations under them."[1]

—HENRY DAVID THOREAU

I was honored and beyond nervous as I stepped to the induction podium at the Naismith Basketball Hall of Fame in September of 2009. Any previous excitement had long since evaporated as the weight of the task at hand bore down heavily in the minutes leading to my acceptance speech.

Seven months prior I was notified that I was a finalist for induction in February during the 2009 NBA All-Star weekend. It was the first time since my retirement that I had even thought about the honor. Selection for induction was nothing I had shopped for and wasn't a goal of mine, but I had heard the label "Future Hall of Famer" applied to me enough on the heels of our second Olympic gold in 1996 that I wasn't completely shocked to be under consideration.

The actual selections came about two months later during the NCAA Final Four tournament, when we were introduced during the halftime of one of the semifinal games in Detroit. My family and I enjoyed the action from a suite high above the court at Ford Field along with three of the four other inductees: C. Vivian Stringer, David Robinson, and Michael Jordan. Coach Jerry Sloan, still in midseason with the Jazz, was absent.

We reacquainted ourselves with "M. J." and "The Admiral," who had his son David Jr. onboard. Young David fit in with our kids as though they had known each other their entire lives. Later, they hooked up to have a lot of fun with pickup games in the hotel gym. They could have easily been mistaken for old buddies from the same neighborhood. It was fun to see them make a connection.

Watching the games in the relative quiet of the suite offered an opportunity for me to get to know Vivian Stringer. It took only about a minute to begin to see why she is such a great coach. Her passion for the game flowed from her as she spoke, and it was quickly obvious that she truly loves her athletes. Coach's commitment to teaching the game and so much more about life resonated in her every word. Listening to her, I was so fired up I wanted to put a jersey on right then and there. I searched out Coach Vivian as often as I could that weekend just to listen. I have since read her book *Standing Tall*[2] and recommend it to all athletes and parents of athletes. She understands adversity and how to battle through difficulties without whining or looking for shortcuts. Her lessons are important for all of us, especially young athletes. She is an amazing lady.

In the suite we were also introduced to our Hall of Fame hosts. We got to know most of them over the weekend but none more closely than Fran Judkins, who mothered us through the process of induction. By the end of the weekend, she had presented to each of us an official folder outlining the requirements with deadlines and restrictions for the upcoming months that would culminate with our induction.

One of the first duties we had to fulfill was to assemble a collection of at least eight items of personal memorabilia for display in the Hall. Almost anything was acceptable: special game shoes, jerseys, uniforms—you name it. I looked for items from every level that I had participated in. It didn't take long to realize how little I had saved from my amateur days. My sparse cache consisted mainly of some old programs, a couple of pairs of socks from high school, and a T-shirt my college coach had printed for me when I was drafted into the NBA. I considered tendering my first leather ball, a gift from Mr. John Brodsky, a family friend and a former Bulldog basketball player. The ball had a rare Burlington-Cedar Rapids label. But I couldn't bring myself to part ways with something that full of memories; I thought it might bear some special significance someday for the kids. Ultimately, I sent a few trophies and milestone game balls and added a treasured memento that would suggest who I am and what I had considered important in my life. The chosen item was a special shirt my wife, Nada, had made for me with each of our children's hand- or footprints in bright colored paint pressed over the left chest. The kids now reside with me in the Hall of Fame.

Next, I had to select a presenter for the actual ceremony who had to come from a pool of current members of the Hall of Fame. A list of those still living was included in our folder. Scanning over the players and coaches, I gained some perspective on just how exclusive this group really was, and the significance of the honor started to sink in for the first time. The list was staggering, with every name a part of the game's storied history. I knew only a few of them personally other than as opponents. After viewing and reviewing the list, one name stood out among the rest, Isiah Thomas.

Even though we had mostly battled each other for years, I had always admired him and felt a natural kinship as little men in a league of giants. He also had greatly impacted my career on numerous occasions. Isiah's unquestioned success helped open the door for me and other shorter players while setting the performance bar extraordinarily high.

I got his phone number from Fran and nervously dialed. Not anxious to identify myself until I was certain I had the right number, I spoke cautiously with his wife. Once security clearances were met on both sides, I offered her my number to give to Isiah. When he and I eventually talked, the request went better than I could have hoped. Along with an enjoyable conversation, he accepted with a vow to help me enjoy the weekend. I felt honored by his acceptance and looked forward to him joining me on stage on induction night.

Our next duty was to compile a list of people who were to receive an invitation to the induction ceremonies. I thought we could just use the Christmas card list my wife, Nada, kept. But it wasn't that easy, due largely to Michael Jordan's popularity. With him as a classmate, tickets were at a premium. There was only so much room at the inn.

The demand for tickets was understandable. Michael had achieved a status clearly above nearly every other athlete in the entire world. From my vantage point, he wore his fame very well. Michael knew who he was and what he represented to a very large audience, including kids. He consistently treated my family like part of his own. He shared time and insights with them—always with class. I had suffered painful defeats at his hands over the years, but I also looked back on some great times at the Olympics in '92, along with the usual seasonal contests. I can only express gratitude to Michael for always bringing his A game. He accepted challenges every year as a true champion. I was honored to be a classmate of his in the Hall of Fame.

To accommodate the increased demand, we were all limited to fifty invitations. I wondered how we could possibly comply.

My immediate family gobbled up the first eleven tickets, which made no provision for Nada's immense clan. We accepted that we could only touch the tip of the iceberg.

I held my breath as I turned in the list, apprehensive about fallout. I knew I had excluded many people. I wish I could have sent out a hundred more invitations, though I wondered at the same time if anyone would really come. Most of my guests hailed from the West Coast, so I anticipated that the cost of travel and the whopping $1,000 ticket prices would curb everyone's appetite to attend. To my surprise, that wasn't the case.

Over the next couple of weeks, I got a taste of the magnitude of the upcoming induction. Phone calls poured in thanking me for invitations. Many vowed not to miss the once-in-a-lifetime celebration. Frankly, I was floored by the response. I began wondering, *Just how big a deal is this?*

That answer was becoming clear. For the first time, the ceremony would be broadcast around the world on live television. The venue itself was moved to Symphony Hall in Springfield, Massachusetts, to allow more seating. Even the Hall of Fame personnel knew they were traveling in uncharted territory.

With preobligation timetables fulfilled and travel details arranged and met, I had one last item to attend to—my acceptance speech. Preparing for my last fifteen minutes in the spotlight took more than a couple of weeks, working around the end of summer fun and the start of school activities for the kids. I have kind of a backward system for drafting a speech. I write down ideas as they come to me, in no particular order. When I begin to like what I have scratched out, I put it into an outline form. (Most people organize their thoughts with an outline and work in the other direction.) I recently had had to scrap another normal habit of writing notes on index cards. A strange thing had happened since reaching my mid-forties. The keen eyesight that I had treasured for four decades had begun to blur, maddeningly. I settled on full sheets of paper with large print in lieu of busting out the spectacles on national television.

I also refused to use the teleprompter they offered. I didn't want my first attempt at using the gadgetry to be in front of millions of viewers. I could see myself squinting at the teleprompter while someone backstage with a perverse sense of humor altered the scroll. I opted instead to trust my own methods. I practiced my speech countless times alone and in front of Nada.

None of these preparations translated into confidence, however. Free throws at the end of even the biggest games seemed much easier in comparison than the task before me. The heavy pit in my stomach was growing. I needed more practice.

Unfortunately, Hall of Fame activities kept all the inductees busy. Interviews for posterity, live appearances, speeches to school assemblies, dinners, and receptions filled the weekend leading up to the induction. The demands of being whisked from one event to another left little downtime or even a private place to practice my speech.

• • •

The dates worked out for my whole family to be able to attend. My oldest son, Houston, joined us late, as his football season at the University of Montana had just begun. A shoulder injury had temporarily sidelined him but provided a day or two to join us in Springfield. His coming completed the weekend for me personally, even though I knew that being injured and separated from his team bothered him. We made the best of the opportunity to enjoy the big event together.

The events of the week turned into a long-overdue reunion as friends and family from Salt Lake, Spokane, the Jazz organization, the broader NBA, Gonzaga, and USA Basketball popped up around every turn. This convergence of people from these different worlds was probably the most fun for me. After his arrival, Coach Jerry Sloan often served as a lightning rod without trying to do so. He not only attracted but entertained these eclectic audiences with great stories and unfiltered commentary. My older sons and nephews still talk about his stories. Jerry held court for hours. Even current NBA players such as Glen "Big Baby" Davis enjoyed listening to Coach.

It's an odd phenomenon when I come across other NBA players, past or present, after being retired for a while. Even if we weren't friends before, a kinship forms with the cooling of competitive fires. We share a unique camaraderie that immediately binds us together. It's not every day that NBA players frequent Spokane, so when I saw them at gatherings such as those in Springfield, it was a special treat.

Most of the weekend's events were a mixture of responsibilities and fun. A reception held at the actual Hall of Fame the night before the induction is a perfect example. The Hall was packed and everyone came handsomely dressed and in good spirits. A live band and a dance floor were surrounded by food and refreshments, setting a festive atmosphere. During the weekend I bumped into several old Gonzaga teammates and their wives. We snapped a lot of pictures and comfortably shot the breeze as only old friends can do. One after another, I continued to see pals from my past and took the chance to catch up on lost time.

As I was enjoying the elegance and nostalgia of these festivities, the evening was interrupted by a clever ruse. A very pregnant young woman approached me to say hello and congratulate me on my induction. I was totally distracted by her beauty and her delicate condition until this "expectant mother" suddenly "gave birth" to the basketball and black marker she had concealed under her blouse. Signing autographs was not permitted at this function,[3] but the miraculous "delivery" didn't spoil my evening in any way. However, concern over my looming speech continued to gnaw at my stomach, so we decided to gather up the troops and head back to the hotel early.

I don't recall all the events leading up to the induction ceremony, but one amazing thing has stayed with me. Two of my longtime friends, Greg Byrd and Steve Brown, were in town. The three of us had attended high school together. Greg and Steve were having lunch, trying to recollect the name of a very large African-American man who was seated at the table next to them in the hotel restaurant. They were convinced he was a former NBA great, but couldn't identify him. Eventually, they worked up the courage to ask him to resolve their memory lapse. Bob Lanier playfully gave them a hard time before confirming that their hunch was correct. After chatting for a while with the two complete strangers, Bob found out that Steve did not have a ticket to the induction ceremony. He excused himself, said good-bye, and walked away. A few minutes later Bob returned and presented Steve with a ticket to the ceremony, free of charge.

Steve was in Springfield on a business trip that coincided with the Hall of Fame activities. He was invited to the festivities but somehow didn't end up with a ticket to the induction ceremony. I had talked to him several times that weekend and assumed that he was there for the event and had a ticket. As it turned out, that wasn't the case. When Greg and Steve later told me their lunch-time story, I was amazed by Bob Lanier's generosity to a complete stranger. I cringed at the thought that Steve would have traveled all that way and missed the ceremony had the former NBA player

PHOTO BY ANDREW D. BERNSTEIN/COURTESY OF NBA

NBA Hall of Fame induction. John's family, left to right:
Mike Stepovich, Nada's father; David; Laura; John; Samuel;
Nada; Lindsay; Michael; Houston; and John's father, Jack.

not intervened. I was grateful to be told about Bob Lanier's generosity. Steve is definitely someone who needed to be there!

• • •

As my family was dressing in tuxedos and gowns for the big night, the pit in my stomach was inching up to lodge in my throat. We left the hotel for the short ride to Symphony Hall in a cream-colored Rolls-Royce. To preserve the regal appearance of our motorcade, our children were asked to ride in a car behind us. There was only one glitch in these perfectly laid plans—Uncle Nick. Everyone has an "Uncle Nick." He is the guy who crashes parties, shows up consistently where he shouldn't, and involves himself in every conversation while inexplicably endearing himself to those who should be most offended. Nada's brother Nick is that guy and was riding with Nada and me in our car. As we rolled up to the red carpet, the first one out of the car amid the camera flashes and bright lights was Nick, smiling and waving like a polished Hollywood veteran. The kids' car pulled in behind the three of us in time to see their uncle's performance. The spectacle of Nick lumbering importantly up the stairs makes me chuckle now, but his grand entrance added a fair amount of tension at the time.

Navigating the sea of people crowding the entrance to Symphony Hall, I recognized the faces of famous people on every side, and I suddenly experienced a feeling of awe. On my left was a veritable *Who's Who* of NBA legends, filling row after row. On my right, family and friends made up the cast of a *This Is Your Life* episode—each standing to say hello as I passed. I felt myself flush, realizing how important this day was to so many people. The pressure intensified as thoughts of my upcoming speech once again intruded.

With my whole world seemingly at my side and the rest of the world tuning in, I listened to a brilliant acceptance speech by David Robinson. Friendly, confident, and seeming completely at ease, he delivered a heartfelt and genuine oration without the aid of notes or a teleprompter. I was so impressed with David that I began to think of twenty ways I should change my own remarks. Sensing my distress, Nada tapped me on the hand, smiled, and whispered, "Yours is good. Just go ahead with it." She helped me more with those few words than she will ever know.

It was finally my turn. I walked up the stairs with my poster-sized notes to face the music before the world. As I was standing at the podium with Isiah at my side, I scanned the crowd through the glare of the lights and realized I was glimpsing a mosaic of my life. There they all were—so many of the people who had helped me to this unimaginable pinnacle of achievement. Nada, my beautiful wife and trusty sidekick of twenty-three years; all the kids, the oldest boys now men; Dad, older but not too old to continue as the family's Rock of Gibraltar; my brother with his wife, Mary Ann, and two of their three grown sons: Steve Jr. and Shawn; my two sisters, Stacey and Leanne, the nearest things to earthly guardian angels that anyone could have. Only Mom was missing from her reserved seat. I am certain she was at our side as always—steady, strong, and proud of her family. Beyond stretched rows of people who had helped me through my life, many step by step, to the actual spot upon which I now stood— too many to thank in my allotted few minutes.

Even with my king-sized notes, I managed to leave out people who were important to me who had been specifically scripted into my outline. For instance, I omitted a group of ladies who have a special place in my life—the Sisters of the Holy Names— who had helped raise me. In fact, only minutes before I left the hotel, I had received a basketball autographed by each sister at the convent with her prayers and good wishes. Though I forgot to acknowledge them in my remarks, I hope they know that I always hold them in my heart. Overall, the speech went well without any major glitches. It helped that the crowd laughed once when I wasn't trying to be funny.

The relief I felt as I descended the stairs from the stage was nothing short of liberating. The smile couldn't have been kicked off of my face. I could barely muster a reserve befitting my tuxedo. I couldn't think of anything but how happy I was to be finished with that speech!

In the wake of my joy, Coach Sloan was walking to the podium. Jerry had to walk ten miles to and from school every day as a boy, but watching him trudge up those stairs, I wondered if this wasn't the longest walk of his life. Probably nobody understood at that moment what he was feeling more than me. I tried to get his attention to give him a grin or a pat on the back, but his course toward the podium was fixed. He was zeroed in on his task at that point. All I could do was listen—and enjoy.

His words were those of a genuinely humble man. With the simplicity of his homespun delivery, he told stories of his life in southern Illinois as a boy and a young man. Everyone in attendance was captivated. I particularly enjoyed one part where he told the audience about playing for the Evansville Purple Aces while glancing up from his notes to deadpan, "Our jerseys were orange." Given everything he and I had been through together, sharing this evening with him made for some very special icing on the cake.

• • •

My 2009 induction into the Naismith Basketball Hall of Fame was an improbable and remarkable event for me. It capped off a career I had not anticipated. I often tell people who dream of being in the NBA that nobody, I mean nobody, was less likely to realize that dream than me. In light of this fact, I usually suggest to them, "Go for it. Dreams do come true."

Following the induction ceremony, all of the Hall of Famers in attendance joined the newcomers on the stage. There were a record number of prior inductees in the audience that night, so the onstage meeting was an historical event as well. Milling around with some of the best players to ever take the court, I canvassed the remaining crowd one last time and reflected on how this night had come to be. Looking out at the people who remained in the audience only confirmed what I already knew: my success was a result of a collective effort. I was the beneficiary of a force much larger than myself. It's only appropriate that I start from the beginning to tell many of the stories that made that honor possible.

CHAPTER 2

A Thousand Feet Deep

S ome of my earliest memories as a child are of traveling across the fertile rolling hills of the Palouse[1]—to Mom's hometown of Ferdinand, Idaho (population 150).[2] I recall as though it were yesterday, all six of us assuming our familiar seating arrangement in our green Plymouth station wagon. My regular spot was the middle of the backseat but with my chin resting on the front seat between Mom and Dad. From there I absorbed the whole adventure hoping Dad would push the speedometer over 100 miles per hour. This was a time before any seat belt laws. My older brother, Steve, would sprawl out with a pillow—unchallenged in the rear trunk space, while sister Stacey, trying to stave off her inevitable car sickness, lay claim to a window for precautionary purposes. My younger sister, Leanne, plunked down without a vote in the remaining spot.

As a boy, I was fascinated by the sheer cliffs and oddly placed stone formations that dominated the landscape in and around our Inland Empire. I later learned that Spokane sits squarely upon a thousand feet of solid basalt that oozed as lava out of cracks in the earth millions of years ago. This thick and impenetrable

"Ferdinand, Idaho, Home of John Stockton's Mother . . . Clemy."

bedrock has provided the foundation for unlikely and incomparable civic events and an uncanny number of individual success stories. The World's Fair transformed the city with Expo '74, resurrecting some of the verve from our boomtown days of yore. Since then, our modest community of approximately 200,000 residents boasts two of the largest outdoor athletic events in the country: Bloomsday, an annual 12K race, has topped 61,000 participants and Hoopfest, which holds the title of the largest three-on-three basketball tournament in the world. Individual Spokanites have flourished disproportionately on grander stages as well. The immortal crooner "Bing" Crosby spent his youthful "White Christmases" in the same neighborhood where I grew up. His house and statue remain features on today's Gonzaga University (GU) campus, where his Christmas music still brightens the holidays. Renowned US House Speaker Thomas Foley also sprouted from the Lilac City. He was a schoolmate of my father at Gonzaga High School. Spokane has also produced an abundance of talented athletes. Mark Rypien, MVP quarterback for the 1992 World Champion Washington Redskins, and Ryne Sandberg, perennial Chicago Cubs All-Star, are among the notables who had their origins there.

These modern athletes were the beneficiaries of a long legacy of success. As early as the first decade of the twentieth century, local players excelled nationally but not where you might think. Because of their relatively recent success, almost everyone is familiar with Bulldog or "Zag" basketball; both the men's and women's Gonzaga University teams have achieved consistent success on the national stage. What most people don't know is that the Bulldogs were a national powerhouse in the 1920s and '30s— in football. The team was known from coast to coast with their standouts placed on equal footing with the likes of "Red" Grange, Ernie Nevers, and "Bronko" Nagurski. My grandfather Houston Stockton gained just such a national reputation on that Bulldog gridiron. He went on to win an NFL Championship in 1926 with the Frankford Yellow Jackets.[3] (Frankford is a suburb of Philadelphia. The Yellow Jackets became the Philadelphia Eagles in 1933 for the price of $2,500 and 25 percent of the debt.) That team finished undefeated, with fourteen victories, six over the Chicago Bears—a record that stood until the Miami Dolphins tied it in 1972.[4]

I didn't know it when I was young, but looking back I see how well-grounded the citizens of my hometown have been for generations, resting upon that thousand feet of solid rock. From this basalt, a remarkable history sprung, of people, places, traditions, and dreams. Much of it centered in my neighborhood, the "Little Vatican."

CHAPTER 3

Family

We don't get to choose where or to whom we are born. We are so fortunate in this country, even in bad times, to have opportunities that many people in the world couldn't imagine. I thank God every day that the stork dropped me in the United States of America, at the home of Jack and Clemy Stockton.

Mom's full name is Clementine Josephine Frei Stockton. She was the youngest of fifteen children born to Clemens Christian and Philomena Uhlorn Frei. Both were German-speaking Swiss nationals. Because he died before I was born, I never knew my Grandpa Frei. I am told he was a small and frail man who was sick most of Mom's childhood. He must have possessed a little scrappiness at one time, however, because he came to America alone at age thirteen, never to return to Switzerland. Upon his arrival he was immediately robbed of what little money he had. He managed, nonetheless, to complete his cross-country journey to Idaho and become one of the successful pioneer farmers on the Camas Prairie.

The name *Philomena* means love of work, so Grandma was

The Frei home in Switzerland.

appropriately named. Raising a family of that size on a farm with an ailing husband must have been a heavy yoke. Thankfully, she was of sturdy stock, living to a ripe old age of ninety-six, with bacon lard as a primary staple in her diet. She prayed the Rosary often over the crops and before meals, as her faith was her true staple. By the time Mom came around, her brothers, many of who were old enough to be her dad, shouldered much of the farm work while Grandma cooked for them.

The soil on their land was a sight to behold. Even our un-

trained, big-city eyes could detect the richness of the earth on the unirrigated farmland. We could almost feel the cool, moist clumps of black dirt just by looking across the fields and breathing the fresh air. In later years, when one of my uncles dug a basement by hand, he bragged, "I didn't come across a single rock."

Philomena Frei, John's maternal grandmother.

Mom had to grow up quickly on the farm. She did much of the work as

The Frei family. Clemy, John's mother, is sitting on the lap of her father, Clem.

her brothers went to war, got married, or otherwise moved on with their lives. Way ahead of her time, as a ten-year-old girl, she drove the tractor, worked in the fields, and milked the cows. As a self-confessed tomboy she did find time to play basketball in high school and was apparently very good.

Thankfully, most of Mom's siblings lived long enough to provide me an opportunity to arrange a special family gathering. In 2001, with the help of an air charter company, Nada and I were able to bring most of Mom's siblings and their spouses to Salt Lake to watch a Jazz game. They enjoyed the sights, sounds, and taste of the city. A chartered tour bus chauffeured these small town folks around our "huge" city. They ate at Jazz owner Larry Miller's new restaurant, the Mayan, where to the amazement of the clan, divers plunged from high perches into pools of water. They capped their trip nicely by watching a Jazz victory, a first opportunity for most of them. My aunts and uncles took pictures on the floor of the Delta Center. Uncle Al even made it back to the training room, where he and Karl Malone chatted like old

Grandmother Philomena Frei.

classmates. He had had a storied life in the service working behind enemy lines (basically a spy) during World War II. If Karl
had known that then, they would still be talking. It was a thrill
for me to see them hit it off, and I know Uncle Al will never forget it. It was also a great feeling to see Mom having such a great
time with all her big brothers and sisters.

Mom remained close to her family long after she left the prairie for the big city. It had been clear to the family for a long time
that young Clemy had certainly inherited Philomena's love of
work, but it was not going to be on the farm. Immediately after
high school, she followed in her big sister Aggie's footsteps and
went into nursing. She moved to Spokane, graduated from nurses
training, and began working at Sacred Heart Hospital.

• • •

Dad's full name is John Houston Stockton. Most people call
him Jack, and his story is entirely different than Mom's. He was
born to John Houston Stockton (who answered to Houston or
Zeb) and M'Liss Finnegan Stockton. He was a Spokane boy born
and raised. He grew up in a house practically on Gonzaga's campus in the shadows of the football stadium on Desmet Avenue. In
fact, in the next eighty years he moved a total of four blocks from

Jack Stockton (right), John's father, in the Coast Guard.

there to his current residence. He did, however, have a couple of adventures along the way that gave him a taste of the rest of the world. In 1945, at the end of his high-school experience, he volunteered for the Coast Guard and underwent training for the invasion of Japan. Dad proudly boasts that "they heard I was coming, so they surrendered."

After the war he was assigned to lighthouse duty in Chesapeake Bay near Portsmouth, Virginia. One of his first assignments was the repair of a frozen and long-since-silenced foghorn. The old timers had tried many methods to resurrect the horn's crucial blare with no success. Eventually they decided to send the new guy up on the roof with a rope around his waist and a hammer in his hand to literally beat the foghorn and its sheets of ice into compliance. Dad struck true with his trusty hammer and released the full force of the horn with its ten-mile range directly into his left ear. He couldn't hear the laughter of his older companions for weeks, but it was assessed a job well done.

While stationed in Virginia, Dad became somewhat of a genealogy student and discovered that the Stockton family tree took root in the counties of Sligo and Roscommon in Ireland, landing several generations later smack at the bottom of the Declaration of Independence.

The signature of Richard Stockton, son of another John Stockton, can be seen clearly and legibly on the Declaration. His penmanship, however, was much better than his reputation. History tells us that he was captured and tortured by the British. As a result, he recanted his loyalty to his new country and pledged allegiance to the king of England, becoming the only Declaration signer to do so.[1]

Was he a traitor, as history tells us, or a tortured patriot? We don't know for sure. Nowadays, Dad is quick to point out with a smile that Richard was actually the brother of our direct ancestor.

After winding through several states and generations, another interesting character by the name of Harling Smith Stockton, believed to be in our direct line, pops up in Missouri, where he was apparently at the center of a great deal of havoc. He was thought to have ridden with Quantrill, the infamous Confederate marauder from Missouri, who burned down most of Lawrence, Kansas. Years ago, on a Jazz preseason trip to Lawrence, I tried to locate some record of this association but was unable to do so. Still, the family lore persists.

A portion of the Missouri Stockton clan eventually mounted up and joined a wagon train headed west. Their destination was the fertile Willamette Valley in Oregon. Mother Nature had other ideas. With winter approaching, the weary travelers chose not to brave both the Rocky and Cascade mountain ranges. They settled in rather than risk the dangerous cold. The wagons had stopped near what is now Parma, Idaho. It was there that my

PHOTO COURTESY OF GONZAGA UNIVERSITY ARCHIVES

*Houston Stockton, John's paternal grandfather, in his
Gonzaga University football uniform.*

great-grandpa met Ellen Glennen of Ireland. They fell in love
and were married, and Great-Grandpa Stockton learned how
to work the rocky and generally inhospitable earth to produce
crops. Parma became their home, and it was here that Grandpa
Houston was born.

• • •

My Grandpa was an incredible athlete. He was powerfully
built, with enormous hands. He attended Gonzaga on a football scholarship and was listed in the program as 5'11" and 195
pounds. He achieved All-American status in the glory days of the
Gonzaga University football program.

Houston and M'Liss were divorced when Dad was still a
boy. Grandpa moved on and eventually started another family
in Bremerton, Washington, where he became a state highway

*Mary Me Stockton Washburn and
Dode Stockton Petragallo.*

Grandma M'Liss Stockton.

patrolman. Perhaps his most harrowing moment on duty came
on November 7, 1940, as Mother Nature flexed her muscles,
infamously buffeting the Narrows Bridge over the Puget Sound
in Tacoma, Washington. Grandpa was directing traffic on the
Bremerton side of what became known as "Galloping Gertie."
High winds caused the bridge to begin undulating, and the span
eventually buckled under the stress, collapsing disastrously into
the waters of Puget Sound. Grandpa was not hurt, but the movie
of the undulating bridge is still a classic disaster tape.[2]

Following their divorce, Grandma M'Liss remained in
Spokane to raise her family. Divorce carried a large stigma at the
time and I don't remember Dad talking much about his legendary
father. He wasn't resentful or angry but simply said, "He wasn't
around much." Dad's maternal grandfather, Michael J. Finnegan,
who ran the Hecla Mining Store in Burke, Idaho, during the
boomtown days, filled the fatherly role in the Stockton house. My
dad absolutely admired and adored him. With Great-Grandfather's
help, Grandma managed to successfully raise Dad and his two

*Michael J. Finnegan, John's great-grandfather
and Jack Stockton's maternal grandfather.*

sisters, Mary M'Liss ("Mary Me") and Dolores ("Dode") in their small home on the campus of Gonzaga University.

• • •

Dad's mother was born Mary M'Liss Finnegan in Green Bay, Wisconsin. I wondered if perhaps she met Grandpa Houston during one of his trips to play the Packers where a wink and a smile convinced her to head to the Great Northwest. Here, again, research ruined a great story. I learned later that the Finnegans migrated much earlier to the mining towns of Burke and Mullen, Idaho. Exactly how M'Liss met young Zeb remains a mystery. Where she came from wasn't important to us. We just knew she was a terrific grandma. We fought for the right to spend the night at her house, playing Yahtzee and gobbling up Gerber pears.

She had her hands full raising her three young children, even with the help of her father. Dad was well-liked and accepted

Jack and Clemy Stockton at their wedding, 1957.

authority, but not without discussion. He was prepared to stand on principle—even in the path of principals. Young Jack took many a "hack" from the good fathers at Gonzaga High School as a result. Father Mullen once ordered eleven hacks for Dad. After seven, he refused to take any more hacks and was told to clean out his locker and go home. As he rounded the corner to home sweet home with the contents of his locker under his arms, M'Liss met him at the porch and didn't let him off the hook. Without discussion, she merely pointed her finger. Eyes down, shoulders slumped, and no doubt dragging his feet, Dad went back to meet his fate. When he returned, Fr. Mullen met him at the door and asked officiously, "Are you going to take those hacks now?" Dad responded with a mix of defiance and resignation, "I am not!" I can only imagine what Fr. Mullen was thinking at that moment. "Put your books away and make up the time you missed after school," were his final remarks on the matter. The good Father surrendered a little bit of himself as the two forged a friendship around these types of standoffs.

After his time in the service, Dad came back to Spokane in the late '40s, where he worked for Kent Cigarettes and later as a Campbell's Soup salesman well into the '50s. Toward the end of that stint with Campbell's Soup, he met Mom. Apparently he hadn't been eating his own chicken noodle soup, as he came down with a bad case of strep throat. His doctor sent him to the hospital. According to Dad, a beautiful nurse walked in and said, "Hello, Mr. Stockton. How are you today?" In his familiar, irritable fashion, he scratched the back of his head and rasped, "Just great. That's why I'm in here!" She immediately left him to his misery and thoughts. Later, when he felt badly about what he'd said, Dad asked another nurse to mediate on his behalf for a second chance with the lovely Miss Frei. Thankfully, due to his intermediary's persuasiveness and, of course, Dad's own overflowing charm, Clemy reconsidered. The rest is history. They were married in Assumption Church in Ferdinand, Idaho, on the 24th of November, 1956, and lived for the only time in Dad's life outside of St. Aloysius Parish. Their firstborn, Steve, arrived a year and a month later, prompting one of Dad's favorite comments, "We were married in November and Stephen Raymond was born in December."

Soon the growing young family was too big for their quarters. Mom, Dad, brother Steve, and sister Stacey (and with me on the way) were headed back to the "Little Vatican"—for good.

In one rather adventurous stroke, the young family took several bold steps. Dad retired from the soup industry, and Mom quit nursing and became a full-time mom. Dad secured a loan for a new car, a new house, and his new business—Joey's Tavern—with a single stroke of the pen. Within two years, my youngest sister, Leanne, would join the foursome in our new house conveniently located two blocks from the "Tav."

In that home, Mom and Dad gave us a good life and the legacy of a fine name. As each of us left home, no fences needed mending, no reputations required burnishing, and no debts lingered. They gave us all of this and some large shoes to fill. Success is too often seen in terms of wealth and fame. My parents had neither, but they are my heroes. Theirs is a true American success story.

PART II

A Sentimental Journey

Endeavor

I set upon a journey and presumed my destination
But scant across my path were things of prior contemplation.
Now, with retrospective sight, I grasp what I couldn't see:
The essence of the trip—converging roads through me.
I conceived a thousand treks under a thousand rubrics more;
From various points of origin, a circle was still in store.
Nothing you can conjure avoids a truth that's crystal clear;
Embark in any direction, you'll finish in the mirror.
I began within a gym, and though I never tried,
Somewhere amid the motion, I finally glimpsed inside.
Through hours of repetition, skills that I could hone
With mates in tribulation, I struggled, not alone.
The hours turned to days, now months upon the road.
My wheels seemed to spin, the truth of things be told.
The place that I set about—still distant—of that I'm sure;
But with all uncertain travel, some unexpected things occur.
The fear to try and fail tuckers out along the way.
The friends who shared the ride most likely there to stay.
To the place from which you left, you can never again arrive.
You've changed and looked inside; you grow because you strive.

—KERRY L. PICKETT

CHAPTER 4

The "Little Vatican"

My good fortune wasn't limited to the gift of family. I grew up in a classic Roman Catholic neighborhood centered around Gonzaga University and the impressive spires of St. Aloysius Church. The streets of this little world were lined with houses filled primarily with a melting pot of Irish, German, and of course, many Italian residents, as the nickname implies. Although much has changed since my childhood, much has remained the same—Dad is still in the family home and many of his neighbors haven't changed since our family bought the house. A brief drive through the familiar streets allows me to travel down memory lane to visit and enjoy dear friends, fond times, and treasured places.

As a toddler, my boundaries were limited to the view of Holy Names Academy, a Catholic girls' high school, and Mission Park. Both were ornately framed by the cathedral window in our living room.

Most days my dad was occupied, but available, at the tavern with his partner and his high-school pal, Dan Crowley. He didn't plug into the family's social calendar, however, until his

*John, his family, parents, and siblings and their children
with the spires of St. Al's in the background.*

shift behind the bar ended, which, on occasion, was after two
A.M., though most nights it was six P.M. on the button. Mom
had turned in her nurse's cap to assume the formidable role of
"domestic engineer," as we liked to tease her. Ever present, she
stayed busy with self-imposed duties at home that far exceeded
the nine-hour workday.

Oftentimes I would work alongside her, listening to the pleasant sound of her voice singing or humming her favorite melo-
dies. Even as we all grew, we spent many hours at home or in the
neighborhood playing and rousting about with what amounted
to an extended family. We were seldom chauffeured to any activity, and there wasn't much disposable cash. The world hadn't
yet become completely organized by adults. Many adventures lay
before us kids, and we were left to figure them out for ourselves.
We did, and boy, did we love it!

The three amigos: John, George Lucas, and Steve "First Down" Brown.

In no time at all, my world expanded to include our entire block. It was about then that most every mischievous undertaking, curious inquiry, or courageous expedition came to include my partner in crime, George Lucas, who lived only a few houses away. Together we would catch bees in the alley, climb every roof that we could, and attempt to start fires with a magnifying glass. We traversed the forbidden wall of Marian Hall like a forty-yard balance beam. It was an old dormitory for Holy Names Academy. The grounds were patrolled by imposing and habited nuns who didn't horse around, so stealth was essential. We also crawled like commandos through the battered hedge that shielded the mysterious neighborhood Flaherty house. It was an old mansion on the corner possessed of a spooky aura reminiscent of Boo Radley's house in *To Kill a Mockingbird*. Wherever we ventured, we knew everyone on the block, and they knew us. We were never "watched" but always seen. That came in handy when George and I actually did start a fire and needed the nearest hose to extinguish it.

John and Leanne visiting with Santa.

Our energy could not be contained for long, and our horizons soon broadened to include new boundaries. The Spokane River with its eerie undercurrents formed a menacing eastern border of the neighborhood. The railroad tracks ran along the river, and the underbrush provided makeshift camps for many real-life hobos. Together they were synonymous with danger. The rest of the "hood" was defined by two busy streets, Hamilton and Mission. These were only for seasoned veterans such as my older brother, Steve, and older sister, Stacey. George and I didn't mind our confinement within the hidden mystery of the neighborhood. We had the park, the tracks, and the fish pond behind Holy Names—complete with turtles and frogs to occupy our imaginations and our time. We also had a gym, an orphanage, and neighbors such as Mr. Shanks, who would give us Nilla Wafers just for knocking at his door. All I needed to do was look both ways before crossing any street and call if I was going to be late for dinner. Our number was Hudson 3-8456, and we dialed it on rotary phones.

John with his grade school teachers and a family friend.
Left to right: Sister Jane, Sister Dolores, Sister Helen,
Sister Phyllis Marie, and Sister Reginalda.

Things became more complicated as I entered first grade. I anxiously awaited my chance to join the big kids and cross the busy streets. Steve, at Mom's insistence, grudgingly walked me to school. His stride was purposeful and would have challenged an Olympic speed walker. I believed his intent was to lose me. With a sack lunch containing a bologna sandwich, a Twinkie, and some Fritos corn chips, I nipped at his heels the entire way. Contrary to my mom's safety stipulations, Steve never used the sidewalk or crosswalks. We crossed Huttons' yard, jaywalked, cut the corner at Defelices', and jaywalked again. Then, down an alley through Stevens' yard and across the parking lot of Geno's restaurant, we continued. Next, we timed the cars in both directions and raced across Hamilton without using the lights. We darted through another alley, crisscrossed Mr. Hare's yard, and completed the journey with a double-jaywalk across Mission Avenue (east and west traffic separated by a grassy boulevard lined with trees). We used the time-and-dart technique previously employed. Steve broke every pedestrian rule I knew in our inaugural walk. Regardless of its illegality, it remained my route of preference. Years later, when I was allowed to ride my bike to school, I actually got pulled over on my green Schwinn Typhoon while attempting to cross Mission without stopping. I simply circled in the street until all the cars passed and then used my momentum to quickly cross. I thought it was safer than stopping and walking, but the police disagreed. The two motorcycle officers mercifully let me off with a warning.

After surviving Steve's trek, I was faced with the prospect of my first day of Catholic schooling. I already knew about the nuns and their legendary stern discipline. They yelled at you, hit your knuckles with rulers, and made you pray all the time. I must have looked like I was about to be fed to the lions as Sister Jane met me at the door with a disarmingly warm and welcoming smile. Could I possibly trust that greeting after all I had heard? As it turned out, I could. Sister Jane, like most of the Sisters of the Holy Names, was one of the nicest, kindest people I have ever been around. They had discipline in their lives that translated to us. They were smart and completely dedicated to our well-being. So, my first-grade year—except for witnessing a few accidents, such as tongues getting stuck to frozen fenceposts and minor bladder issues that always seemed to occur next to me—went off without a hitch as did the rest of my grade-school tenure, with a few exceptions.

In the second grade I became embroiled in a Campbell's soup label contest controversy that never went public. Miss Lorenz, one of two lay teachers who taught me, was constantly urging us to think of someone besides "me, myself, and I." She entrusted me with the honor of tallying the coupons accurately. I, however, took a more selfish, dishonest route, and won the competition by a landslide. We had a big ceremony without a recount, and I

John with his silver tooth, 1971.   *John with his silver tooth, 1972.*

was awarded a doll with a pretty pink outfit for my trouble. I'm certain Miss Lorenz knew that the coupon totals did not match the numbers I had submitted and crafted the prize accordingly. I hope she knows today that I got the message, and I appreciate her sending it.

• • •

My year outside the classroom didn't improve much. It started with a crash that had to break Mom's heart. Stacey had taught me to ride her bike on the sidewalk, where my friends and I had become fairly proficient at jumping curbs, skidding brodies, and riding double. We thought our skills merited building a ramp for test purposes. I seconded the motion and took over the construction project. The ramp that I engineered was made from an eight-inch two-by-four propped at an angle on a rock. For all of you engineers out there, this makes a perfect brake. Like any good inventor, I volunteered for the test run. I rode hard and fast with the required precision. I hit the ramp and when the bike abruptly stopped, tumbled face-first over my handlebars, badly chipping my newly arrived front tooth, which a prominent silver cap would cover for the next six years.

An ensuing disaster was a perfect complement to the tooth

incident. I was babysitting my four-year-old sister Leanne who had stuck toothpicks upright in the carpeted stairs as an obstacle course for Mom when she returned. After a gentle chastising, we cleaned up the toothpick course together. Convinced the stairs were clear, I bounded down the steps, driving one of the small wooden spikes deep into my bare foot. Undetected by X-ray, the tiny spear festered for six months until it had to be surgically removed. So, by the age of seven, I had literally tested my mettle from head to toe. I wasn't done yet.

I faced for the first time the loss of a friend. Joseph Kosek tragically drowned in a pond behind Gonzaga. It was devastating. Afterward, we saw his mom every day in the drug store next to Dad's tavern. These were both happy and sad reminders to each of us. Fittingly, my year of full-body injuries ended with a stifling bout with pneumonia. I was an awfully sick kid. Doses of harsh antibiotics mixed with mom's homemade peppermint bark pulled me through, and I survived to begin grade three.

A daily highlight during my primary school years was my walk home, which usually included a visit with Dad inside the tavern that was deliciously outside the letter of the law. To me, Dad and I were secret partners in a thrilling daily caper. He shrugged off any concern, saying, "If I get a ticket because my own kids come to see me . . . well, so be it." Sometimes Dad would give us twenty-five cents to go across the street to the Dairy Freeze to get a large order of fries. They had a pinball machine there, but we knew if we wasted the quarter on that beautiful siren of a machine, there would be no fries and no more quarters. This was a quandary of the highest magnitude.

The Martieris owned the Dairy Freeze, and they had heavy Italian accents. Mrs. Martieri was always really nice to all of us kids. One day I paced on the sidewalk in front of the order window until she finally called out in her understanding and compassionate tone, "Johnny, you look-a hun-ngry. Would you like-a an ice cream-a cone?" I never turned her down. Her accent was music to my ears, especially with an offer like that.

Some days I would run straight home. In an excited rush to greet Mom, I was usually guilty of slamming the door and yelling, "M-o-m, I'm home!" On days when Dad had the swing shift, Mom would try to shush me and the door so we didn't disturb Dad's nap. The swing shift meant that Dad would have to work from six A.M. until lunchtime, then come home to stay until after supper when he again donned his bartending apron until closing time at two A.M. He needed his afternoon snooze, and we didn't want to disturb him. As you might expect, despite Mom's diligent efforts and our best youthful intentions, we constantly woke him. To the best of my recollection he only erupted twice out of about a thousand door slams. His bark on these two occasions made up for the 998 he had ignored. When we heard that bedroom door swing open, we scattered like shotgun pellets behind the nearest pieces of furniture, hoping to avoid the tongue-lashing. Thankfully, we were never devoured as he showed remarkable tolerance for our youthful thoughtlessness.

• • •

Mom kept a tidy house. She worked at it every day. She obviously had other skills that she sacrificed for the sake of our team. I still consider her to be the best mom and housewife ever! She possessed a beautiful singing voice, although she didn't think so. Mom would harmonize with songs on the radio or chirp unaccompanied. Her voice was warm, calming, and made you feel good inside when you heard it. I spent a lot of time with her around the house. She wasn't bossy. She invited me to help. I assisted her in cooking, cleaning, painting, and even wallpapering. I learned how to do all of these things under her encouraging eyes.

I was the chief assistant on grocery shopping missions to the IGA across from the tavern. Mom didn't need a written list as she managed to get most everything we needed once a week from memory. Mr. Kissinger, the owner, often included complimentary maple bars for the two of us. We would borrow the station wagon from Dad to bring the groceries home.

Mom and Dad were great at finding individual time for all of us kids but it was often in the flow of their workday. I think that is something that is missing in our modern culture: kids working with their parents. It was both enriching and fun, and provided time for some pretty good talks.

I was a momma's boy even though Mom didn't think so. I would often wait for Dad after work at the Tav and ride home with him. If I had my trusty Schwinn with the rack on the front, we would ride home double.

Then there were Sundays. An opportunistic early bird like me would get up with Dad and walk down the dirt alley to help open the tavern. Aside from getting to put out the clean ashtrays, wash glasses, and brush the pool table, I also got to run the floor buffer, a monster machine with a rotating head that moved from side to side and polished the floor. In the hands of the untrained, it would buck and bounce, pounding the stools and booths. Dad rushed me through the tutorial to avoid disaster.

After this voluntary work detail, it was off to church. Our cleaning attire and overall appearance was understandably a bit less than suitable for mass. Dad would lead me through the side doors where the priest, ushers, and altar boys prepared. We would sit behind the main altar in a circular hallway with five smaller altars where the young priests practiced saying mass. As we observed these ceremonial inner workings, I couldn't wait for the honor of being an altar boy. I finally got my chance in the sixth grade, following once again in the footsteps of my brother. I was, at a minimum, "gung-ho" in the performance of my duties. I would call the older boys and offer to serve their masses as well as mine, even the six A.M. service, to rack up the merit points in order to earn my KOA (Knights of the Altar) patch in record time. I wasn't quite as angelic as this might sound. My altar boy days ended less than a year later with a minor controversy. Ironically, my supervisor thought I had missed a shift, which I hadn't. After some fruitless negotiation, I resigned.

• • •

Most of my early association with basketball was with my brother. When Steve and his friends played, he took me along for one reason—I was little enough to drop through the top of any chained doors. Often in the dark I would have to scurry about the gyms at GU, Bishop White Seminary, St. Al's, or Gonzaga Prep to find a door or window unencumbered by chains to let my older accomplices onto the forbidden hardwoods. They seldom let me play, so I dribbled or shot baskets on the side thinking I was lucky to be there. It wasn't until I received a red-white-and-blue rubber ABA (American Basketball Association) ball for Christmas that things changed. The older guys, even the college students, thought it was cool. They would let me play if I let them use it. It was a no-brainer. When alone, I would shoot in the driveway, sometimes after shoveling snow. I know today that this was valuable in my development. Shooting in winter gloves wasn't very effective; but I enjoyed shooting enough to be willing to endure the elements. That was the revealing part.

ASSISTED

Moving inside to play basketball required leaning on our neighbors, the Sisters of the Holy Names. I had soon worn a path from our house to the front door of the Academy. Once inside I would scamper up the carpeted steps to the office, hoping to reach Sr. Ann Herkenrath or Sr. Mary Anne McGee. Both possessed the "Holy Grail"—the keys to the gym. As their names echoed from the page through the hall speakers, I would listen for the sound of their heels clipping down the hall. I can't ever remember them turning me down or denying me access.

Bouncing from gym to gym, on sidewalks, streets, and driveways, I wore the nubs off of that colorful ball. Every year for Christmas I would receive a new one just as the threads started appearing on the old sphere.

My competitive athletic adventure began for real with an unanticipated twist in the summer between my fifth- and sixth-grade years. I had begun as Steve's diminutive breaking-and-entering man and continued as a bartering pipsqueak sporting a worn ABA ball. The twist began with a chance meeting—a meeting with someone who had never stepped inside our neighborhood: a Hoosier, a big Hoosier.

CHAPTER 5

Patterns in the Park

The summer of 1973 was flying by in customary fashion. The long days were filled with swimming, bike riding, and appropriate youthful mischief. Sometime around late August I had a chance encounter in the park—about a hundred steps from my front door—with three strangers who had never before set foot in our neighborhood. The meeting would profoundly affect all involved for the rest of our lives. Over the next thirty-nine years my relationship with these people blossomed. I still don't accept coincidence as an explanation.

My two closest friends, Steve Brown and George Lucas, were with me in the park that day. We were running football patterns when we spotted what appeared to be three GU students. They fit the general description of students who arrived around this time every year. With their scraggly, tattered, and hippie-ish look, they were not particularly impressive to behold, but had a definite air of athleticism. The uninvited threesome offered to throw us passes. Suspicious that this was a ploy to abscond with our football, our patterns were understandably short at first. An hour and a half later we were still joyfully running bomb after bomb.

Coach Kerry Pickett, John "Shakey" Blake, and John "Sully" Sullivan, circa 1978.

These guys could really throw a football, and we could run all day. We were made for each other. We hadn't known these three men before this day and probably would not have remembered them were it not for a fateful decision on the part of the largest and scariest of the trio, Kerry Pickett. The very next week, partially dragooned, he offered his services as our coach at St. Al's.

• • •

I didn't know it at the time but Dad had assisted young Mr. Pickett and his wife earlier in the week. The two had come to town looking for a job and stopped at the tavern. As it turned out, Dad helped them find work and housing in the neighborhood. He did, however, exact a bit of a quid pro quo when he learned that Coach Pickett had played basketball and football in college. Apparently an agreement was struck, and the big redhead was to become our sixth-grade basketball coach. His "staff" would come to include his wife and law student partner, Virginia, and the other two park quarterbacks, John Blake and John Sullivan. "Shakey" and "Sully" had recently moved up from Phoenix. Sully was beginning law school, while Shakey, having returned from two tours of duty in Vietnam, would go where the wind blew for a spell. The friends from Phoenix and the Indiana couple had met only a few days earlier. The four had found work at the now-extinct Forum Tavern only a block down from Dad's place.

Between shifts at the bar and law school, the foursome formed a formidable alliance to catapult the St. Al's B-squad basketball team to some renown. Coach Pickett spent three hours per night, six days a week preparing us. His sidekicks assumed the duties of concessions, event management, and refereeing as they prepared the St. Al's cracker box as if it were Madison Square Garden. When the ball was tossed up for tournament games, Dad was often at the microphone. His role there was probably part of their pact, and needed about as much arm twisting as it took Pickett to command the bench. Sully and Shakey were mostly behind the whistles, while Virginia was astride the popcorn and Kool-Aid.

In the next three years, I learned more about basketball, life, and myself than at any other time in my life. Things outside the lines included personal hygiene, team Christmas caroling, and book reports on Coach's classic favorite novels for less than stellar grades. I think it is safe to say that we were held to becoming better people. I have never been pushed physically, challenged mentally, or tested emotionally more by anyone else. I was in for quite a ride—a ride that would have to wait for basketball to begin because it was football season.

• • •

I loved football. It was easily my favorite sport. This was not an inherited trait from my famous grandpa. The big allure was the helmets, cleats, and shoulder pads that made us feel like warriors. It was also partly that my brother had played and was good at it. His mentor had a voice and a name perfectly suited for football—Coach Linebarger.

Coach Bob Linebarger was a St. Al's fixture. Underpaid and overworked, he doubled or tripled as coach, PE teacher, and school disciplinarian, armed with a very large hack paddle. Although imposing to us as second graders, Coach also had an incredible feel for kids. George and I fell in love with the game as his ball boys long before we ever donned a pad. When we got our chance as sixth graders, we thought we were the big boys.

• • •

One afternoon before the sun set on the gridiron season, I came face to face with our basketball future. It peered over the panes of opaque glass through the clear window at the top of the classroom door. No one had ever done that. We sat motionless as the penetrating and remorseless eyes of a shark surveyed the room from behind wild and unruly red hair and beard. When the bell rang, Coach Pickett strode with intense purpose into a St. Al's classroom for the first time, in tattered and worn jeans, an XXL Indiana T-shirt, and boots that had seen better days. Our meeting was terse and serious. Our practices would be worse.

Hoops began immediately following football season. The basketball practices were long, intense, and legendarily miserable. Parents were not invited. They probably weren't planning on coming anyway because most had to work, so that luxury wasn't available.

It was prior to Title IX, so girls' sports were nearly nonexistent. This meant we had the gym entirely to ourselves, and three-hour practices were commonplace. Jam-packed into the posted daily practice schedule were fundamental repetitions of every variety.

PATTERNS IN THE PARK

Practice ended with "hallways"—a medieval torture master-minded by an evil conditioning genius. St. Al's school is almost a block long with the gym at the bottom of one end. The hallway course began as we exited the gym's interior doors. We would run the length of the lower hallway to the cafeteria and climb two flights of stairs. So as not to be cheated out of the building's final thirty yards, we hooked left in the upper hallway to reach its most distant end. We then ran the entire length of the upper hallway, touched the other end, tracked back to the center, down the stairs, then retraced our steps back to the gym—that was "one." A course of well over two city blocks, not counting stairs, this training regimen seemed over the top after three hours of practice. In no time at all, however, this torture turned into a source of pride and a badge of honor that offered incomparable conditioning as a lifetime reward,

The B-squad that first year under Coach Pickett included two Mexican exchange students, Pedro and Gerardo. They preferred being called "Peter" and "Gerry," because we butchered the true pronunciation. Peter found a home at our house—in my bedroom, but not without some struggles. We fought about everything, including the Alamo, and learned many derogatory names for each other before the dust settled. By the end of the year, however, we were as close as brothers.

Peter's cousin Gerry was plump and too heavy to play basketball. Besides, the sport was brand-new to him, but Coach found a spot for him and set some conditioning goals. As we all ran our "hallways," our rallying cry became "Cien, Gerry," which means one hundred (pounds) *en español*. Gerry took ownership in that distant goal, along with the team and Coach Pickett. When Gerry's parents returned in the spring, they didn't even recognize their svelte son. Coach helped us to realize that being part of a team is much larger than statistics and playing time. Gerry, even with very few minutes of actual playing time, became an indispensable member of an undefeated team.

There was no place to turn for sympathy or relief from Coach's demanding routine of preparation. As I said, Dad kind of liked the brash young Irishman and his methods. Our jaded view of him never wavered until games began, and we started reaping the fruits of our labor. Our schedule was limited to other parochial school B-squads who simply weren't as prepared and nowhere near as conditioned. Scores consistently soared into the sixties, with our opponents laboring to reach double figures. Coach set up more challenging practice games against older teams. At time-outs, Coach continually pointed out that the score did not matter. We owed our opponents our best effort so they could gauge their progress as well.

That year I began to learn that whether you are ahead or behind, concentrating on the quality of your performance is the essence of competing. Winning makes it fun, and if you master competing, you will win most of the time. The preparation process makes the experience fulfilling. No preparation means no foundation to build on in the future. Additionally, it is hard to build character or inner strength without demanding regimens, hard work, and trying times on the practice floor. Often, in today's models of equal playing time without reference to practice or performance standards, I think kids are robbed of valuable tools to confront life's real circumstances. Competitive athletics should be a metaphor for real life. In today's world, we seem to be skewing the relationship to our children's disadvantage by making rules that bypass the investment and go directly to the dividends. If everyone gets a trophy, the only winners are the fragile egos of the parents.

I didn't fully recognize it, but I was beginning to learn lessons that were shaping my life. It wasn't that I hadn't heard them before at home; I had. But they were being cemented in my mind forever because of the source. I was learning that good people come in all kinds of packages, even loud, scary, foreign packages.

I also began to see that working hard hurts but that I could endure a lot of pain as well and keep going. You can train yourself to not get tired. I came to appreciate the mental aspect of fatigue. Finally, I learned that self-esteem (not that I had ever heard of the term at that time) cannot be given. Self-confidence is earned by accomplishing things through your own efforts—things previously beyond your reach.

• • •

As winter turned to spring, basketball gave way to baseball. Sports in those days didn't overlap. The "round ballers" put away their sneakers, dug out their mitts, and headed to baseball practice. Generally we were all more adept at baseball than other sports because Little League baseball was the only game in the summer. By age six we knew every rule, pickoff play, base-stealing technique, and strike-zone subtlety. If you couldn't catch a fly ball, stepped out when the ball was pitched, or threw "like a girl," life was rough. These shortcomings were inexcusable within the ranks and punishable by ridicule or banishment from the neighborhood sandlot.

It was under this peer pressure that my career in youth baseball unfolded. I had some ups and some downs in these years. As a six-year-old, I had the misfortune of wetting my pants while playing right field. Unfortunately for me, our pitcher didn't see me jumping up and down and crossing my legs out there. He kept walking batter after batter until the dam finally broke. It would have been worse if we had been decked out in fancy white pinstriped uniforms like kids today. As it was, we wore a team jersey, hat, and blue jeans. The dark blue denim pants mitigated my embarrassment—a little. The hat (actually a helmet) and the jersey had to be returned at the end of each season.

Six years later things improved dramatically. As a twelve-year-old, I pitched a perfect game. The book read: "No runs, no hits, no errors, and no walks," and I made the newspaper. That was cool. The best part about Little League was that after winning a game we would all pile in the back of a pickup truck and head to A&W for a frosty mug of root beer. On the way we would turn our hats backward so they wouldn't blow off and then sing "Ninety-Nine Bottles of Beer on the Wall" all the way there.

Today this would be a jailable offense for the parents who okayed it and for the driver as well. As much as I want my children to be safe, I wonder what we are losing in the name of safety. Can we be too safe? Is there any limit to what we are willing to give up in order to ensure safety for our children? Should we keep kids in booster seats until they can shave? I am quite sure the car seat companies would lobby for that. I think it is a shame what we are willingly surrendering for the illusion of safety.

As eighth graders, most of us had now played basketball for Coach Pickett all three years. We had great confidence in ourselves and each other. No matter how high Coach set our goals, we had learned by this time that we could reach most of them. This was especially satisfying in light of the fact that we were not a handpicked group of all-stars but instead a bunch of mutts from the same tiny neighborhood grade school. We had simply learned to outwork the competition.

Around this time Coach Pickett introduced Steve Brown and me to his Sunday league. This was a group of coaching friends fifteen to twenty years older than we were. They played without fail on the day of rest. The combatants had some impressive résumés, and the games tended to be for keeps. Brownie and I didn't always want to go but were *nudged* into doing so, as Coach would swing by to pick us up anyways. We quickly learned the meaning and consequences of game point. If we shot the ball, we knew it had better find the mark. We had to *earn* the right to shoot in Coach's game! If we gave up an easy shot without fouling at game point, we faced a dismal fate. Defense, hustle, and passing would keep us in the game, not shot attempts. As we learned how to play, we could participate more fully.

Coach Pickett's reach extended to track that spring where I enjoyed one particularly exhilarating experience as a member of the St. Al's track team. When the gun sounded for the mile race, the presumed winner was obvious to everyone. He was clearly a veteran, armed with real spikes, experience, and a stride worthy of his six-foot frame. In contrast, I toed the line in my sneakers on the cinder track, having never run an official race. I had, however, watched Olympic races many times on TV. I vowed to draft behind the leaders and try to kick to victory at the race's end. After two laps of drafting behind the lengthy favorite, I spotted Coach Pickett sprinting across the infield in my direction. He had taken a good angle of pursuit, something he had taught us in football, and I knew he was coming for me. After a startled double take, I heard him shouting, "What are you doing? Pass this guy and start running!" Remarkably, he wasn't panting following a sprint of his own. Obediently I bolted to the lead as we entered the turn. Passing on the outside of a turn meant I had to run farther than the wily veteran in the inside lane. Nevertheless, I took the lead for good and won going away for a new Parochial League mile record of five minutes, eight seconds. So striking was the victory that it remains for my dad the number-one athletic accomplishment of my life. The hallways paid off!

There's no better venue for enhancing your mental toughness than long-distance running. Pitted against a competitor who wants to win as much as you, the race often becomes a game of cat and mouse. To win you must push, stretch, deny, and reconfirm your own limits in order to go beyond those of your opponent. With no teammates and no obstacles, your heart and preparation are all that stand between victory and breaking. Each moment on the verge of surrender, you press a little harder until the other runner fails to respond. It's a battle as much against yourself as your opponent. Winning a long-distance race is a mental, as well as a physical, triumph—which is tough to achieve in any arena.

By the end of my eighth-grade year, I had learned a lot about athletic competition. The lessons I learned have stayed with me for a lifetime. I have never since looked at a challenge with fear. The unparalleled self-confidence and self-esteem I gained through my demanding junior-high athletic experiences gave me a leg up in the upcoming years.

A common thread that wove through these early competitive years continued to be my family and their support. What I looked forward to the most was being around my brother, Steve. Four years older, with a driver's license, he was mobile. I always wanted to do anything that he wanted to do. Consequently, we played a lot of catch, and he could throw curves, knucklers, sliders, and fastballs. I was equipped with a vintage catcher's mitt that barely resembled today's version, its sparse webbing affording little or no protection. I would brace myself firmly in a crouch while Steve signaled the pitch before letting it fly. My brother was an all-league pitcher in high school and unsympathetic towards my mitt problems, which meant I had to elevate my game a titch just to survive.

What I lived for above all else was the chance to play hoops with Steve in the driveway. Casual shooting usually gave way to a game of one-on-one. He toyed with me mostly, but occasionally I would get close. That wasn't a good thing as it usually resulted in scraped knees and torn jeans as he would drive me into the fence or onto the driveway. One bloody night I ran to the steps, a few short feet from where Mom was washing dishes, and called him every bad word I could think of at the top of my lungs. Mom never flinched, pretending she didn't hear me. Perhaps it didn't register that I could say such things. I then ran into the house and told Dad what Steve had done. His response, controlled and matter-of-fact, was, "Maybe you shouldn't play with the big boys." After a few more huffs and puffs, I was back out the door for round two. My final record against Steve was about a thousand losses to one win. We quit playing each other after the one win. It was probably a healthy decision for both of us.

It wasn't all blood and guts in the driveway. We actually had some pretty good times as a family on a less intense basis. Occasionally after dinner the whole family would play "Around the World" or "H-O-R-S-E." Stacey had a loud guffaw similar to that of Johnny Carson's vaunted straight man, Ed McMahon, on their classic *Tonight Show*. This resulted in the whole neighborhood knowing that the Stocktons were having a blast in the driveway.

These early experiences with competitive athletics and family activities combined to prepare my buddies and I, who were just a summer away from the halls of Gonzaga Preparatory High School. We were about to become Bullpups.

CHAPTER 6

The Life and Times of a Bullpup

An Assessment

A brief look into the rearview mirror to see where I stood in the summer before ninth grade would reflect a very small, undeveloped boy, under five feet tall and weighing less than a hundred pounds. I had big, even gawkish, hands and feet for a boy my size. Despite my physical disadvantages, I possessed some real natural instincts for sports, things such as anticipation and guile. I also had my share of competitiveness that I believe to be an inherited talent that was honed in the driveway with my brother.

Another asset I possessed that aided me was an overactive curiosity. Any of our household repairmen could attest to this as I was draped over their shoulder their entire service call. I learned by watching, and I was always in the way, watching. The basketball floor was no exception. Whether on the bench or in the stands, I tried to pick up and absorb other people's techniques so my strengths were not as obvious as my weaknesses.

Mom and Dad were realistic in terms of my future in sports. They saw what I saw in the mirror. But behind closed doors they resolved to raise money and make the time to provide me with opportunities in high school. I know now that they believed that each season would be my last hurrah. Thankfully, they didn't inform me of this at the time.

I did have two additional assets that were quite real—my sisters, Stacey and Leanne. They became, for me, major motivators with their individual forms of encouragement. Looking back, I see what a constant source of support they were. They always made me feel I was the best player in the league. The biggest competitive carrot driving me forward remained the prospect of beating my older brother, Steve, at anything. I never took my eyes off of that target.

Summing up, I think it's fair to say that I had no delusions of being better than anyone but knew I was good enough to get into almost any game and contribute. In spite of my physical deficiencies, I continued to dream big and compete hard. Even when I felt I was in over my head, I could usually hear Dad's words echoing in my mind: "That just makes it a fair fight."

My classmates and I graduated from eighth grade with unparalleled intelligence—or so we thought. My own subtle chinks, though not apparent to me, must have been painfully obvious to Dad. He didn't hesitate, when he felt the situation warranted, to nudge me in the correct direction. I remember one time outside the tavern while sitting on the hood of our car, talking with Dad, a friend of his walked by and said hello. I responded but remained seated. Immediately, in a guiding tone that wasn't open to questioning, Dad directed me, "You get up off your rear end when you meet someone." I knew he wasn't joking, so I popped to my feet, held eye contact, and gripped the man's hand. Meeting people correctly has proved to be an indispensable life skill that I learned in a few seconds as a hood ornament.

Dad didn't seem to find the humor that I did in many

circumstances. Bragging about having to stay after school or re-ferring to my mom, even jokingly, as my "old lady" were just a couple no-nos that invited a swift and sure punishment.

More often than not, the punishment for any disrespectful behavior was to be confined to quarters; good old-fashioned spankings had long since fallen by the wayside. I hated being grounded worse! So, being eager to free myself from the chains that my own big mouth usually wrought, I would volunteer for weeding in hopes of having my sentence commuted. Dad got a lot of yard work done that way, but it was torture for Mom to have me underfoot all day. I had too much energy to keep cooped up for long. Still, they usually held their ground long enough to improve the landscape around our house before they turned me loose ahead of schedule.

• • •

I took a break from these homeschooled character adjust-ments to attend Gonzaga Prep's Summer Basketball Camp. It was the only camp I had ever attended. It cost twenty-five dollars and went for twenty-five days. So, every day for five weeks, I pedaled Steve's heavy yellow ten-speed the mile or so to Prep early each morning to participate in both the grade-school and high-school sessions.

There, I enjoyed instruction from G-Prep legend Terry Kelly. He was widely considered to be the best player to have ever played in the league. I tried to absorb every word he said during his guest appearances. Terry's backcourt mate, Mike Kelley, was at camp every day and took me under his wing. I followed him around like a young pup and copied his every move. Mike and I took on all comers in two-on-two and won many Slurpees—the standard wager. Payment was tendered at the nearby 7-Eleven right after camp. The icy concoctions slid down easily for winners and losers alike. My colored tongue was a credit to Mike's skills. He really didn't need my help but let me hang around and learn from him.

• • •

Toward the end of that summer, my world was rocked. Mom and Dad packed up my brother and pointed him three hundred miles west to the University of Washington. I had developed, like many little brothers, a kind of a love/hate relationship with him. I had taken so many beatings at Steve's hands—not all on the court, I might add—that the thought of his absence was in some ways appealing. He also had talked me into doing many of his jobs, such as cleaning the birdcage. He paid me with broken stuff like a ham radio set that I thought was neat only because it belonged to him, though it never worked! Still, I was heartsick when he left. As they were getting into the packed car, I took off on my green Schwinn Typhoon barely saying good-bye so he wouldn't see me cry. Steve called me back to cheer me up and raise my spirits. I thought he was all right after all and was surprised he didn't hate me either. Looking back I see that he was the best big brother a guy could ask for. He made nothing easy, but he always looked out for me while including me in many of his exciting adventures.

As summer closed, I think I was better prepared to begin high school—at least in Dad's estimation. I was off to Gonzaga Prep with its high academic standards and strict Jesuit traditions. The school was focused on excellence in education with the declared mission of turning every student into "a person in the service of others." As nice as that sounds, and as important as that has become to me, it meant absolutely nothing at the time. I primarily wanted to play sports and share in the storied athletic traditions.

I don't think I needed to be told that my school work had to be a top priority. Still, the reality was that sports were what motivated me.

The first bell was still weeks away when football practice began. This is a great way to start high school, because you have more than fifty guys you know pretty well before you set foot in the hallways. Even though I had an inkling my gridiron future was preordained to be a one-year hitch, I kept my options open. I played backup quarterback behind my friend Steve Brown. I discovered that playing QB can be a painful experience for a flyweight. On every down in practice, our large and powerful center seemed to enjoy snapping the ball through my hands and into my stomach. I began most plays with the wind knocked out of me. This occasioned a quick move to cornerback where we were supposed to run as fast as we could and hit people with our heads . . . on purpose! That didn't work too well for me either.

I did have one chance to be the hero in the ninth-grade championship game. With time running out, I dropped a sure interception and touchdown that would have broken the 0–0 tie. A "pick" might have changed my life in a direction toward football. As it turned out, this was the last time I wore a Bullpup football uniform. Although I had decided that the gridiron was likely no longer in the cards, that freshman squad with our tattered jerseys, worn pads, and chipped helmets still brings back fond memories.

• • •

When basketball tryouts began, I couldn't believe how many guys battled for twelve spots on the freshman squad. The range of abilities was dramatic. I thought I would make the team but wasn't holding out for much playing time. Surprisingly, I ended up as a starter on a terrific team. We finished our freshman season as promising, undefeated league champions.

My first year of high school sports closed on the baseball diamond where I started at shortstop. As I had hoped and prayed, I was now thoroughly entrenched as a three-sport athlete at Gonzaga Prep. No longer a tenderfoot, I had earned my first stripe. I had survived my initial high-school challenges—and had a lot of fun doing so.

• • •

That summer I was invited to play AAU basketball with some Prep teammates and city rivals. We won the qualifying tournaments in the state, making us eligible for the National Championship in Frankfort, Kentucky. I think that event was the only national tournament at the time. Qualifying was a groundbreaking experience for a team from Spokane.

The Kentucky countryside was as beautiful as its storied basketball tradition. As the games began, we saw great teams and players from all across the country. I played sparingly but enjoyed the experience. Shortly after our return to Spokane, I received the Burlington-Cedar Rapids ball from Mr. Brodsky. He must have grown tired of watching me wearing the nubs off my old red, white, and blue ABA balls. I thought that ball was the most beautiful thing in the world, and it wasn't even brand-new. I cleaned my gift regularly with saddle soap, and I never let it hit the ground outside. Nobody has ever treasured a gift more than I did that ball. It got used for many years! I still have it as a reminder to me how precious a single ball was at a time when there weren't many around.

• • •

I finished the summer playing baseball. Somehow there had been no scheduling conflicts with my basketball tournaments. It was clear to everyone that my swing would never be a threat to the Ruth and Gehrig legends. As things turned out, I would play only two more years of baseball at Prep.

With the benefit of 20/20 hindsight, I can see that events were funneling me towards basketball. In an ironic twist, our football team's success my sophomore year aided me in making the varsity basketball team. As a spectator I thoroughly enjoyed the Friday Night Lights. Week after week, win after win, I watched our football team as they fought their way to the state finals. I was oblivious at the time to the fact that this success might limit the number of basketball hopefuls.

To get as ready as I could, I "laced 'em up" at G-Prep, sneaked into GU, and on weekends joined Coach Pickett's crew, often at Fairchild Air Force Base just outside of Spokane. Gini's brother Bill was a Marine captain living on base while he attended law school. He got us onto the high-security grounds and into the high-level basketball games. The competition there had a level of athleticism that we seldom found in town.

I was well prepared for tryouts but still had no illusions of making the team as a sophomore. The auditions began with a couple of returning members of our team still occupied with the state football championship. It still didn't dawn on me that their good fortune was mine as well. I tried my hardest to impress the new varsity coach, Terry Irwin. I made an effort to win every sprint and every drill. It sounds corny, but I did the same thing throughout my nineteen years in the NBA. Winning all the sprints after practice can make up for a lot of errors during practice. Coach must have agreed as I avoided the varsity cut list along with my St. Al's compadre, Steve "First Down" Brown.

With a new coach and a young team, we owned just an average record by midseason. I think Coach decided it would be a good time to start grooming me for next year and inserted me into the starting lineup. I gained valuable experience. In a game against North Central High School, I had a chance to play against Spokane's baseball legend, Ryne Sandberg, who was also a football star and a very good basketball player. The radio announcers in that game made fun of my size-twelve shoes, calling them "gun boats." At 5'6" with a 115-pound frame, I remained eligible to play in a grade school backfield. The shoes, by the way, did look odd.

I knew where my bread was buttered. I passed a lot and seldom hoisted a shot unless I was pretty certain it was going in—a Sunday League lesson with Coach Pickett. Dribbling only as necessary, I could transport the ball under pressure from point A to point B effectively. The years I had spent practicing dribbling by weaving between the basement barstools with the lights off were paying dividends. I also made a habit of knowing who could shoot and trying to get them the ball as often as possible.

We managed to reach the playoffs that year, which offered a little promise for our young and coming squad. My sophomore season had been a better beginning to my varsity career than I could have possibly imagined. Coach Irwin and the football team had given me a chance to fulfill my dreams, but I couldn't let the momentum stop there. I wanted to keep getting better.

Within weeks of the season's end, I passed my driver's license test and was behind the wheel. It took only a few days to get myself into a major pickle. I was so excited about driving that I wanted to give anyone and everyone a ride. Eventually a pal of mine, Mario Mediate, asked me for a lift home, and I enthusiastically obliged. Unfortunately, I overshot the landing zone and had to backtrack on the dirt road behind his house. Fortunately, my copilot and partner, George, had taught me a foolproof technique for navigating on loose gravel. With my teacher at my side, we began to slalom back and forth until sudden panic jumped into my hip pocket. I slammed on the brakes as Dad's gold Oldsmobile Vista Cruiser station wagon swerved and careened off a humongous curb. The curb saved me from wrapping the battleship around a massive locust tree but also popped two tires, ruined two rims, and disrupted the alignment. After delivering Mario safely home, I drove the hobbled vehicle down to a nearby tire store.

After much deliberation, George and I came up with a plan. He ran home, emptied his piggy bank, and returned with enough cash to buy two rims and fix a flat. It was all he had, so it had to work. I called Dad and told him that I had gotten a flat, and they couldn't fix it. I added that the tire guy thought we needed a new set . . . all true. After replacing the tires and the rims, I had to destroy the evidence. I backed up to the beautiful Spokane River and rolled the residual broken wheel and popped tire down the bank into the depths. To this day, I can't believe I did that. Every day, like a telltale heart, my desperate and illegal disposal of the evidence beats on my tree-hugging conscience. I didn't summon the courage to tell Dad the truth for almost twenty-five years. I was still nervous when I broke the news at age thirty-nine. Better late than never, I guess, although the deception isn't a proud moment in my life.

Thankfully, driving remained largely uneventful for almost a year after this incident. Then came a double whammy. I received my first speeding ticket while driving home from a party. When I found out there was drinking going on, I left and began the drive home. Within minutes, a set of flashing police lights appeared in my rearview mirror. Where is the justice in that? I had done the right thing, and I got punished! Perhaps it was poetic justice for the swerving, lying, tire-in-the-river caper.

Shortly after that I rear-ended an old Buick while driving Mom's Toyota Corolla. The collision didn't even knock the dust off the Buick's bumper, but the Corolla sustained considerable damage. My parents had bought the second car when Steve began driving to school and practices. It was still Mom's car, however! And we had to ask her permission to drive the car. In a practical sense, we (the kids) were the primary pilots, but Mom and Dad retained the right of refusal regarding our privilege to drive the car.

I knew I had to tell Dad about this collision. I worried about it for hours. When he saw the damage, he managed a signature head scratch before asking if anyone was hurt. "No," I replied. "Were you horsing around?" he asked. "No," I echoed (not this time, anyway). "Well, the car is only a tool. Take it and get an estimate tomorrow," he replied. I was surprised at his soothing and thoughtful response but shouldn't have been. Dad was at his best when things went badly. Even today, at eighty-four, he rallies when we need him the most.

My relief was erased a month later when Mom and Dad informed me that due to the ticket and the accident I would have to pay for my own insurance. The premiums would reflect my recent driving record. I was going to have to mow a lot more lawns and shovel a lot of snow if I wanted mobility. My lack of protest might have surprised my folks. I think they expected some negotiation at least.

I often wonder how my friends and I survived our early years behind the wheel. Our brushes with injury or even death come back vividly now when my own children drive off behind the

Mother-son dance, Gonzaga Prep, circa 1978. Left to right: John and Clemy Stockton, George and Mrs. Bernie Lucas, and Steve and Mrs. Ella Brown.

wheel or as passengers in a friend's car. I automatically recall one frightening night when someone must have been watching over me and my friends. Our driver that evening, without notice, had to quickly slam on the brakes, which resulted in a perfect 180-degree spin in the middle of a three-way intersection. When the smoke from the tires cleared, we peered out from our unbuckled perches to see that his Suburban had come to rest about eight feet from a concrete wall that protected the freeway far below us. We were lucky that night, and many others as well. I pray that stupidity isn't hereditary.

• • •

My hair-raising exploits didn't curb my growing enthusiasm for basketball. Coach Pickett continued to include Brownie and me in the Sunday League as well as trips to the Air Force base to take on all comers. At that time Coach was still one of the best scorers I had ever seen. Brownie and I were just along for the ride and in the process I learned the rules of the courts. These were great times that also provided a pretty steep learning curve!

• • •

The summer before my junior year, we made another quest for an AAU national championship. This time we were headed for Huntington, West Virginia, under Coach Pickett and his pal Mark Bowman. We triumphed again in the qualifying tournaments. I learned a little something, however, in the town of Moses Lake, Washington—something that stuck with me throughout my career. Our game schedule for the qualifier had been changed without notice. At the last minute, my teammates and I learned of the change from another team staying in our motel. The coaches and our parents were at dinner, so we had to literally run to the gym. I felt sick and had a fever, so the team and I decided that I would coach. Eventually, Coach Pickett made his way to the gym, where he stormed to the bench, disregarded my ailment, and put me into the game. We were down by fifteen points at the time.

I had a great game, and we pulled out a win. Frankly, my stats had little to do with the win; our attitude just changed when our fearless leader arrived. I did learn, however, that I could play when sick. Sniffles, hangnails, or little bruises can keep some players out of the lineup for days or weeks. That night I learned that I could actually play better if I was slightly ill. Maybe I concentrated more. I don't know for sure. I do know that this tendency held up throughout my career. I also learned to brace myself when quality opponents announced they were sick. They usually put together a gem of a game against us.

For the second year in a row, we were going to AAU Nationals. For over three weeks before the trip, we practiced every morning at six o'clock. Coach managed to incorporate "hallways," his famous running regimen, at the larger high school. One of the guys on the team, who was unaccustomed to Coach's ways, tried to avoid the running by hiding in a locker at Prep. Upon discovery (and cheaters always got discovered) he was sentenced to hard aerobic labor. By the time we left for Huntington, he was perfectly trained for a marathon. (He actually went on to run several marathons as an adult and later became a successful college basketball coach.)

We received some added domestic training along the way as well. Coach Bowman and his nine-month-old daughter Sarah joined us each day at practice. Players not involved in a drill were assigned babysitting duties. We rocked her and gave her a binky or a bottle when it was warranted. As you might expect, the trainees occasionally lost track of the crawling speed demon. The alarm whistle would blow and a search party would bolt to nearby steps and doorways. One time we eventually found her under the bleachers, caked in black soot—or whatever you call the smorgasbord of filth found under bleachers. By the time we finished basketball/marathon/babysitting training, we felt prepared for anything we might face in West Virginia. Boy, were we wrong!

We opened against a Chicago team that was pictured in the program as a ragtag bunch. We found out looks can be deceiving, as several future Division 1 players took the court. One was a guard whose picture was haphazardly stuck in with the team as though it was an afterthought. For three quarters we battled and pressed the Windy City squad, managing a tie. As the fourth quarter began, their photoshopped guard, Isiah Thomas, took matters into his more than capable hands. He dribbled through and around our press, feeding big men for dunks as if it was a layup drill. At 5'9" he added some dunks of his own to his cache of steals and blocked shots. Foreshadowing his later fame, the diminutive guard was everywhere. He repeated his act, and then some, in the championship against a highly touted seven-footer, Earl Jones, and his DC teammates. Isiah blocked the towering figure's skyhook—twice—and dunked on him at the other end. Thomas was the best player I had ever seen, and he was about my size. To say that he raised the bar for me would be a gross understatement. I had played well but finished the day stunned. Normally I would have brushed it off and gone on to the next activity. But on this day Coach Bowman had to retrieve me from a dark motel room and redirect my attention away from the amazing Chicago guard who changed my basketball world. Eventually I rejoined the crew and managed to get kicked out of the pool for high-altitude acrobatics—backflips off of the lifeguard chair and the gazebo.

The next day we lost again to another loaded team from Colorado. This concluded the tournament for us. All that remained was an educational trip to Washington, DC. As we approached the Capitol, we stopped near Sharpsburg, Maryland, at Antietam—which is the site of one of the deadliest battles in the Civil War. We learned that in one day, over twenty-two thousand casualties occurred on that battlefield.[1] The tragedy and the significance of those sacrifices were not as palpable to me then as they are now. Still, it caused us to pause and reflect about how easy we had it. Our worries had been limited to making jump shots and layups—theirs had been a struggle for freedom and life itself. Many of the soldiers in that battle were young men our age. The significance of this was not lost on our team.

• • •

At last, my senior year was at hand. I gained still another invaluable lesson outside the classroom. Toward summer's close, I decided to try a local gym with a tough reputation in search of the best competition. The facility was known as the East Side Youth Center (ESYC). I had heard they had great games, but I had never ventured to the gym, considering myself an unwelcome outsider. Even though I remained under the impression that it was an "all-black" court and that I might not be welcomed, I thought I would give it a try. With my Burlington Cedar-Rapids ball under my arm, I walked into the ESYC. As I passed through the game room on the way to the gym, all action stopped like a scene from a movie. Every sound and activity came to a halt. A lone ping-pong ball was left to bounce unattended as all eyes shifted to me. By the looks of it, this was an all-black venue after all. Feeling a little uneasy, I continued into the gym where I got the same reaction. Shoes quit squeaking and games ceased to be played; a dead silence filled the gym. I guess they weren't expecting an ivory guest.

As play resumed, I took a seat and asked, "Who's got next?" I was picked up for the following game and went on to have a great time. The play, as it should have been, was just about basketball. The court at ESYC had the same rules, intensity, and camaraderie as every other place I had played. I'm not sure I have ever had more fun playing than I did that day. The experience and the lesson have stuck with me. I was happy to learn that Spokane didn't have gyms that were "all anything." I have never been in a game where color mattered. The only question is always, "Can you *play*?"

THE LIFE AND TIMES OF A BULLPUP

• • •

My senior team finished solidly but without any earthshaking accomplishments. I did break the city scoring record, and the whole team signed the game ball. (That ball currently resides in the Naismith Basketball Hall of Fame.) College scouts weren't exactly beating down my door. I received interest from only three Division 1 schools: University of Montana, coached by Mike Montgomery; University of Idaho, coached by Don Monson; and Gonzaga University, coached by Dan Fitzgerald. I visited these schools with the notion that there was no way I was going to Gonzaga. It was too close, too familiar, and I was tired of getting kicked out of the gym.

This intense recruiting "battle" boiled down to this: Contrary to my knee-jerk declaration, I didn't want to leave home and the benefits of the world's greatest mom. So, on Easter Sunday, 1980, without prompting or significant thought, I blurted out to Mom and Dad, "I want to go to Gonzaga." They were openly happy with my choice. To their credit, during the process they had never hinted at a preference. The decision was mine to live with, good or bad.

My high school Bullpup basketball career formally closed at the state basketball all-star game. I played there with two future teammates and friends: Dave Clement, a forward from Burien, Washington, who, like me, was already signed at Gonzaga; and Bryce McPhee, of Tacoma, Washington, who would sign after favorably impressing Coach Fitzgerald, who had watched the game. The question now became could I run with the big dogs just down the street?

CHAPTER 7

A Walk across Hamilton

My higher education began before my first trek down Boone Avenue into a Gonzaga classroom. I had taken a construction job in the summer of 1980 that was quite an eye-opener. Officially I was a card-carrying laborer, although I was immediately tagged with the sarcastic label of "college boy." Sporting new work boots, clean and unscarred, with matching hands, I fit the bill. With that bottom-of-the-totem-pole designation, I experienced some "interesting" situations.

I began as a Shop-Vac operator on a school building project, where my assignment was to suction up a stubborn and recurring puddle from a concrete floor nearly every hour of every day for two weeks. Its source was rainwater that fell from the roof directly into the future elementary classroom. A quick repair of some flashing would have saved me some damp, monotonous work—and the company about two weeks' wages. My insights remained unspoken, and the problem persisted.

Another assignment pitted me against a second-story room stuffed to the ceiling with construction debris. My job was to make it disappear. The garbage was headed to the landfill via the "big" dump truck, with me behind the wheel. A little green behind the ears, I managed to successfully deposit my load but forgot to engage the emergency brake as I hopped out of the cab to talk with the attendant. As we completed the paperwork, the empty behemoth began rolling backward. I was able to run it down and avoid disaster, but I was permanently labeled "dump-truck deficient" and forced to surrender the keys to the big rig.

A couple of weeks before school and basketball were to begin, I decided it was time to give my notice. I scheduled a meeting before work to inform the owner and to thank him for the job. Surprised to see me at his office, he made a couple quick calls then immediately fired me on the spot—for "lack of productivity." I didn't need a college degree to figure that one out on my own, although his reason for firing me is a mystery that baffles me to this day.

I didn't fight the judgment, nor did I present my case, because the timing was perfect. It gave me the extra week that I had already been looking for to get ready for basketball

I did, however, have a sick feeling about being terminated. I felt as though I'd let down the company and the people who had helped me get the job.

• • •

As I stepped into my first class of my freshman year, I spotted a beautiful girl named Laura Stepovich with the word *History* colorfully written on her notebook. I decided to plunk down next to her in the first available seat. She was seated near the door, which helped my decision. "Hello" was as much conversation as I could muster until some weeks later. The ice was finally broken when I looked out the door one morning and saw a carbon copy of Laura walking by. After a couple of awkward inquiries, I found out the

The Stepovich twins, Nada and Laura.

pedestrian was her identical twin, Nada (Nādă). We finally had something to talk about besides history.

By midterm I felt comfortable enough to ask Laura if I could borrow her class notes, and she generously consented. Organized and legible, her notes were perfect for my study habits—bare-bones memorization. My notes, on the other hand, were scattered and disorganized. I couldn't effectively listen to the teacher and write at the same time.

As promised, I swung by her dorm room to pick up the notes, where I was formally introduced to her mirror image. Suddenly nervous, I nabbed the notes and quickly departed, offering thanks on the move.

I soon found out Laura had a boyfriend. That was okay, as she was probably out of my league anyway. So, I "settled" for her twin sister. At least that is what I like to tell people. (Actually, this "settling" bears little resemblance to the truth, but it makes a good story.) After twenty-five years and counting of wedded bliss, I still think I made the right choice—or the right one chose me. This whole story comes later. It was time for basketball—the reason I had come to Gonzaga.

• • •

My freshman year we had a senior-dominated team. Don Baldwin was our no-turnover, no-nonsense point guard. He didn't look impressive athletically, but he always seemed to succeed. Don teamed up with a couple of characters named (Hugh) Hobus and (Ken) Anderson. These guys were like Pierce and McIntyre on *M*A*S*H*. They always pushed that fine line of authority with comic bravado, but they were also tough guys and reliable players.

Our coach, Dan Fitzgerald,[1] was a larger-than-life character and one of the most interesting people I had ever met. He brought his extensive knowledge and irrepressible Irish personality to the court for each practice. He walked in talking, walked out talking, and talked all the way through any meeting you had with him—luckily his stories were often spellbinding. Coach even talked when he drove. Everyone buckled up in his car, and it had nothing to do with the law. While driving, he would spend more time looking and gesturing to the backseat while delivering one of his gems than he did watching the road. I think Coach drove by Braille, listening for honks and relying on the rumble strips on the road's edge to stay in his lane.

• • •

Practice always began with one of the many "Fitz-isms" I would hear over the next four years: "The best thing about freshmen is they become sophomores." Actually, our freshman class was very good, but thanks to Coach's ego-stifling observations and some humbling lessons at the hands of our elder teammates, we didn't suspect we were very good at all.

Whatever the case, we, just as all freshmen do, had a lot to learn. Playing successfully on the road at the Division 1 level was first on the list. Part of that challenge was living on $12 per day for meals. The players often pooled our resources just to secure a dozen powdered donuts for a shared, high-powered breakfast of champions, saving the bulk of our funds for the all-important pregame meal. That didn't always work out very well. One time I was scurrying out of Kentucky Fried Chicken with my supper when I caught my foot on a curb and performed a face-first dive across the asphalt. My box flew out of my hands and busted open, spilling the entire feast. Scraped and dirty, I could only watch helplessly as an enterprising seagull swooped down and took my biscuit, adding insult to injury. Some of the older fellows generously offered to chip in to buy me another entrée, but I was too steaming mad to eat—or even talk, for that matter.

Food wasn't the only road hazard. I learned quickly just how difficult it is to win on an opponent's home court. In an overtime game at Loyola Marymount University, our senior forward Ed Taylor had to sink a couple of free throws to clinch the win. The catch was, in LMU's old gymnasium, students could easily reach the bars that supported the backboard and basket. And they weren't opposed to some unauthorized gymnastics. Eddie was shooting at a moving target! Somehow he found the bottom of the net—a valuable lesson from a senior leader about adjusting to conditions on the road.

We finished my freshman season with a 19–8 record and naïvely assumed we had a chance at making the National Invitational Tournament (NIT). We didn't get a sniff.

• • •

John playing for Gonzaga University; Blair Anderson (#35) trailing the play.

There were, however, some interesting sidebars to the season. Oddly, my greatest contribution as a freshman hoopster was actually made off the court in Dr. Carriker's history class. Whenever he had a freshman basketball player in class, he employed a fun and generous tradition. However many points that player scored in the game immediately prior to the final exam would be added as extra credit to *everyone's* final exam score. Normally this gift proved to be of little significance since freshmen didn't usually play or score enough to greatly impact anyone's test score. Fortunately for students in this class, a small NAIA school from Montana was slated for the contest before the final exam. It was a mismatch from the start, so Coach emptied his bench. Though I had played regularly in most games, I got significantly more time in this one. I tallied eighteen points, to the delight of all my classmates, who were grateful for the boost.

ASSISTED

• • •

During the summer between my freshman and sophomore years, I was introduced to weightlifting and our trainer-turned-strength-coach, Steve Delong. In 1981, weightlifting was just starting to become a mainstream training aid for basketball players. Prior to that time, the practice was frowned upon in the world of hoops. Conventional wisdom held that too much bulk ruined your shot. Steve believed otherwise and was determined to change all that.

Mr. Delong was also fairly new to the game my freshman year but seemed like a gnarled veteran. He looked like a mustachioed drill sergeant. He was expressionless and seldom spoke. He quickly gained favor with Fitz because he could be trusted with *any* responsibility. His duties ranged from trainer, nurse, and psychologist to carpenter, bus driver, and mechanic. Overworked and underpaid, he never complained. I avoided him my entire freshman year, even when I was hurt. That was fine with him; he hated freshmen. It was also fine with me; he was intimidating.

The weight room was becoming his territory as he welcomed me and my backcourt mate, Tim Wagoner, into his lair for the first time that summer. In the beginning, the process was extremely painful. I couldn't bench a hundred pounds nor do a single chin-up.

By summer's end, I could confidently bench 135 pounds ten times. Chin-ups were also no longer a chore. On the basketball court, bigger guys no longer casually bumped me off-course. I could use my newfound speed and explosion to my advantage. Weight training became one of my most beneficial and enduring habits—one that contributed positively to the rest of my career. The confidence gained by doing the work yourself is probably the best aspect of weight training. When you see and feel the benefits, you begin to believe in yourself.

• • •

I only had to walk back across Hamilton Street for my sophomore year to begin. The Stepovich twins had a much longer journey but reappeared no worse for wear to begin their second year. Nada and I saw a lot of each other "by chance" in and around Kennedy Pavilion (KP). She played volleyball in the fall and because KP was the only gym on campus, our paths often crossed.[2] I guess we were dating, but it was hard to tell. We didn't date during the season, nor in the summers, and I certainly never spoke of having a steady girlfriend. All I know is that Nada invariably returned in the fall with her web woven a little more tightly than when we had parted. That at least is my version of events.

• • •

School continued to go well, as I actually felt I was growing up. One sign of this was my newfound friendship with Professor Tom Gilmore. He taught Eastern philosophy, which included Buddhism, Taoism, and Hinduism. He was an authentically bohemian eccentric who had me thinking seriously about topics beyond my previous horizon. I wasn't planning on philosophy as a career, but I loved learning and opening up my mind to new ideas and thoughts, especially ones I had previously considered ridiculous. Professor Gilmore was, in large part, responsible for that growth.

The Jesuits certainly shared a hand in my progress as well. In one of my classes, I found myself seated in front of a priest who was notorious for giving athletes a hard time. I hoped for the best but prepared for the worst. When I received my grade from my first essay I noticed Father Siconolfi had circled the word *it's* (I had used it as a possessive pronoun, rather than the contraction for "it is.") and scrawled in the margin the anguished words, "I wept when I read this!" I learned that Father was just passionate about literature and had a good sense of humor. He was fair but demanding and became one of my favorite teachers.

• • •

Even while Nada and I were officially dating, I remained pretty secretive about her with essentially everyone. This was partly due to my shy nature and partly to avoid the incessant questions. My MO was revealed in one funny incident with Coach Pickett and Gini. It was my birthday, and going out to dinner with them had become an annual tradition for the three of us. They always asked me if I would like to bring a date, and I had always declined. On this evening they picked me up as usual and headed to the restaurant. When we were about a block from my house, without explanation, I suddenly snapped, "Take a right," followed equally abruptly by, "Take a left," and ultimately, "Stop." Coach Pickett responded with catlike reflexes to my directions. I jumped out of the car, ran into the dormitory, and, to the amazement of my hosts, reappeared shortly with Nada at my side. I felt as though I was treading water, so the introductions were as short and terse as my directions had been.

As we drove the forty miles to Wolf Lodge, a rustic steakhouse near Coeur d'Alene, Idaho, the conversation was limited. Bringing Nada had temporarily set me back. When we arrived at the restaurant, however, I was in no way inhibited from putting on my customary eating exhibition. For starters, I dazzled my date by consuming several Rocky Mountain oysters, a local

Nada Stepovich playing volleyball for Gonzaga University.

delicacy. I then proceeded to wolf down forty ounces of steak before moving on to Gini's leftovers. This was also a delicious tradition. I added a massive Idaho baked potato, baked beans, some deep-fried bread, and topped it off with dessert. I wasn't showing off, as this was standard operating procedure. Nada seemed unaffected by my gargantuan appetite and displayed a hearty appetite of her own. We both had had a very nice first off-campus date—with other people present to boot! Even so, I remained essentially hush-hush on matters concerning Miss Stepovich and myself.

• • •

Moving from the classroom back to the school of hard knocks, I secured a summer job at Washington Water Power, our local utility company. This turned out to be my favorite summer job, as almost all of my coworkers were college students. Our boss, Scott Morris, was a former GU student and gym rat from the days when I was sneaking into GU by myself. The job itself matched my personality. As part of an energy saving program, we wrapped hot water tanks with insulation. We were paid on an escalating scale based on performance. The more we wrapped, the greater our wage per hour. Hustling door to door, crisscrossing the county, climbing into crawl spaces, closets, and wherever, we pursued our quest to blanket the most tanks.

It was dirty work that provided its share of adventure. A revolting example of this occurred as we were passing a fellow wrapping crew while driving down the street. We tried to stop them to say hi, but they forcefully waved us off before halting. From a safe distance, they pulled over to inform us that they had just come from an elderly lady's home that housed twenty or thirty cats in the basement—unattended. It was so dark they couldn't see the plague that had befallen them. The fleas and stench eventually overwhelmed them. The crew was on their way to the hospital where they could be sprayed down and their clothes literally burned. They told us later that they had felt something beneath their feet and thought it was just basement dirt—instead, it turned out to be several layers of the cats' "deposits." Talk about hazardous duty!

There were many other strange on-the-job encounters that summer. Once I was invited into a house and escorted downstairs past a room filled with live, ceiling-high marijuana plants. The windows were sealed and blue lights were humming. I was no expert on the subject, but I knew they weren't cornstalks. The homeowner said he trusted me because I looked the part—so much for his judgment. My judgment, however, proved to be only slightly better. I quickly wrapped the tank, increasing my rate of pay, and made a rapid escape, choosing to remain mum regarding the crime scene I had seen.

The incident put me on edge for some time. Days later when I entered the home of some obviously ardent Billy Graham supporters, I treaded warily. Signs advertising his ministry peppered the yard, front window, and the bumper of their car. Inside the house there was a lot more of the same. Strangely enough, I felt more at ease in the cornstalk house. Just as I feared, the homeowners immediately engaged me in a religious conversation. "Are you Christian?" was the polite but ominous question. Without hesitation, I blurted, "No, I'm Catholic!" Now that was bright! Catholics are Christians, but I think I got my point across to the residents. I didn't want to discuss my soul or anyone else's while I was elbow deep in fiberglass.

Everybody on this job could have used a little of the reverend's forgiveness from time to time, as pranks ruled the day. A classic prank was insulation theft. Each morning we stuffed our individual trucks full of tank wraps. Making the big bucks, however, required a second trip to the warehouse to reload. Time was money, so crews working nearby but away from home base sometimes took advantage of a coworker's full truck, trading empty scraps for the lush pillows of wrapper's gold. My partner Fred and I fell victim to just such a dastardly attack one morning—but we knew who had done it. Immediately we returned to the warehouse, which was stacked to the ceiling with hundreds of rolls of fiberglass. We quickly reloaded our truck. Then one of us (I'll never tell who) climbed the stack of wraps all the way to the top with the culprit's ten-speed bike hung over a shoulder. At the summit a perfect knot was tied, suspending the bike from the rafters. By day's end the pyramid of wraps had dwindled to nothing by virtue of the day's labor. When the prankster returned, his

Bryce McPhee and John at Gonzaga University.

Schwinn was a dangling ceiling ornament some twenty feet from the ground. Victory was ours.

• • •

Comic pranks, summer workouts, and life without a girl-friend came to an end as I began my junior year with the optimistic notion that we should have a pretty good team. The guys had worked hard that summer, and we were all getting better as we matured. We *felt* ready to make a leap forward, but I think we still pictured ourselves as blue-collar players without the pedigree to be champions. Franklin Roosevelt once said, "The only limit to our realization of tomorrow will be our doubts of today."[3] I believe deep down that was probably true of us.

There was, however, one game that year that permanently changed the way we thought about ourselves and the way people thought of Gonzaga basketball. The transformation began on our final journey back to Chicago to sacrifice ourselves to the mighty DePaul Blue Demons. They were nationally ranked, undefeated at home, and had blasted us in the previous two meetings. They were confident of their pedigree. We didn't really expect to change that and paid only lip service to the possibility of an upset. We found out, however, that strange things can happen any time you "lace 'em up."

As I recall the game, our big guys, Bill Dunlap, Jason Van Nort, and my roomie on the road, Bryce McPhee, were playing very well in a low-scoring affair. With less than ten seconds remaining, we were down by one point and had the ball under their basket. Coach Hillock, who had taken over admirably when Fitz resigned his position after my freshman year, called time-out and carefully mapped out our closing strategy. Expecting pressure, he designed a play to advance the ball quickly and get a good shot early enough to have a chance at a rebound. At the sound of the referee's whistle, Bryce inbounded the ball perfectly, leading me to open court. Amazingly, most of the press was behind me as their defense broke down. My eyes lit up as our forward, Dave Clement, broke away for an uncontested layup—but this was far from a sure thing.

Dave had nicknamed himself "The King of Composure" our freshman year, after a less-than-composed effort in our Blue/White scrimmage. He vowed to all mankind that day never to revisit his frantic, nervous behavior. He had kept his promise with uninterrupted success for the previous couple of years. As I reflexively lofted the ball over the remaining defender into The King's waiting hands, I prayed for his continued composure. Panic set in (mine) when I saw him relapse and pick up his dribble too far from the hoop. This left an awkward distance to shoot the layup. To avoid a traveling violation, he jumped prematurely—off the wrong foot—turning the sure "gimmie" basket into a prayer. The ball came off the backboard hard as the clock ticked towards zero. As I sprinted toward the basket, hoping for a chance to

John playing basketball at Gonzaga University.

tip the ball in, I was suddenly blocked out of the play by a very large Blue Demon. What I didn't know was that The King had recovered from his "brick" and miraculously reappeared on the other side of the basket to tip in his own miss, over the top of both me and the defender, as the horn sounded. It was the most incredible play I had ever witnessed. Over the years, in my mind's eye, I rerun Dave's tip-in in slow motion whenever I feel I need a pleasant memory.

That night at the hotel, the lines were buzzing with congratulatory calls. The next morning, upon returning to Kennedy Pavilion, student intramurals stopped to give us a rousing cheer. It was apparent that this was more than just a big win. It was a monumental victory that raised the bar of our own expectations, shined a new, special light on Gonzaga's program, and piqued the basketball interest in our community.

Due to great coaches and players who have believed, Gonzaga

has since gone on to achieve considerable basketball notoriety. Twelve years separated that game in Chicago from the start of Gonzaga's run of great teams, and I like to think that Dave Clement's tip-in might have been the spark that led to igniting the Bulldog flame. I know the win changed the way we thought of ourselves.

• • •

Throughout my junior year, the classroom continued to provide humor and lessons not found in the pages of a textbook or inside the lines of a basketball court. One experience involved a study group friend and a test of character. Lori Abraham was also a varsity basketball player as well as an eventual housemate of the twins. I saw a lot of her, and we became best of friends. As fellow business majors, we crossed paths daily in the classroom. This particular semester we had both missed our final exam in Mr. Sladich's marketing class due to basketball travel schedules. Professor Sladich wore many hats during his forty-six years at Gonzaga. He was a highly regarded campus fixture. On this occasion he had graciously permitted us to reschedule the exam.

Lori and I arrived together over Christmas break for the makeup final. Without ceremony, Professor Sladich handed us our exams, closed and locked the door, and left us alone to our challenge with only these parting instructions: "Bring this to my office when you're done." As the door latched shut, we looked at each other and smiled. With our notes and textbooks within arm's reach and unmonitored discussion opportunities available, it appeared we were poised to ace this final. But after a couple of inquiring glances, we made a silent agreement that we would not betray the trust Mr. Sladich had placed in us. Instead, we buried our heads and went to work. It was a good moment for both of us—one that has paid dividends for many years. Later we admitted to each other that in earlier years we might have buckled under the temptation. We hadn't, and we were proud of ourselves. Lori and I learned a lot about trust and responsibility being around Harry Sladich.

The classroom wasn't all about deeper lessons. In Fr. Bargen's speech class, we learned while we laughed—often at ourselves—as we wrestled with public speaking. Father quickly made it clear that to be successful the speaker must know his topic. With that in mind, I delivered two gems, if I do say so myself. One was a demonstration speech on tapping a beer keg. Using props acquired from Dad's tavern, I expertly tapped the stainless-steel barrel and drew a glass of golden malt beverage. The schooner had a perfect head. (Actually, I could have done this by age eight having watched Dad over the years.) Throughout the speech Fr. Bargen audibly chuckled in the back of the room. His evaluation of my speech was an exuberant A. He vowed that if I had offered him a taste test, he would have added the plus!

My second successful oration was a descriptive speech I had drafted from my Wolf Lodge experiences with the Picketts. First, I graphically described the texture, taste, size, and shape of a Rocky Mountain oyster. Nobody in class seemed to know what they were. After confessing that I initially thought these were actually some sort of seafood that came from mountain streams, I divulged my secret: "These are, in fact, the testicles from unsuspecting bulls who give their all for our enjoyment." Amid the sounds of people gagging and groans of disgust, I heard the uproarious laughter from Fr. Bargen in the back. An enthusiastic A was again his verdict. For the first time in my life, I was actually enjoying public speaking.

Coach Pickett had forced me for years to speak at the banquets of whatever team he was coaching at the time. Those were some of the worst days. My stomach would churn and my palms would sweat all day until the banquet ended. Public speaking was never something that came easy to me. Coach would not cut me any slack, and I couldn't get away from him. Mom and Dad wouldn't intervene either. Though giving a speech in public never became easy, I got better. Even today I still have those miserable sensations and minor discomforts when I speak publicly. I do feel confident, however, that I *can* speak when I have to. There is nothing worse than the prospect of jumping into the water if you know you can't swim. With the help of these early uncomfortable experiences with Coach Pickett and Father Bargen, I know I can at least dog-paddle to the shore.

Most accomplishments that we take pride in don't come easily. In a situation unrelated to basketball, someone once told me, "You wouldn't understand (my struggle), because everything came so easy to you!" Without protest, I smiled and accepted the compliment. Inside, however, I noted how mistaken peoples' perceptions can be. I guess we all assume that the other guy has walked an easier road without the benefit of taking a single step in his shoes. I think this is a common mistake. Successful individuals often make their journey appear easy though usually it comes from tens of thousands of hours toiling, working, tinkering, or even playing at their chosen endeavor.[4]

In my case, I have no doubts I was born with some gifts that meshed well with athletics and specifically basketball. I would have loved, however, to have been 6'5" with a forty-inch vertical leap—because those guys *must* have it easy. Much of my success has come from many hours of hard work, but I readily admit practice was most often fun and never a drudgery for me. One thing is certain, I spent many lonely Friday and Saturday nights shooting, sometimes in a snowy driveway. I didn't feel as though much came easily.

. . .

Summer workouts again included attacking the weights with Steve Delong—more furiously than ever. By my senior year, the drill sergeant had become a dear friend and adviser. We called him "Doc." He was probably more demanding than ever because he knew how far we had come and how far we could go.

Steve was the glue that held athletics together at GU at that time. He taught us that we could survive, and even thrive, in humble settings. Coach Jerry Sloan used to tell me, "You have to ride the old yellow school bus once in a while in order to really appreciate things." Well, we had a lot of appreciation, because we rode in an old blue military bus or a hobbled van with bent axles. It was usually driven by Doc, because he could fix the old warhorses with wire and a pocket knife if necessary. Coach Sloan would have seen our circumstances as "character building"—and they were.

. . .

There is something very special about a senior year. I had heard this from the coaches and older players from day one. When that time finally arrived for me, I understood them for the first time. An air of confidence flooded over me that was as palpable as it was unexpected. The light went on, and the game started making complete sense. It was getting easier. Shots that I wouldn't have attempted a year ago I now took without hesitation. I believed every shot would find the bottom of the net. Every pass felt right. I knew what my opponent was trying to do before he did it. The mind-set just happened. Of course, I still missed shots, threw bad passes, and got beat on defense, but not as often. When you have that kind of faith in yourself, you simply perform better than you ever thought you could. I sensed the same shift in my senior comrades. I had never been so confident in myself and in my team. We felt prepared for anything that came our way.

• • •

Our senior season began with such hope. We were good and deep. Then, shortly after our annual ten-mile warm-up run and our first few weeks of practice, we experienced some disheartening defections. One starter and a couple of backups inexplicably left the ranks.

Shorthanded but not entirely broken, we arrived in Portland, Oregon, for the prestigious Far West Classic tournament in the middle of a treacherous ice storm that crippled the city. Upon arrival my roommate, Bryce McPhee, probably our best player, was informed by "Doc" that he was done—out with a fractured fibula. We were now down to eight.

We regrouped and played inspired basketball at the venerable Classic. Out of the chute, we tamed a highly regarded Robert Morris squad. Later in the tournament we would get another try at our neighboring nemesis, Washington State University, coached by George Raveling. Only weeks before, we had lost to them on a heartbreaking last-second shot. I thought at the time it was my last chance at them, and that was a crushing blow. Being a local boy and losing all four years to the "Cougs" was beyond disappointing. In truth, few people but us expected that we would win those contests. Washington State's one-sided victory column hid a spirited rivalry.

If we could cash in on this rare second chance, the win would be almost as big as the DePaul victory a year earlier. The game

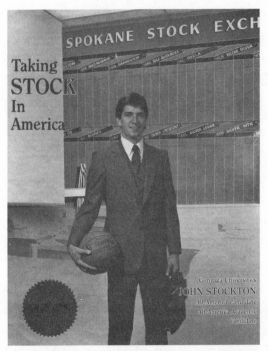

The "Stock Report," 1984, written by Dale Goodwin.
The suit was rented for the photo shoot.

unfolded in an ominously identical fashion to our earlier loss. It again came down to the wire as play stretched into overtime. Having fouled out in regulation, I helplessly watched the extra period with a dreadful sense of déjà vu. As before, we were up by a point with seconds remaining. At the other end of the floor, Chris Winkler, the same heroic shooter responsible for our earlier loss, released an eerily similar dagger from the same spot over our same defender, Jeff Condill, at precisely the same final tick of the clock. This time J. C. found enough stretch in his long arms to cause the shot to fall short. This was a sweet, sweet victory in a time-honored venue. Our center, Jason Van Nort, had performed incredibly in the overtime, and J. C. solidified his status as an up-and-coming star for the Zags.

• • •

J. C. had come to Gonzaga during the summer as a displaced veteran from Southern Illinois at Edwardsville. They dropped their program, leaving his game homeless. At a time when I was away at my brother Steve's wedding in Butte, Montana, Jeff had come out to Gonzaga to look at our campus. I had to rise early in the morning after a late-night reception just to make his acquaintance. I blew through the mountain passes like the ancient flood waters from Lake Missoula to get back and work out with this Midwestern orphan. The audition began the moment I returned. After some spirited games, a roundtable hoops discussion followed. Jeff had a fearless "show me" attitude and loved to compete, even if it was just in a summer pickup game. He knew he would fit in nicely with our team and we were likely to become good friends.

Despite our remarkable play in Portland, we didn't win the event. The Oregon Ducks made sure of that. If my memory serves me correctly, Blair Rasmussen, a future NBA seven-footer, combined with a teammate to make nineteen of twenty shots, which insured that our Cinderella slipper wouldn't fit after all. Regardless, we seemed to capture the hearts of the Portland fans who rallied around our shorthanded team. I was selected MVP of the tournament. To say I was surprised is an understatement since we had finished third. Only about five of us stuck around to watch the final game between Oregon and Oregon State and the all-tournament selections. Even my parents had returned to the hotel. It was quite a thrill to see my teammates' reaction to the announcement. A prestigious list of previous winners, all of whom filled NBA rosters, added luster to the moment. That was the first time that someone actually mentioned my name in the same paragraph with the NBA.

ASSISTED

The euphoria soon subsided as our wheels nearly fell off completely with yet another crippling injury. Jason Van Nort, our second leading scorer, tore his ACL. We were down to seven and needed a practice player. To remedy this situation, our staff dipped into the intramural pool for a boost. Being a small school, it was unlikely they would find Kobe Bryant working over the student population. So, they settled for the next best thing, Gino Cerchiai. Standing 5'7", he courageously accepted the call and joined the squad. He would never have passed anyone's eyeball test but filled in admirably for us. Gino worked hard and was a good teammate. We all appreciated his efforts. Eventually he made a brief appearance in a league game to the delight of the fans and his teammates.

As the season progressed, we were flying by the seat of our pants, a new experience for all of us. Individual creativity flourished without the threat of bench time. We only had two subs, so Coach couldn't realistically pull anyone out of the game. Scratching and clawing, we were somehow perched atop the WCAC and poised to win the conference with four games remaining.

The last straw was a case of bronchitis I contracted late in the season. The illness cost me valuable practice time and fifteen pounds. I played in our remaining games but only feebly. J. C. rallied us with a monster game against Santa Clara, but that was our last real hurrah. We limped, coughed, and crutched our way into a fourth-place WCAC finish. To this day, I'm very proud of our team's effort. Nobody gave up.

The coaches around the conference must have appreciated our predicament as Gonzaga was well represented in the All-League selections. I was named Player of the Year despite our fourth-place finish. My Bulldog teammates took great pride in that accomplishment. I was given the award, but *we* had earned it.

It is hard to believe that a season so cluttered with disappointment and individual tragedies could also provide incredible opportunities for one lucky person. Fate deals some strange hands. I was in no position to complain.

• • •

After a relaxing spring break I returned to campus and was forced to hit the ground running. Unexpectedly, I had received a phone call that ignited a string of events and opportunities that would propel me to the NBA draft in late June of 1984.

In the spring I attended every class that my travels would permit. Although I missed class more often than I preferred, I managed to maintain a decent grade point average. This was due to a number of factors. Our fourth-year business classes were focused on team skills and group projects, so it was my good fortune that my classmates carried me. I also need to thank my teachers for their consideration during my absences. I hoped that I had earned their understanding by my history of never skipping classes. In any event, I graduated on time with a 3.3 GPA.

The unexpected call I had received came from the NCAA. They were preparing the Emerald City for the Final Four at the King Dome. During the tournament they hosted an all-star game. Elite players from around the country who weren't fortunate enough to make the finals were invited. Ricky Ross from the University of Tulsa had backed out suddenly, and they needed somebody to replace him. I was only 270 miles away and could leave immediately. In business school they teach, "Location, location, location." The maxim was true in this case as I was the most available option. After a quick, forty-five minute flight, I joined the *Who's Who* of college basketball. A few of the highest rated players didn't attend this game on the advice of their agents so as not to adversely affect a presumed lofty draft status. I, on the other hand, was trying to *establish* a draft status. The all-star game went well as far as those types of contests go. Our team, the West, tried to play together, which made it an enjoyable experience. I played pretty well and managed a few points and a couple of assists. Truth be told, however, I drew more attention with my defense, which included a couple of blocked shots. I logged that little bit of information about getting attention for defense and then enjoyed front row seats for the Final Four games.

Bobby Knight was the color commentator for that all-star game. As it turned out, Coach was the skipper of the 1984 Olympic Team as well. I don't know if one thing led to another, but when I returned home, I received an invitation to the Olympic Trials in Bloomington, Indiana. Even if my play in Seattle had nothing to do with the invite, Coach Knight at least knew who I was.

However the invitation came to pass, it was a dream come true. I immediately informed my family, friends, coaches, and teammates. I was a little surprised that I just couldn't wait to tell Nada. She was student teaching at the time at St. Al's grade school just blocks away.

Uncharacteristically, I searched Miss Stepovich out in the teachers' lounge. She appeared at the door with a shocked look on her face. I immediately shared the good news. I also told her of my nearly fatal mistake of almost throwing out the invitation. The envelope it came in looked like a sweepstakes notice. Given my eagerness to share the good news and her excitement on hearing it made it apparent to both of us that maybe there was more to the relationship than we previously thought. Time would tell.

I boarded the plane for Bloomington, surrounded by well-wishers as I set off in search of a lofty dream.

. . .

The University of Indiana is a huge and beautiful campus, but there wasn't much time for sightseeing. As I recall, more than seventy-two athletes convened on campus, each hoping to fill one of the twelve spots on the Olympic roster. I never considered the odds. I just got ready to play. Three grueling two-hour practices a day would test the hearts and minds of the hopefuls. The first practice divided us by position. This was a real *Who's Who,* but, truthfully, I didn't notice. My nose was to the grindstone as I picked up full court and dogged the ball for ninety-four feet every play. The afternoon practice combined guards with forwards, adding beef to the equation and ramping up the competition. The evening practice was all-inclusive. Nearly every big name in college basketball and a few from the pro leagues in Europe were in attendance. Again, I was oblivious to everyone's pedigree. When I called home, I was invariably asked about Michael Jordan, Patrick Ewing, or Chris Mullin. "I don't know," was my response because at that time, I only knew them by the random numbers they were assigned for the tryouts.

Practices were intense, which was appropriate considering the level of competition and the prize at stake. After nine grueling practices in three days, one very good player declared in the locker room, "Just cut me and put me out of my misery!" Those of us within earshot shared an empathetic chuckle. Fortunately, I was holding up pretty well but had no idea how the staff viewed me among the multitudes. My first inkling came when the coaches culled the herd by cutting about fifty athletes. I barely flinched at the news that I was still part of the remaining squad. I took little notice of who had gotten cut. My attention remained focused on the next practices.

Three-a-days persisted, only with fewer numbers, which increased our individual repetitions. On the bright side, I started to get to know some of the guys I had been toiling with and against during the tryouts. I met Karl Malone at a lunch table, and we hit it off immediately. Open and friendly, his Louisiana charm welcomed conversation, and I obliged. He was an underclassman at the trials but was comfortable with everyone, and I really enjoyed being around him. Charles Barkley also sticks out in my mind as he held court regularly at meals. He seemed to know everybody personally. Chow time was extremely entertaining as the "Round Mound of Rebound" seemed to have reserved energy stores for his comedic routines.

That segment of the tryouts ended with another cut. Again, I don't recall knowing who was released at the time. I do know that I was invited back as one of the final twenty players for the US Olympic Team.

Unfortunately, the next stage of the tryouts began the evening prior to my college graduation ceremony. So, the night before I left Spokane to return to Bloomington, I went to my last college dance. The band played "Johnny Be Good" as a parting good-luck wish. Once again, I was sent off with enthusiastic and touching support that I hadn't expected. I knew I carried the hopes and dreams of many Spokanites and fellow Bulldogs as I boarded the plane back to Bloomington.

Only two of the remaining twenty players hailed from the West Coast: Leon Wood[5] from Cal State Fullerton and me. We arrived together after our long flights but late for the first practice. Coach Knight had already begun his introduction to zone strategies when we stepped on the floor. Having missed a portion of practice, I leapt at the chance to participate when the opportunity presented itself. Being in the front of the line and jumping at any opportunity to play had always helped me in the past. As it turned out, I should have watched this time and waited awhile until I understood the system. I wasn't horrible but had missed the point that Coach was trying to make. For me, practice ended much better than it began with some two-on-two matches that paired me with Chris Mullin. Chris was a delight to have as a partner. The St. John's phenom seldom missed a shot and could really pass the ball. I followed the same technique that had won me so many Slurpees at G-Prep with Mike Kelley—that is, set screens and roll to the basket. Chris did the rest. I don't think I'm misstating the facts when I say we were undefeated against some unbelievable duos.

As we gathered the next morning for another grueling practice, a shrill whistle blast silenced the bouncing balls and we gathered around Coach Knight at Assembly Hall, University of Indiana's arena. We scrimmaged more with fewer bodies, and I learned why everyone agreed that Jordan and Ewing were so good. It was a joy to play alongside them.

Following practice, we broke for lunch. As I took my first bite of fish sticks, the coaches entered the room unannounced and, five days earlier than expected, announced their choices for the 1984 Olympic Team. My name wasn't on the roster. I tried to absorb the news without outwardly flinching, but finishing the meal became a struggle. Sitting motionless, I heard Coach Knight point out to those of us who had been cut, "If someone else was coaching, you might have made this team. However, if someone else was coaching, you might not have made it this far." Truer words were probably never spoken. Disappointed beyond belief, I couldn't argue his logic. It felt a little like getting fired from my construction job all over again, only much worse. My loftiest dream was shattered. It had been within arm's reach; now it had evaporated.

• • •

I packed my bag and boarded the van to the airport along with some pretty fair players who had suffered a similar fate. Terry Porter, Maurice Martin, and I were entertained by Charles Barkley's monologue all the way to the airport. He didn't seem too upset. Unlike the rest of us in the van, Charles knew that his future was set. He was a cinch to be a top-ten draft pick for the Philadelphia 76ers.

I boarded the flight about the time my classmates were receiving their diplomas in Spokane. Having missed graduation and lost out on a dream in the same day, I was deep in thought on the long journey home. Arriving at the gate at Spokane International, I was greeted by a loyal friend of Mom and Dad's, Mr. Zinkgraf, who was backed up by a crowd larger than either of my send-offs. Embarrassed about being cut, I hadn't expected this kind of a homecoming, and I sheepishly worked my way through the crowd of supporters not saying much. I can't describe the intense gratitude I felt toward everyone who came.

I went to Jack and Dan's for the last remnants of the graduation festivities. This included Nada, Laura, and their roommate Lori Abraham, who commandeered a prime booth to celebrate with their parents. I decided to join them along with my own folks as we all merged into a single group following some mass introductions. Mom and Dad were both at the Tav that night. It was their custom on graduation weekend to be on hand to say good-bye to the departing students. As always happened, Dad had developed a rapport with many students—a relationship that often began when, as freshmen, they had tried to sneak into the tavern as underaged drinkers and that developed into genuine friendships as they came of age. Dad broached the generation gap better than anyone I have ever known. He knew everyone's name, and the young people admired and respected him as a genuine friend.

The evening played out in a relaxed fashion. I thought my parents had only known about Nada for a few weeks. I say "I thought" because they astounded me throughout my life with what they did know. Often it felt as though the whole world reported directly to Dad any news on my siblings or me. In any event, I don't think they suspected a girlfriend until I accidentally let the cat out of the bag with the help of Ma Bell.

I had called home collect from the Olympic Trials to keep everyone current on the news in Bloomington. Immediately following that conversation, I again dialed collect but added "person to person" for Nada Stepovich. This ensured that the person you were calling was at home and willing to accept the charges. With no cell phones or calling cards, this was the only reliable method of communicating without carrying a roll of quarters in your pocket. The problem was that I accidentally redialed Mom and Dad's number instead of Nada's. My heart sank when Mom again answered and the operator barged in with her well-rehearsed spiel: "John Stockton calling 'collect, person to person' for Nada Stepovich." I couldn't hang up, and I couldn't explain.

• • •

It was getting late in the game for Nada and me as we sat in the booth at Jack and Dan's. With college officially over, graduates tended to go their separate ways. My future was completely uncertain. Nada's immediate plan involved returning to Fairbanks to begin paying off her student loans by securing a teaching job. In Alaska at the time, 10 percent of a student's debt could be erased annually if they brought their skills back home and put them to work. Since most of Nada's family lived in Fairbanks, her decision made sense.

So, with separation looming, we both agreed that we wanted to find out if our relationship merited more time and effort. Nada decided to stay in town a few more days with my promise that I wouldn't ignore her the whole time. Since she said "the whole time," I figured I could live up to that bargain. She was not a high-maintenance girl.

Over time Nada had proven herself. Early in the spring I invited her out for a nice steak dinner on my dime. I chose a new restaurant that wasn't too pricey, mostly because they were running a two-for-one promotion. After a delicious meal, I busted out my coupon. She wasn't the least bit offended. In fact, I gathered that she thought it was an intelligent and practical ploy. To stay within their budgets, Nada and her housemates had been dining on Top Ramen all year, so this was a feast for her. She appreciated my frugality almost as much as the hearty meal. We could have eaten much better had I just invited her home. That wouldn't have cost me anything. Except in my mind it would have implied something, something I wasn't prepared to admit—yet.

Nada's first visit to our house took place on that holdover weekend. Mom was painting the kitchen and had enlisted my help. Dave Clement volunteered, bringing personality and height to the project. At 6'8", "The King" could easily roll and brush the ceiling without the use of a ladder. Mom giggled at just how simple he made the process appear. She had grown fond of Dave over the past few years as he always managed to knock on our door right around suppertime. Mom would unfailingly invite him to dinner, and he always accepted with perfectly rehearsed reluctance. Utilizing impeccable manners, he devoured mounds of food as he spread the praise like butter. Between bites he would carry on with comments such as, "Mrs. Stockton, that was the most incredible food . . . !" If you remember the show *Leave It to Beaver*, you can see he had a little Eddie Haskell in him.

From the onset I was committed to the project until it was completed, which meant the entire day. Suddenly that morning I remembered my commitment to Nada. I phoned her immediately and invited her to join our work crew. Responding to her first invite to the house, she arrived in minutes and comfortably donned some old family paint clothes. Unfazed by the odd date, Nada shined in this glamourless work environment. She blended admirably with The King, the messy paint splatters, and, of course, Mom.

From a pragmatic point of view, Nada had all the outstanding attributes of a prospective spouse. To begin with, she could catch and throw a football. She also wasn't spoiled rotten and could mix comfortably with the fine dining set as well as the Top Ramen crowd. This Alaskan didn't require constant attention and could work with the best of them. The icing on the cake was that she even looked good in old paint clothes. One might think that all of these qualities should have sealed the deal. I can only say that I wasn't quite ready, and Nada was probably in the same boat. We did, however, decide that our story deserved more time to unfold.

Even though our future together was far from settled, Nada and I talked a lot about marriage, having kids, religion, and life in general. We didn't discuss these topics as though they were items on a punch list preparing to march down the aisle. Instead, these discussions tended to be more philosophical, as we stumbled across subjects and problems that might arise if we ever did tie the knot.

• • •

Nada and I appeared to be a good fit. Her family history might explain why. She came from great stock. Nada was born in Fairbanks, Alaska, as the eleventh of the thirteen children of Mike and Matilda Stepovich. She missed the top ten, following her twin sister, Laura, by only a few short minutes.

The twins' father was born Mike Anthony Stepovich on March 12, 1919. He was the son of "Wise Mike," a tough Yugoslavian immigrant and one of the pioneer gold miners in the Fairbanks Creeks area around the turn of the century. Gold mining was a well-established and lucrative business there at that time and persists to this day. When young Mike decided he wanted to go to law school rather than follow in his father's successful footsteps, Wise Mike colorfully expressed his disapproval with the comment, "Mike, take care of your feet, 'cuz you certainly don't have a head!" Young Mike shrugged off the warning, opting to make his own mark in the political world rather than in the frozen soil.

His boyhood years were spent living with his mother, Olga, in Portland, where he developed into an outstanding baseball player. In fact, scouts from the Boston Red Sox came to his house to try to sign him and two of his teammates, Johnny Leovich and Johnny Paveskovich. Olga was born in the old country and saw no future for Mike in athletics. When he was given a choice between college and the Red Sox, her motherly opinion was clear: "What do the Red Sox know?"

Apparently quite a bit: Paveskovich went on to enjoy a Hall of Fame career and became a household name; the baseball world

A WALK ACROSS HAMILTON

Mike Stepovich, last Territorial Governor and first State Governor of Alaska.

knows him as Johnny Pesky. He legally shortened his surname so all the letters could fit in the box score. The Pesky Pole, a landmark in Boston's Fenway Park, remains today as a testament to his contribution to the Sox. Leovich, however, gave Olga a .500 batting average. His only claim to fame was that he finished his career going one for two in a single game for the Philadelphia Athletics in 1941 before joining the US war effort with the United States Coast Guard.[6]

Mike was destined for greatness—in time. He initially attended the University of Portland but completed his undergraduate studies at Gonzaga. Later, he acquired a law degree from Notre Dame. He moved back to Alaska following a hitch in the Navy to practice law and learn the art of politics.

In 1957 he was appointed Territorial Governor of Alaska by President Eisenhower. A year later, at age thirty-nine, he graced the cover of *Time* magazine when he led Alaska into statehood, remaining as her first elected State Governor.

The Baricevic family. Standing, left to right: Kenneth, Matilda, Cecelia, Elizabeth, and Ferdinand. Sitting, left to right: Kata (Katarine) and Louvre (Lawrence) Baricevic.

• • •

Nada's mom, Matilda Zorka Baricevic, was born in Portland, Oregon, in 1922 to immigrant Slavic parents, Louvre and Kata (Lawrence and Katarine) Baricevic. Matilda was one of five children—two brothers and two sisters. Louvre worked for the city's St. Vincent Hospital where he was the chief engineer. Exceedingly capable, Nada's grandfather built their impressive family home on land he had acquired over time from St. Vincent. (The family actually shared a driveway with the ambulances!) The home still remains within the family.

Neither of Matilda's folks spoke a word of English in their house as they staunchly clung to their Slavic heritage, which remains important to the family to this day. The Baricevic children were left to learn English on their own at school.

Matilda, along with her siblings, attended the Cathedral School run by the Holy Names nuns. The kids were so bright that as soon as they gained a command of their adopted language, the nuns immediately bumped each of them up a grade. Their academic prowess continued as they all graduated from college and many had successful careers after earning PhDs—quite a feat for any children of immigrant parents. For women at this time, these accomplishments were even more extraordinary.

Matilda graduated from the University of Oregon and took one year of law school. She gave up the law to pursue social work for Catholic Charities. Talented and energetic, she stepped away from a blossoming career to rear thirteen children. She considered her successes as a mother the highest possible achievement.

• • •

Following her holdover painting weekend, I drove Nada home to Medford. I spent a couple of pleasant days getting to know the Stepoviches in their element. In addition to enjoying great company and spirited discussions, Mrs. Stepovich and I had a great time baking pies. We used fresh fruit from the orchard, and she taught me some of her tricks along the way. She could really cook! It wasn't uncommon for her to have a couple of pies in the oven as her fresh homemade bread cooled and dinner for fifteen was being served. Every bite was a treat.

One of their dinner traditions, however, threw me for a loop. They ate very late at night, usually between nine and ten o'clock. I was used to eating dinner at six o'clock sharp after Dad's shift. At my first meal with their family, I was so hungry I could have eaten skunk on a platter by the time the food arrived. To make matters worse, dinner, when it finally arrived, came in the form of "zuppa," a Yugoslavian soup which is essentially a broth containing rice-sized pasta known as piti-piti. It seemed quite a bit less than a hearty meal. Half starving, I slurped down about nine bowls thinking that was dinner. When I finally came up for air, Matilda was bringing in meat, potatoes, and vegetables; basically everything I would have included in the soup. *Better late than never*, I thought as I filled up on the late-arriving meal—a little wiser.

The next day I drove back to Spokane alone as planned. Nada and I agreed to exchange occasional letters but made no further commitments. My immediate goal was to try to play basketball professionally. That summer would provide exciting and unexpected opportunities.

PART III

Perspectives of a Professional

Perspective: The Flight of a Sandpiper

Shall I fly beside a road or soar a bit beyond,
Glide above an ocean or hover 'round a pond?
A matter of perspective how you go along
Pathways are rather certain, an old familiar song.
Walk within the pace, and the view is self-restrained.
To go as others have, the limit's pre-ordained.
No risk to march in step—the same monotonous sounds
Things are nice and cozy if you never leave the grounds.
The journey in the lead, a different matter now
Nothing's quite for sure, no directions how.
In the quest to stay ahead, you set yourself apart;
It's a little tougher go, takes a little bigger heart.
The plateau's for timid souls, an easy place to stay,
The summit's in the clouds; the climb is every day.
Peaks become the valleys, new mountains there to find
Boundaries pass away, limits are in the mind.

—KERRY L. PICKETT

CHAPTER 8

Guardian Angels

After graduation, making a team in the NBA was still a long shot, but the idea wasn't as farfetched as it was prior to the Olympic Trials. Many of my friends and supporters were furious with Coach Knight for cutting me and keeping his Indiana freshman, Steve Alford. I understood his decision and appreciated what he and the selection committee had done for me. He provided me an opportunity to play and be seen at the highest competitive level. The fact that he kept me as long as he did was a massive boost to my NBA chances.

The Olympic Trials didn't provide the only leg up on my journey toward the NBA. Opportunities continued to pop up, seemingly out of thin air. Maybe a guardian angel was working overtime. In hindsight I can see a series of improbable events that took me on an unlikely path I could never have imagined. Whatever the source of the helping hand, I am grateful to have had it.

• • •

As I mentioned, the Far West Classic was the first time I showed up on any NBA radar screens with anything other than

111

a passing blip. The event was a premier holiday tournament and being selected MVP was a nice feather in my cap. Slowly but surely I added to my résumé and gained momentum as opportunities to enhance my draft chances continued. As opposed to the more highly touted college players, I played in every event I could find. This included a lucky break in being a last-minute replacement for the all-star game at the Final Four in Seattle in 1984. In addition to valuable exposure, I received the added bonus of gaining a highly respected advocate. Jack Gardner, the retired Hall of Fame coach of the University of Utah, was working as a scout for the Utah Jazz at the time. He watched the game in Seattle, was impressed with my play, and passed that on to the Jazz. I guess you never know who might be watching. In my case, Coach Gardner was and provided the biggest assist of my career.

I played in as many predraft camps and tournaments around the country as would have me. I was invited to play in the WIT in Lewistown, Montana, and another tournament just down the road in Malta. My teammates and I, which included future Houston Rocket standout Jim Petersen, bunked on mattresses thrown on the floor of vacant houses in the small towns and ate for free at the local diners. The experience reminded me of the basketball barnstorming days of yore.

I had to dip into my own pocket to get to the next tournament in Portsmouth, Virginia, but was well taken care of by my host family, Don (Mr.) and Mike (Mrs.) Taylor from the moment I arrived. The teams were selected ahead of time and I was treated to the honor of being coached by former Boston Celtic and Hall of Fame legend Dave Cowens. Coach Cowens seemed to trust me to make good judgments, especially at the end of games, which capped off a wonderful experience.

Back home in Spokane, the man who recruited me to

Gonzaga, Dan Fitzgerald, took calls on my behalf. He had worn many hats for me over the last four years: coach, mentor, tutor, friend, and advisor. He was perceptive, so he could sort through the scuttlebutt coming out of the various NBA front offices and try to clue me in accordingly. Apparently George Karl, then the head coach of the Cleveland Cavaliers, had been most open about his interest in drafting me. In future years, whenever we crossed paths, he would often joke, "Remember, I was the first"; and he was!

The Portland Trail Blazers, with their legendary coach, Jack Ramsay, also showed interest and took some action. They flew me to Portland for a workout and a psychological evaluation. Evidently I passed, because they indicated they intended to select me with their twenty-sixth pick early in the second round. Things were starting to get exciting.

Whenever I was home, Fitz would set up a personal "combine." He assembled some local high school stars together with my Bulldog teammates, J. C. and The King, and ran me through the ringer while constantly rotating fresh players against me. Using demanding drills as the platform, he was the master at subtly tweaking my techniques to achieve large benefits. I couldn't have had a better mentor to prepare me for the challenges ahead.

Whatever reputation I had developed as a player wasn't enough to elicit an invitation to the premier predraft event in Hawaii. Only the highest rated players were on that list, and understandably nobody dropped out of that event. I was invited to the next best thing, though, the Chicago predraft camp. It was akin to the modern combines. We were weighed and measured. Our jump-reach was dutifully recorded. Mine was thirty-three inches. It is the only testing stat that I remember. Chicago was different than the other camps, because we actually practiced with the team we were going to play with all week. We were placed under the guidance of Coach Fred Carter; some guys called him "Mad Dog"—but not me. I surely wasn't going to irritate anyone with a nickname like that. He ended up being a demanding but helpful and pleasant man who coached and worked in NBA basketball circles for many years.

I stepped into a great situation in Chicago. We had a gem of a team. Two players who stick out in my mind were Jerome Kersey, out of Longwood University in Virginia, and Kevin Willis, out of Michigan State. Both were thoroughbred athletes and great basketball players; they were special. It didn't feel as though any of us were trying to market, or "show" ourselves. We played relaxed, undistracted, and unselfishly through an undefeated week. Undoubtedly, we helped each other into the league as each of our projected draft positions improved following camp.

I had a moment in the presence of Utah Jazz coach Frank Layden that week but didn't realize it. I was boarding an elevator at our two-towered hotel, which seemed to have about a hundred floors per tower. I employed normal elevator etiquette: push the button, look straight ahead, and offer no conversation. Coach Layden was apparently behind me the whole time, sizing me up. Years later he confessed that he had scanned me like "a piece of meat," assessing my height, sturdiness, length of arms, and so forth. Whatever his thoughts were, he kept them to himself until draft day. We never spoke, because I never knew he was in the elevator. This was pretty amazing because Coach was a very large man in those days; I must have been in my own little world to overlook him in such a small space.

As draft day approached, I remained hopeful but not anxious. Fitz confirmed Portland's intention to draft me with their first pick in the second round. I was merely hoping for a chance to try out. If that materialized, where or with whom would be frosting on the cake.[1]

• • •

With Trail Blazer mania on the brain, I waited for the announcements on draft day. Fitz poked his head in at the house to tell me, "Keep your eye on Utah." Apparently they had called him earlier—only once—to ask a few questions but never followed up. I didn't even know where they were positioned in the draft.

Many friends and neighbors crowded into Mom and Dad's house to watch the event. The interested mob inched closer and closer to our lone TV set as the first round progressed into the teens. I was trying hard not to anticipate anything. Fitz's tip, however, spiked my interest in Utah, who was up next. The commissioner approached the stand and announced, "With the sixteenth pick of the first round, the Utah Jazz select . . ." I took a deep breath, ". . . John Stockton of Gonzaga University." The house erupted. I bolted outside and lingered around the driveway trying to make sense of what had just happened, so I missed the reaction of the Utah crowd, which was not entirely favorable. Moments later the phone rang. It was "Hot Rod" Hundley, the voice of the Jazz, calling from the Salt Palace to congratulate me and to let me know that the fans were saying, "Who?" not "Boo!" after the announcement. I think it was probably a mixture of both from the Utah faithful, but it didn't matter. I never heard their reaction. I'm not sure I heard anything for quite a while.

The rest of the day was like walking around in a dream. I remember feeling as though I was a spectator in a tremendous celebration. People weren't clamoring to shake my hand. In fact, their focus wasn't on me at all. The elated group was caught up in the joy of the moment; someone they knew had been drafted to play in the NBA! That occasioned quite a party that day at the Stockton house. There was a genuine sense of happiness that seemed to deeply reach everyone present.

Many of the people there had traveled with the St. Aloysius team eight years earlier to the grade school championships in Seattle. They were happy for me but also for themselves because that's how it was in our neighborhood. When *anyone* did well, everyone knew they were part of that success. These friends, neighbors, teammates, and coaches had each played a direct role in me being drafted that day. It was pretty special to share the experience with them.

• • •

Fitz capped off the celebration with a quick press conference in Kennedy Pavilion at Gonzaga. He proudly presented me with a T-shirt that read "Forever a Bulldog" and displayed the logos of both GU and the Jazz. That shirt currently resides in the Naismith Basketball Hall of Fame.

After the press conference, Fitz recommended that I ask the Jazz for some game tapes. This seemed like a good idea since I didn't know much about the team at the time. Ultimately I did ask for the videos, which turned out to be a coup of sorts. When the media searched for information about the Jazz's first round selection, they discovered that I had asked for the tapes and were duly impressed. Apparently nobody had done that before.

The rest of the blanks concerning the unknown kid from Spokane were filled in by Jazz coach and general manager Frank Layden. He proudly announced with his Brooklyn accent, "He's Irish, he's Catholic, and his Dad owns a 'bah' (bar). What else is there?" I knew Salt Lake was largely a Mormon community and

John, far right, getting ready to scuba dive at Coach Kerry Pickett's mountain cabin. Looking on, from left to right, are Jeff Condill, Stacey Stockton, Nada and Laura Stepovich, and Steve Delong.

wondered if those comments might work against me as I didn't understand the relationship yet. I never needed to worry about that as I would soon find out from my own experiences.

Within a few weeks I was invited to Salt Lake City to attend a banquet honoring the '84 team as the Midwest Division champions. The town was still abuzz from their unexpected and sudden success. One of the young public relation guys who I would get to know well over the next two decades, Dave Allred, hosted me for most of the day. Assistant Coach Scott Layden took time before the banquet to drive me through Big Cottonwood Canyon. The tree-filled gorge was stunning and located only minutes from downtown Salt Lake City. It was easy to see why Scott was so inspired by the spectacular canyon! Over the years I would retrace that route many times with visiting family and friends.

Following our drive, Scott and I prepared to join the

*John playing for the Utah Jazz with Mark Eaton
and Bobby Hansen (in background).*

celebration. Before the gala began, Coach Layden introduced himself to me. He was warm, welcoming, and funny from the start. Our conversation was short as Coach was wearing many hats that day and had to keep moving. I also met a couple of future teammates as well, men who would become two of my best friends, Mark Eaton and Thurl Bailey.

Mark was as striking as the mountains. Listed at 7'4" and 290 pounds, with shoulders as wide as the key, he tended to grab your attention immediately. Equally impressive and immediately obvious was Mark's gracious demeanor. Completely comfortable in his own skin, he was both intelligent and personable right from the start. He made me feel welcome in Utah and fortunate to be on his side. I immediately knew I would like my new home.

That was further confirmed moments later when Thurl Bailey made his way over to me. An impact rookie the prior year, he was a relative newcomer himself. Before joining the Jazz, Thurl had

Thurl Bailey at the John Stockton School of
Basketball talent show, circa 1991.

been a star for North Carolina State where he was coached by the irrepressible Jimmy Valvano and had won a national championship. He greeted me with his trademark handshake (he would actually snap his fingers around your gripped hand while shaking it) and proceeded to treat me as he would a younger brother. Completely under Thurl's wing from that point on, I met a lot of nice people and felt very much at home.

As the banquet ran its course, I was officially introduced. After standing most of the time next to Thurl, who stood 6'11", I must have raised more than a few eyebrows when I stood and waved like the other guys did. At 6'1" and 175 pounds, I think they were all looking for more of me.

I returned to Spokane armed with film of the Jazz games I had toted back from my visit. Fitz set up additional workouts to help me prepare. NBA teams don't wait for a player to get ready; either he is or he isn't. Windows of opportunity are easily missed. I had been drafted, but I wanted to make sure that when called on, I could perform. My preparation formula was simple: Fitz would furnish the know-how, and the rest was up to me. I resolved that my conditioning would never be an issue. I intended to be in the best shape of anyone on the team. That much was within my control. I was going to be ready.

There was, however, one small remaining hurdle to contend with: The uncomfortable business of my contract! League rules prevent any player from attending camp without a signed agreement. Through my agent, Jim White,[2] I found out that negotiations with the Jazz had stalled. Normally, a first round draft choice tends to get slotted monetarily between the guy in front of him and the guy in back of him, and the dollar amount is generally guaranteed. In my case, the Jazz were forced to play differently, saddled with unique financial constraints at the time. As a result, they had grudgingly offered me two years guaranteed at the NBA minimum salary of $75,000 per year. It was a lot more money than I could have made working for a living. (In truth, I would have played for free.) Nevertheless, they had drafted me with their first round selection, and we thought they should play by the rules.

Because of these negotiation difficulties, the Jazz rookie camp began without me in September of 1984. Technically, I was a holdout. To make matters worse, Coach Layden got on the then-fledgling ESPN channel and emphatically announced, "His replacement is in camp right now!" Coach was playing hardball. Armed with my new business degree, I decided to resist the threats, holding firm that their offer was ridiculously low. I refused to budge. The truth was that I was scared to death, fearing I had blown my chance to play in the NBA. I told Jeff Condill after a preseason workout, "I think I'll have to go to Europe now. I'm done!"

The next morning the Jazz finally buckled under the strain. They raised their offer by a whopping $5,000. I agreed on the spot. The deal was struck at eighty grand. With all the high-level finances behind me, the time had come to pursue the unimaginable—actually playing in the NBA. I sold my "Vette" (Chevette), packed my clothes, and moved out of Mom and Dad's basement for the first time in my life.

My contract was guaranteed for two years, but I felt certain it would be only a one-year hitch. I didn't doubt my own ability at that point but was convinced the Jazz would soon realize their mistake and send me packing. Everything was based from that point forward on that notion. I would save money and live sparsely so I had something to show from the whole experience. It was a mind-set that worked for me. I would practice and play as if there were no tomorrow. In this hunkered-down mentality, I was oddly comfortable and relaxed about the challenge. The way I saw it, I really had nothing to lose.

However, a lot of people were counting on me. I didn't want to let any of them down. I wanted to make them all proud. My foot was in the door and if failure greeted me, so be it. I would have had some great experiences, lessons, and a little financial starter kit to show for my efforts. But I was ready to give the NBA my best shot.

CHAPTER 9

A Foot in the Door

"Act as if everything depended on you;
trust as if everything depended on God."[1]

—St. Ignatius Loyola

W hen I arrived in Salt Lake City for my rookie season, I was immediately whisked away to have a physical examination performed by the Jazz medical team. Mostly this was standard operating procedure—giving blood, supplying a cough here, providing a sample there—but with a couple of twists. While submerged in deep water, the players were asked to climb onto a scale and exhale aggressively in order to determine our lean body mass or body fat. Following the "baptism," as the therapist, Moe Forsyth, referred to it, we were directed to a treadmill with monitors attached to our freshly shaved chests. The medical staff wanted to ascertain our levels of cardiovascular health and conditioning. Because of these shaved areas, we looked like mangy dogs as we began the stress test.

Apparently I made an instant impression when I asked, "What is the record time for this treadmill exam?" It wasn't supposed to be a contest. Most guys ran only as long as required to complete the workup. Some worked a little longer so as to not look lazy. I looked at it a little differently and wanted to win both the body fat and stress tests, whether anyone else was trying or not. In the years to come, Karl Malone and I competed for the lowest body fat until we both got below what the staff thought were safe levels for a season of competition. Each of us teetered between one and three percent. As for the treadmill test, I broke the existing record that year and my own record in each of the seasons that followed. That is, unless Dr. Shields had been stroking my ego for nineteen seasons.

Russ Shields is the extraordinary physician who administered the treadmill test. I trust his skill and judgment to this day. I still remember him pretending to be irritated by having to wait until my run was complete. My best guess was he enjoyed watching my personal battle with the machine.

The rest of the day, and most of the next week, was spent at my new home away from home, the Salt Lake Hilton hotel. The Hilton housed all of the Jazz hopefuls throughout training camp. I bumped into Coach Layden there in the gift shop where he offered me a bit of sage advice that I held dear throughout my career: "Don't change who you are. Don't start growing a beard [as if I could!], buying fancy cars and jewelry, and playing the part." Taking his wisdom to heart, I didn't change hairstyles, lifestyles, or even the length of my shorts for two decades. If nothing else, I was coachable.

While in residence at the Hilton, we were armed with a real per diem—fifty dollars. This was a significant raise from the twelve-dollar poverty line at Gonzaga. I took the liberty of splurging for real meals at the hotel's Mexican food restaurant—every day of camp.

Turbocharged with tacos and enchiladas, I boarded the shuttle for the first time to our Westminster College practice facility with the other rookies and free agents. When we arrived, even before I could lace up my sneakers, I was directed to an office in the upper corner of the balcony of the old Payne Gymnasium to sign my contract. Although it was only a formality, and a subdued one at that, it was an exciting moment for me. I had a foot officially in the door and hoped the rest of me would follow!

Scurrying down the antiquated steps, I entered the world of the NBA. In the confines of that old gym it didn't seem too different from what I was used to—until practice started, that is. Every player was great—the best of the best from where they hailed. I began learning from the first whistle: how to move, get open, and shoot lay-ins at a distinctly different level. In drills, especially full-court drills, some of the veterans, glad to avoid extra running, volunteered their place in line. As a result, I sometimes ran drills two to three times more than most of my senior colleagues. I absolutely loved it; the more the better. Even as I aged, I never gave up my spot in line. I tended to enjoy and look forward to practice.

Shooting was a primary focus of nearly every session. The drills were intended to be performed at high speed and with great intensity to mimic the game environment. The theory is, if athletes train at game tempo, their actual shooting percentages will mirror those in practice. I agree. The catch is, it's nearly impossible to duplicate NBA game speed in a practice. The full-tilt competitive gear is special and can't be readily summoned in the practice environment, but you can come close.

I received a little taste of that battle speed and intensity in our initial scrimmage. The first time I touched the ball, Rickey Green, the Jazz's veteran point guard, picked me in the backcourt. He led the NBA in steals the prior year, so it wasn't as though I was his only victim. Moments later, Jeff Wilkins blocked my first layup attempt. He did this with emphasis (and "extreme prejudice," I might add). After practice I asked him, "What should I do in that situation?" Without really considering my question, he barked back with the gruffest voice he could muster, "*Pass the ball, Stock!*" Wilk was pretty decent to me after that, and it proved to be good advice.

My conditioning yielded unexpected benefits. I wasn't tired, so I picked up the offenses quickly, being able to focus on the plays rather than fatigue. I played well that day and throughout camp, despite the embarrassing opening scrimmage. When asked about my game, Jerry Eaves, Rickey's backup the year before, told the coaches, "He can play." He was recovering from knee surgery at the time, and I was competing for his spot. So it was surprising to hear, years later, that he had given me that plug with the staff.

Back home, Mom and Dad must have been dying for any information. Since cell phones were still ten to fifteen years away, calls home were made sparingly. I did call Fitz to let him know that I didn't think my NBA teammates were *that* awesome. The truth was, they were awesome, but I felt it was possible for me to compete at the professional level.

Personnel decisions were made quickly. Cuts to the squad were hard on everyone. Scott Layden performed the distasteful role of the Grim Reaper. Before practice he would walk up to a player and say, "Coach would like to see you in his office." We all knew what that meant. In his office, Frank confirmed the bad news and gave his honest assessment to the player: "I think you are not an NBA player," or "Perhaps if you were stronger or a better shooter you might be NBA caliber," or even, "You are definitely good enough, we just don't have a spot for you right now." The guys always seemed to appreciate Coach Layden's wisdom and candor.

I felt bad for everyone who met this fate. I had become friends with these guys. The whole notion of a dream lost bothered me, and I empathized with each of them. After observing my reaction to one of these decisions, John Drew, a veteran scorer who had been through a few of these situations, grabbed me by the arm and said, "Just be glad it ain't you, Rook!" Truer words were never spoken. Still, I tried to wish them luck while concentrating on my path forward.

• • •

Our first preseason game was against the Kansas City Kings, soon to be the Sacramento Kings. Within fifty steps of checking into the game, I heard someone in the sparse crowd holler something about me belonging in the CBA (the Continental Basketball Association). Next, Larry Drew, no relation to John, picked my pocket in the backcourt. It sounds like a broken record: I get in, and I get picked. I was, however, learning in the process and was far from a turnover machine. Point guards who are don't last long. When I lost the ball it was usually to a different player with a different technique. The same thief seldom got me twice. Meanwhile, I cached their techniques to try on others. I wanted to employ everything that worked against me on opponents. It was particularly satisfying when, on rare occasion, I could return the lesson to the teacher.

Learning was one of my strong suits. I gained a lot of knowledge through playing but might have absorbed even more while watching intently from the bench. I focused largely on our all-star point guard, Rickey Green, and the man he was guarding but also picked up tidbits from all the players who earned playing time. Each trip up and down the court is stuffed full of countless nuances that mostly go unnoticed by the season ticket holders. These were the very things I learned to notice. That's what experience provides—a memory bank full of the tendencies of each player and then being able to instinctively apply the knowledge without conscious thought. I found that thinking in the heat of battle merely clogs the processors and slows reaction time.

Every night the best basketball players in the world were my teachers. Without writing down a single note, I compiled a mental video library on everyone in the league. The whole process of watching and learning was interesting—it excited me. I began acquiring a better feel for the game while becoming a fan in the process. My appreciation for the athletes and players grew as I came to better understand the nature of the game. Every night from the best seat in the house, I marveled at the talent on the floor.

Whenever I sat on the bench, I was genuinely immersed in the game. I wasn't pouting or whispering to teammates about playing time, and I wasn't scanning the crowd for friends or movie stars. My attention stayed between the lines. I was aware of foul situations and had acquired a feel for the significance of "time and score." I gained a sense of what the coaches expected and when— so I was ready when they called my name. When Coach looked down the bench, he would see my eyes staring right back at him conveying the message, "I want to play." He never had to call me twice, wait for me to tuck in my shirt, or take off my warm-ups. Even when playing meant filling in the last thirty seconds of a blowout, I was eager to oblige. It was an honor to play at all.

• • •

Historically, the Utah Jazz traveled a lot in the preseason. My rookie year was no exception. Our excessive tune-up travels culminated with the Hall of Fame game in Springfield, Massachusetts, against the mighty Boston Celtics. Bird, McHale, Parish, Ainge, and Dennis Johnson formed the core of one of the best teams of all time. I don't recall for sure the outcome of that game, but I doubt it went well.

We flew the entire next day across the country to Seattle for opening night at the King Dome. We wore our green uniforms for the last time in an opening loss to the Sonics.[2] Adding insult to injury, I was informed after the game by an announcer that I cost someone a million bucks. As it turns out, had I made my otherwise meaningless three-point shot at the buzzer, a fan would have collected the promotional prize.

The only good news about my early travel experience was that I got reimbursed for riding in the coach area of the airplane. It was part of the league's collective bargaining agreement that players must ride first class. NBA legs don't curl up very well in economy class. The head coach was able to bump someone to the cheap seats, but the team would have to reimburse that player the difference in the cost of the ticket. Usually, that someone was me. My legs fit fine, and I was glad to have the extra money.

I sensed that I needed every penny, as job security had not yet become a reality. The full extent of my wary thriftiness was displayed in my selection of housing. I bargain shopped for a one-bedroom apartment in Midvale, Utah. At a $125 a month, the small, below grade, furnished flat was the cheapest place I could find near our practice facility. I purchased the bare essentials to set up my bachelor pad: bedding; cookware, which included a pot and a pan; a couple bowls, and a plate or two with partnered utensils. While setting in my winter stores, I swung by the local discount food chain and purchased a case of Nalley's Chili, cereal, milk, and enough ingredients to craft a poor man's batch of Mom's lasagna. I carefully divided her family-sized dinner into fourths and froze it for the months ahead.

With my cupboards stocked, I connected with civilization. I

hooked up the phone, selecting the cheapest plan available, which permitted about fifty local calls per month and no long distance. I withheld getting a TV set until late January to watch the Super Bowl. Occupying my "suite" in the large complex was like living in a basement. With my apartment nestled between two other units and practically underground, the ambient temperatures stayed pretty constant, so I didn't turn the heat on in the apartment. I liked sleeping in the cold and wore my sweats when I was up and at 'em. Even though my living quarters were pretty Spartan, I never felt like I was roughing it. But after hearing me sniffle through most of January, Thurl Bailey came over and made me turn on the heat! "Spend it, Stock. You can't hide your money under a rock." I wasn't convinced.

My conservative lifestyle was a direct extension of my natural tendency toward saving money. Everyone knew I was pretty tight. Dad used to say, "Tighter than the bark on a tree." This trait literally paid dividends down the line. My needs were simple: they were limited to food, housing, and gas, and I was able to save a substantial part of my salary for a rainy day. Later, when I needed cash for important things, such as a home, I was able to afford the purchase without borrowing. I knew that having a house bought and paid for would put me way ahead in the financial game.

Another financial policy that yielded returns was paying my taxes—on time! I had received all kinds of advice about zeroing out my taxes and taking part in risky tax shelters. This financial strategy, by the way, zeroed out some pretty big bank accounts around the NBA a few years later when the tax shelters were disallowed by the IRS. Fortunately, I had followed the counsel of my tax attorney in Spokane, Gary Brajcich. Gary came highly recommended by Fitz, who was convinced of his abilities and integrity. I soon trusted him as much as I did Coach Fitzgerald. His conservative approach may have cost me some extra tax dollars, but I sure slept well and probably saved a lot on the back end by not having to pay penalties. Eventually I would reluctantly loosen my purse strings, but not before my job and home were secure. The only sure way to accomplish both was to succeed between the lines on the NBA's hardwoods.

For transportation that year, I piloted a used Toyota Corolla graciously supplied by the Jazz and Wagstaff Toyota, a team sponsor at the time. I drove that car all season without realizing it was my responsibility to license and insure the vehicle. Thankfully, over the next eight months, I was never stopped by the police nor involved in an accident. When I hear stories about young athletes doing stupid things, I think back to those days and try not to be too judgmental. I was very stupid and very lucky. It was dangerous and could have turned out badly. These days I consider it my responsibility to point out such things to young people. They may find it intrusive or too "old school" to apply to them, but I feel that they need to hear it.

The final cuts had now been made to our roster for my rookie season, and I had survived. Many didn't. I saw a lot of great players miss the cut over the years and wondered why.

Techniques and approaches for making a roster varied greatly. Many players were convinced they had to show the coaches they had skills, could shoot threes, and could score. Most of the time, they proved that they couldn't, at least not at that level. Everyone present was skilled or they wouldn't have been there, so rebounding, blocking shots, and the ability to guard people seemed to be a common denominator among those who stuck. The NBA already had lots of guys who could rip the nets. Unless the player was a high draft choice, the organization probably wasn't looking for a scoring machine to fill up the stat sheet. What they were looking for in most cases were pieces to an existing puzzle—players who might eventually grow into legitimate stars. At the other end of the spectrum, some guys were too unselfish. This strategy usually didn't succeed either. Production is absolutely required in order to succeed. Reversing the ball and screening out are great things, but not if the player fails to create a scoring opportunity for someone else or never actually corrals a rebound. Everyone must bring something to the table and contribute.

Others met their doom simply by reading and believing the local newspaper. Speculation about available roster spots and cuts often crushed the competitive spirits of guys who otherwise had a real chance. Many terrific basketball players wilted in the face of these unofficial reports. Coach Sloan would tell us, "Don't cut yourself!" Writers don't pick the team, but players who read the paper and buy into the printed word can't help but display a defeatist attitude. They cut themselves! I have come to the conclusion that, just as in life, you have to be yourself when trying out for anything. The best you can ever be is yourself. If you try to be someone else, you will likely fail. The best approach, I think, is to compete at every drill as though it is the world championship. Stay within your abilities but display those abilities as well as you can.

I determined that if the Jazz were going to cut me, I wanted to make their decision brutally difficult. My own strategy employed my time-honored method of defending every inch of the ninety-four-foot court every second I was in the game. I figured if everyone was bigger and better than me, then by picking up full court, I could get them so tired they might not want to shoot by the time they got to the offensive end of the floor. I also tried to be a great "help" defender using the Minute Man approach—avoiding frontal assaults and causing havoc where

I could. Thanks to Fitz and the tapes, I knew the offense, so I could concentrate on transporting the ball up the court securely without burning much time on the shot clock. I took only wide-open shots I was certain I would make. Otherwise, I was looking to put the ball into the hands of players who could score. With a lineup of Dantley, Griffith, John "The Gunslinger" Drew, and Thurl Bailey, it didn't appear the Jazz had drafted a six-foot point guard to try to outscore those guys.

I played a respectable eighteen minutes per game my rookie season, largely because I did what had gotten me into every rat-ball or pickup game since grade school. I passed. Rickey Green, "The Fastest of Them All," as our announcer Hot Rod Hundley had tagged him, pushed the ball with tremendous speed. We were the second-leading scoring team in the league that year largely because of the pace Rickey set. He was a good passer, and the rest of the team had to match his speed if they wanted to score. Frank Layden used to say, "A great point guard and a great scorer go hand in hand . . . just not into the showers." If the big guys know they will get a pass, they will run like greyhounds. I mimicked Rickey to the extent that I could but looked mostly for the scorers.

Right or wrong, I felt as though the Salt Palace crowd liked and appreciated the way I played from the start. It seemed they looked forward to my short stints as an enthusiastic backup with full-court pressure and lots of passing. Coach Layden voiced his approval by commenting, "Passing is contagious, and this kid makes us want to pass." Since that time I have noticed that teams that enjoy passing and like watching their teammates have success tend to be good. They play with a relaxed and patient tempo that is hard to ruffle and hard to guard.

That first season passed rapidly. We won our last game in San Antonio, finished at .500, and secured a playoff spot. I finished with an honorable mention on the All-NBA Rookie Team. The voters must have factored in my ability to carry equipment onto the airplane, pick up the veterans' bags, and perform other playfully demeaning rookie duties. During the playoffs I jokingly rebelled, saying, "All the rookies went home before the playoffs started, and I'm not carrying anything!" The bold pronouncement fell on deaf ears.

NBA teams have lots of ups and downs in a season. The Utah Jazz was certainly not an exception. As my first year began, a contract dispute sidelined our leading scorer and one of the league's all-time point producers, Adrian Dantley. When "A. D." returned, he was a pleasure to watch. He scored on anybody of any size at any time. Every night was a clinic on using the body to protect the ball, different shot deliveries, and multiple tempo changes. Adrian was a scorer.

Unfortunately, that same year another teammate essentially ended his career because of drug issues. Not having any exposure in that arena, this was an eye-opener for me. I watched as my teammate and friend fell victim to this curse. After returning to the team following a suspicious absence, he appeared helpless to resist his demons. He said as much when he sorrowfully speculated that given the choice between a million dollars and a handful of drugs, he would choose the narcotics. He gave up more than cash that day as his career ended. Deep in my mind I heard the echo, "Be glad it ain't you, Stock."[3]

That year we also experienced a coaching change as Assistant Coach Phil Johnson took the head job at Kansas City. Jerry Sloan was coaxed away from his home in southern Illinois to fill the vacancy. I was nervous at first. Jerry was renowned for his toughness, and his handshake at our introduction confirmed he could probably back up the reputation. Things worked out in the years to come with these men, but at the time it was strange to make the change.

The final loss of the season came at the hands of the high-scoring Denver Nuggets in the second round of the playoffs. Coming off a stunning first-round, game five victory in Houston, we headed to Denver without the services of Mark Eaton, our unassailable defensive mountain. Mark had hurt his knee in the Houston series. The high-scoring Nuggets, led by Alex English, Dan Issel, Calvin Natt, "Fat" Lever, and "T. R." Dunn, soundly defeated us in five games, ending our season.

The playoffs are a reward for regular season efforts. Everything is magnified: the energy, the excitement, and the intensity. Once I experienced that special atmosphere my first season, I was hooked. Losing in the playoffs, however, is final and also painful as the agony of defeat is also heightened. The reality of the season is that all but the champions walk away disenchanted. The end is abrupt and little time is wasted clearing out for the summer. As a rule, we met the morning after the final game of the season to turn in gear, clean out lockers, and handle any remaining business.

Coach would address the team one final time, then turn the floor over to an assistant, the general manager, or occasionally the owner for their thoughts on the season. At the conclusion of this, rookies were normally dispatched for their final duty: going to go get burgers for the entire team and staff. While we were gone, Coach Layden would meet with each player according to seniority. In these meetings he often gave select players his "Frank" opinion on their successes and failures as well as needed areas of improvement. When appropriate, he might also comment on a player's future with the team. If I recall correctly, his comments to me that year can be nicely summarized as, "You need to work on everything this summer." I was anxious to get started.

A FOOT IN THE DOOR

• • •

Following our playoff loss in Denver, I followed the lead of some of our veterans and hopped on a flight that night to Salt Lake. In the NBA, they say a "team has their bags packed" when facing imminent defeat, and it looks like they have thrown in the towel. I didn't, so I had some ground to make up on my return. I packed my bags and cleaned my humble abode throughout the night. I made our final team meeting with time to spare, completed my duties, and said my good-byes. I boarded the first flight out to Spokane that afternoon and played in a pickup game that evening. Obviously, basketball had not turned into a job for me. Seven months and nearly a hundred games of basketball hadn't dampened my enthusiasm for playing. If anything, playing with and against the best basketball players in the world had only increased my appetite. I was eager to share and show what I had learned with my friends and family as well as improve according to Coach's advice.

During that summer the house next to Mom and Dad's became available. I decided to purchase it, although I was still quite comfortable in my basement room at home. I saw absolutely no reason to move out for the summer, so I didn't. My sister Stacey offered to move in and make me a landlord with Nada as her summer roommate.

Nada spent that summer in Spokane working for Pickett and Pickett, attorneys at law, and living with Stacey. We had concluded that she should move to Salt Lake City in the fall if we intended to go forward with the relationship. Both of us knew that the move would involve a leap of faith on her part as I would be her only friend and companion until she could begin substitute teaching. She decided to jump.

When we arrived in Salt Lake for my second year, Nada and

ASSISTED

*The Stockton houses; Jack and Clemy's on the left,
John and Nada's on the right, circa 1988.*

I acquired separate apartments in the same complex. Mine was "comped" as a promotion for the new enterprise. Hers, however, was full price, and she wouldn't let me help with the rent. Her twin sister, Laura, stepped up to the plate to supplement Nada's substitute teacher's salary, which didn't match the rent.

I eventually proposed. I had planned an elaborate dinner as the backdrop. En route to the restaurant, the highway patrol felt I was a little too eager, so they presented me with a speeding citation. After the incident I was too irritated to go through with the proposal. I planned a second attempt after a Jazz home game. We ended up losing, so the mood wasn't right then, either. Ultimately I settled for an evening in front of the TV in sweats. Nada was sick and bundled up, hardly a vision of beauty. I wasn't dressed much better but that was normal for me. I fished the ring out and proposed. She accepted and spent the rest of the night admiring the ring and calling everyone she knew to share the news.

I must have been on a hot streak because Karl Malone arrived in my life that same year. He had been a landmark choice in the summer's draft and would profoundly affect my career and the Jazz for years to come. Unbelievably, he was passed up by twelve teams on selection day. Projected to go in the top five, he

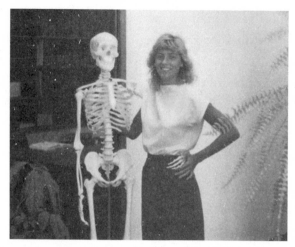

Nada Stepovich, summer intern at Pickett and Pickett law office, circa 1985.

had slipped down to us at thirteenth. Perhaps there are still a few GMs kicking themselves over that one.

Karl and I had a chance to get reacquainted when he flew to Salt Lake for introductions shortly after the draft. We spent most of the day walking around Hogle Zoo, just outside downtown. We spent an entire afternoon uninterrupted. That was a pleasant surprise because Karl really sticks out in a crowd. We picked up right where we had left off at the Olympic Trials in 1984, and I knew we would become friends. I had no idea, however, what a great player Karl would become.

Once the season started in the fall, it became pretty obvious he was special. The NBA didn't seem like an adjustment to him at all. In terms of confidence and carriage, Karl seemed like a star from the outset. His strength, speed, and skills were extraordinary for a rookie—or even a veteran. In short, Karl was the real deal. His first season, he was named to the NBA All-Rookie team, but Karl was just warming to his task. He worked harder in the weight room, on the track, or wherever exercise could be performed than anybody I had seen. He improved his skills yearly, working hard to eliminate flaws such as poor free-throw shooting. Karl remedied weaknesses quickly and without relapse. He took pride in playing defense as well, improving his technique and dominance each season.

Karl possessed a hallmark trait of most great players: a phenomenal work ethic. Gifted to be sure, what made him great was his labor and obsession to improve. Nobody outworked him and nobody improved from year to year the way he did. Karl wasn't going to wait his turn to crack the starting lineup. He would soon define the power forward position for the Jazz and the NBA.

Without really appreciating the changes, some major pieces in my life had fallen into place. I was looking forward to my future.

CHAPTER 10

Wedding Days

Planning and preparing for a wedding is a lot of work. As the big day drew closer, my bride and I came to an understanding. My only job would be to show up for the ceremony!

Nada went home to Medford a month or so before the wedding to assist in the preparations. The reception was going to take place at her parents' home. I remained in Spokane performing a steel siding facelift on our future nest with my old buddy J. C.

J. C. always brought adventure to any project. On this one, besides his nail apron and a hammer, he was sporting a neck brace from a recent moped accident. With no OSHA reps on site, we managed to electrify the siding and pound our thumbs into submission. Although we usually flew by the seat of our pants, on this project Jeff took a harrowing fall from a tall ladder, adding to a long résumé of survival stories. Despite our inexperience, we completed the job in time for the wedding.

With the house restoration completed, I chauffeured Mom and Dad over the long journey to southern Oregon to witness Nada and me tying the knot. We stopped at one of the most incredible places I had ever seen, Crater Lake. It is preserved largely in a pristine condition and is a spectacular vision to behold.

The Stockton family, circa 1986. Front row: Clemy and Jack.
Back row, left to right: Leanne, John, Steve, and Stacey.

We hit the ground running in Medford as the large wedding party and guests began flooding into the Rogue Valley in anticipation of the event. Nobody was disappointed. By night's end, "my people" had found "Nada's people" at a joint called the Sandpiper Lounge. The two sides merged seamlessly into one large group for the entire weekend.

So many circles of family and friends on both sides of the aisle were represented. Mom's relatives had traveled the long distance from Ferdinand, Idaho, and Dad's sisters made the trek, along with many other friends from Spokane. Salt Lake was also well represented. Nada's guests hailed from around the globe—from London to Alaska, and from DC to the Slavic old country. This made for an unusual but interesting blend, to say the least. In fact, Dad sternly warned Coach Pickett not to let things get out of hand. "We are not going to look like a bunch of hillbillies," he instructed. The jury is still out on whether Coach succeeded or not.

Initially everything went perfectly, because I had no duties. My patience and self-control would be tested, however, at my first assignment, the wedding rehearsal. Scheduled for 4:30 P.M., Nada and the bridesmaids were still a no-show at 5:15 P.M. Without cell phones to update their status, they were declared AWOL. The temperature had dropped—to about 100 degrees—and my groomsmen were very thirsty, perhaps due to the activities of the previous night. I gave the nod to adjourn to a local watering hole knowing we could just "wing it" the next day if need be.

Suddenly the missing persons appeared, and we rushed through our training under the stern direction of a couple of Nada's older sisters. One of the directives imposed upon me by the drill sergeants in dresses was: "Project your vows loudly enough for all the church to hear." Personally, I felt as though my vows were between Nada and me, and I had no intention of projecting anything! Plus, I was gagging (just a little bit) on one of the lines in particular: "My family will be your family." The Stepoviches are great, but there are fifteen of them, not counting in-laws, aunts ("tetas"), uncles, and grandmothers ("nanas"). Given the clan's size, a rewind of the last two hours provided a touch of concern over the upcoming merger. I suddenly had a lot of potential bosses whom I wasn't eager to welcome for the long haul (or short, for that matter).

Amazingly, despite all of the tension building between the parched and the tardy, the pot never came to a boil. A fair amount of steam was released when I apparently promised "my love and *infidelity*" during the practice ceremony. It was a Freudian slip that cracked up both sides of the altar within earshot. It was a

The Stepovich clan at John and Nada's wedding. Front row, left to right:
Michael, Melissa, Andrea, Laura, Antonia, Maria, and Christopher Stepovich.
Back row, left to right: Peter, Nicholas, Mike, Matilda, Nada,
John (Stockton), James, Theodore, and Dominic Stepovich.

good thing we stayed for rehearsal after all. I got it right when it counted! *Fidelity!*

• • •

All hands were present and accounted for the next day as the ceremony began. The temperature again soared to a hundred and ten degrees. I could feel the beads of sweat rolling down my chest under my shirt while standing at the altar. Inside I was cool as a cucumber, knowing I had made the right choice. I was willing to commit for life. Nada was stunning in her mom's wedding dress as she walked down the aisle. I didn't notice another soul as she approached until my trance was broken momentarily by Nada's dad. Performing his duty of giving away the bride, he shook my hand, smiling a little too much, and said, "Thank you, my boy!" *Just*

Jack and Clemy Stockton at John and Nada's wedding, 1986.

Nada and John's wedding, 1986.

what did he mean by that? I wondered. It probably had something to do with her student loans that he was transferring to me that very moment. With the ceremony completed and our postvow duties attended to, we took a romantic ride to the reception for the first time as man and wife—in a car packed with relatives!

The celebration was truly incomparable. All of the preparations had been made by Nada's mom, Matilda, and her relatives. A Croatian family friend barbecued a lamb (and a pig) on an outdoor rotisserie to complete the incredible menu. It was an amazing spread of home-cooked food that fed over four hundred people. Fresh salmon from Alaska, baron of beef, shrimp, roasted turkey, salads, pastas, and homemade bread and desserts completed the feast. The scope of the entire smorgasbord was staggering. I have never seen anything like it before or since. The labors of love performed by Nada's family to make this a special day were impressive and moving. The affair gave me a different insight into her family and made my whispered vows considerably more palatable.

Nada and I didn't get to enjoy the fruits of their labor much. We were tugged, pulled, hugged, and photographed to death. I guess that's standard for a bride and groom, but I had had enough

Left to right: best man Steve Stockton, maid of honor Laura Stepovich, John, and Nada.

attention for one day and was ready to leave the reception. I must have had a look of irritated intensity in my eyes because John Blake grabbed me by the arm and said, "Hey, Stocks, it looks like you could use a beer." John had become a good friend since his quarterbacking days in Mission Park some fourteen years earlier. I accepted his offer because I was used to him grabbing and holding me at Sunday hoops, and because I was also sure he could whip me if I didn't. He saved the day, because by then we hadn't even cut the cake or had our ceremonial first dance. Shakey had come through in the clutch.

A half hour later, with those duties completed, the band played a couple of polkas and the party was underway. The dance floor (the basketball court) was buzzing all night. Everyone from grandparents to small children meshed styles and shared space. We ended up staying late to see the all-age diving competition into the pool once the band called it a night. I am so glad we stayed.

We flew to San Diego for our honeymoon the following morning. The week was spent hopping from Disneyland to Universal Studios to Sea World and the San Diego Zoo. We

John and Nada in the Wasatch Mountains.

bounced around between a number of hotels, highlighted by a stay at the historic Hotel Del Coronado.

Our last stop took us south of the border to Rosarito, Mexico. The uncrowded beach there was spectacular, and the food was unbelievably good. We enjoyed our first vacation together, but I was glad to return to US soil and home sweet home.

Reality set in immediately upon our arrival in Spokane when Mom asked me if I wanted any help moving my stuff out of my room in the basement. I hadn't really thought of that. Of course, moving out was a necessity, but I couldn't see the same urgency that Mom did in packing up my stuff. Reluctantly, I complied and transported my life forty paces north.

• • •

Nada settled into our home as I restarted my workouts. I hadn't played basketball, lifted weights, or done any running for more than two weeks. It was the longest break I had taken from my routine in quite a while and a pretty leisurely one at that. I

John and his father, Jack, at Crater Lake.

knew it was time to get back to work. Cleared to play without his neck brace, J. C. and I tried a game of one-on-one that couldn't have been mistaken for basketball. I took my second vow that month: to never let my conditioning lapse again.

I kept that promise. Steve Delong and I worked up a pretty effective regimen over the years that became a habit. In addition, the activities I chose for recreation, such as mountain biking, water skiing, and playing other sports, fit into and enhanced my conditioning by design.

In terms of specific preparations for my third season, Steve Delong had it wired. His theory was and is, "Players are pretty good without me, but if they get hurt getting stronger, faster, or better, then my efforts are counterproductive." I trusted his training methods, and I improved in most areas, per Coach Layden's year-end suggestion.

• • •

Being a married man, unfortunately, didn't propel me to instant stardom. My path to the status of starter proved to be slow but steady. I saw the floor for tip-off only five times my rookie season. The first two were especially memorable. Without the services of our injured point guard, Rickey Green, we had back-to-back games against the Pistons and the Bulls on the road. We faced off against the Pistons at Joe Louis Arena, because the scoreboard had fallen, I believe, at the Silverdome. At the alternate site, I matched up against Isiah Thomas and "The Microwave," Vinnie Johnson. I recall trying to flap the unflappable with full court pressure until the final minutes. I pulled back when Rich Kelley grabbed me by the jersey and towed me backward to play solid half-court defense. Apparently I was just wasting energy, because it didn't even bother those two. I played forty-eight minutes without goofing it up, and more important, we won the game. The next night against Chicago, I played another forty-eight minutes. Only this time they tried presses and traps to take advantage of my inexperience. I handled the pressure pretty well and contributed to another nice win. I was exhausted, as I was averaging only about ten minutes a game at the time, but the temporary promotion was a lot of fun.

In my second year, Karl's rookie season, I earned the starting nod thirty-eight times until a nine- or ten-game losing streak precipitated a change back to "The Fastest of Them All," Rickey. Coach told me he felt that I had hit the rookie wall just a little later than others.

By year three I was slated to start opening day versus the Mavericks. Prior to flying to Dallas, the team was required to attend an appearance in downtown Salt Lake for an antidrug campaign. These appearances were mandated by the team and the league. Although many teams didn't insist upon them, the Jazz did. As time ticked by, the need to toss a couple coins in the parking meter became obvious. I rushed out to the car to ante up, only to roll my ankle on the uneven curb. Afraid to tell the trainers of my injury and the surrounding circumstances, I matched up against Derek Harper in Dallas as scheduled and looked bad. Derek could make a player look bad on a good day, so this wasn't pretty. I went zero for six in a convincing loss. I could almost picture Coach Layden in the coaches' office. He was leaning forward in his chair with a disappointed smile on his face, gravelling out the words, "He isn't ready; maybe he never will be." My minutes steadily increased, but I didn't get another legitimate chance to be the starter until four games into the next season.

Ironically, Coach regained confidence in me during a playoff loss to Golden State at the end of my third season. We were up two games to zero in a five-game series when the injury bug bit Rickey again. He had absolutely owned "Sleepy" Floyd up until that point. When Rickey went down, Sleepy woke up and got on a roll. I played nearly every minute of the next three games and played very well, but we lost three in a row to the Warriors. I was surprised that Frank actually singled me out following the disappointing loss, saying, "Incredible stamina, terrific effort." His tone was subdued but sincere as he pointed at me. I didn't feel completely at fault for the loss, but I think we would have won easily if Rickey had stayed healthy. In the NBA there is a fine line between winning and losing. Sometimes it is as simple as a slight change in confidence. A player can't let an opponent feel good about himself, even for a moment. Every single play is important, because a single play can boost or erode confidence. Once players of this caliber taste blood, it is hard to stop the frenzy and regain an edge.

• • •

By now Nada had experienced some of the best and some of the not-so-best aspects of being an NBA wife. She handled the disappointing losses such as the playoffs without flinching, even though they hurt her nearly as much as they did me. These abilities in an NBA wife are underappreciated. They are often in the spotlight one moment and rudely pushed aside the next. A glamorous pose for photographs with her husband can be interrupted by a shove from an insistent autograph hound or a knock on the noggin by a news cameraman setting up for an interview. These women need to have grace, humility, and a sense of humor—Nada did.

• • •

With Nada seven months pregnant, we celebrated our first anniversary in August following my third year with the Jazz—*not* in a romantic vacation spot, but in an Alaskan lake cabin with Nada's family, with no running water and an outhouse a mere twenty paces from the back porch. Nada has seven brothers: Michael, Peter, Christopher, Dominic, Theodore, Nicholas, and James. All are very good water skiers and always eager to provide a brother-in-law with a *lesson*.

Growing up in my neighborhood didn't include much lake time. I had barely dabbled in skiing, but the stories of the brothers' prowess were legendary. Still, the competitor in me wanted to show off some raw, untapped ability of my own. I wriggled my way into their wetsuit, and confidently zipped it shut. The problem was, I had it on backwards; the zipper goes in the back. Amid the chuckling on the dock, I redeemed myself by successfully dock starting, on one ski, on my first attempt. We skied virtually all day and night. Many people don't realize that the sun barely sets in the summer in Alaska. At three in the morning, we would take a ski run as if it were late afternoon. It was hard to sleep in the sunlight anyway, so off we would go.

I was eager to impress my tutors on every run. I fearlessly attacked the water with sharp cuts and strong pulls as advised. The

John scores against Kareem Abdul-Jabbar.

lake fought back with a vengeance. In a flash, my ski tip dipped, sending me cartwheeling at breakneck speed through, across, and under the dreaded wake. Normally when someone crashes and burns, the boat circles back loaded with excited smiles and good intentioned ribbing. In this case, the speed and impact of my fall generated genuine concern. "Are you okay, John?" they inquired, hoping that I was. "Yes," I lied amid burps of infused lake water. My knee hurt . . . a lot. Standing in about five feet of water, I couldn't put any weight on that leg. *This can't be good*, I thought while electing to wade back to the cabin to avoid revealing my injury.

A fair amount of self-discussion took place on my paddle back to the dock. It continued as I sat alone on the edge of the platform, contemplating my stupidity. Basketball, I felt, was certainly in jeopardy. On Frank Layden's desk lay an unsigned contract that would extend my career by several years, all of which I had risked by waterskiing in the Alaskan wilderness. After about an hour and many prayers that might have been tough to understand between all of my self-incriminating insults, I decided to face the music. I hesitantly tested the leg, putting one foot in front of the other and pacing gingerly back and forth across the cedar planks. To my amazement the knee was fine. Was it the hydrotherapy, or had God heard my prayers? I don't know, but I scratched one of my nine lives from the available lot. I had been lucky.

Waterskiing, despite this ordeal, became a love of mine. Not only did I continue to enjoy it, but it became part of my summer workout with Doc's blessing. As a form of training, I found it to be second to none in terms of body and core strength development as well as muscle toning. Six aggressive ski trips a day matched even the most brutal of Steve's weight-room gems. I often couldn't hold a glass of water at the end of some days, but it was fun, the type of fun that reaches deep inside you and sticks there as a reserve for when things in life get tedious. Waterskiing was a treasured gift from Nada's brothers that we have shared with family and friends ever since. It has been a blessing that has continued to give me and my family great joy and often peace.

• • •

As I noted, my growth as a player and a person seemed to be slow and steady, without noticeable spikes or declines. I looked to begin my fourth year, happy to be a member of the Jazz organization—with two good legs, that is.

CHAPTER 11

Fatherhood

"Every child comes with the message that
God is not yet discouraged of man."[1]

—RABINDRANATH TAGORE

I had always wanted to be a father. More precisely, I wanted to be like my dad. That wish came true in March of 1987 when Nada and I officially learned that she was pregnant. My natural curiosity jumped into overdrive, and I tried to participate in every aspect of the experience. I went to every checkup, including that first visit where I marveled at the "squish, squish" sound of the baby's heartbeat. Dr. Kent Rasmussen, our ob-gyn, was himself surprised to hear the beat at such an early date.

We looked forward with excitement to our scheduled visits with "Dr. Ras" for more than his medical skills. Following each appointment in Salt Lake, we treated ourselves to a burger at Hires Big H Drive-in, famous for root beer and carhops. It was one of the few eating perks Nada allowed herself, as she was committed to keeping her girlish figure. She ate well and often but chose mostly healthy and home-prepared food. She even scolded me one time for abruptly pulling into a taco joint—at her request! "You can't just feed me every time I mention food!" she barked. "Do you want me to weigh a thousand pounds?" I surely had a lot to learn.

FATHERHOOD

• • •

As the due date approached, I had a lot more to look forward to than my fourth season. Only a year before, as newlyweds, we had bought a nice two-bedroom condo. We had been anxious to start accumulating home equity instead of paying rent. Our friends Sonny and Kathy Tangaro, both Realtors, provided not only their professional services, but helped us with every conceivable detail to get us moved into our new abode in record time. They made it easy for us.

I had met the Tangaros during my rookie season. The Utah Jazz owner at the time, Sam Battistone, wanted me to meet some Gonzaga people so I would feel more at home. I squirmed at the notion of meeting anyone at that time who might expect more than "hello." Nonetheless, introductions took place, at Sam's insistence, outside of our Salt Palace locker room following a game. The Tangaros brought two college friends, Joannie and Duane ("Dino") Semerad. The four had attended Gonzaga-in-Florence (Gonzaga's study abroad program in Italy) together. In short order I found out that Dino had grown up only a block away from me in Spokane and had also attended St. Al's roughly ten years before me. I had passed within a stone's throw of his house every day on the way to school, but we had never met. Our neighborhood connection made for a relaxed start to a long friendship.

These two couples took great care of me before Nada arrived, and afterward a friendship between the six of us was solidified around Sonny's remarkable cooking and hospitality. His Italian "Roni" feasts were renowned for their taste, portions, and for the relationships they fostered. He never had to invite us twice. Our relationship with these four people blossomed and grew over the next twenty years. We came to think of them and their children as family.

ASSISTED

We leaned heavily on both of these families as the stork approached—a little too heavily in one case. Sonny had told us about an interesting technique to test the alertness of the child in the womb: "When your wife is in the tub, grab a big spoon and tap the side of the tub. The baby will move around instantly." He didn't say how hard to tap, so with the largest spoon in the condo, I "gonged" the side of the tub. Child and mother both reacted as though a bomb had gone off, causing way more discomfort than the experiment was worth.

As training camp and our preseason schedule wore on, thoughts of possibly not being available for the birth were never far from my mind. Games and practices offered a welcomed break from these concerns. I had concocted a vision of speeding to the hospital and being stopped by a traffic officer who would forgo writing a citation in favor of providing an escort to the hospital, in Hollywood's finest tradition. Under the circumstances, I was willing to settle for just being there.

Considering this was our first pregnancy, Nada stayed remarkably calm, right up to the final hour. A late-night phone conversation from Boise, Idaho, following an exhibition game on the eve of the birth, offers a glimpse of Nada's mettle. I was thinking out loud whether I should rent a car and make the six-hour drive that night, or chance traveling with the team in the morning. Nada calmly reassured me that she would be fine. "Sleep and come home with the team" were her final confident words on the subject.

By the time we reached the Salt Lake City airport the next morning, Kathy Tangaro had already assumed the honor of driving Nada to the hospital. (She claims that she didn't even speed!) I eventually found my way to the maternity ward at LDS Hospital. Confident by then of my timing, I bounded into the room with some well-rehearsed, smart-alecky remarks, ready to perform my duty. Unfortunately as the scene unfolded, the techniques I had learned in the Lamaze classes were appreciated about as much as my jokes. The gentle caressing, the coaching, and the rest of the textbook had to be thrown out the window. Nada instead focused on a jar of Harding Lake water from her beloved Alaska to get her through the pain.

Nada felt at ease under the care of Dr. E. Kent Rasmussen and LDS Hospital. It seems ironic that two, going on three, Catholics ended up there, but the service could not have been better. The hospital even provided a Catholic priest on staff! Nada's stay in the hospital was a testament to her faith in Dr. Rasmussen. Her belief in him was confirmed as he sat many long hours through all of our children's arrivals. We both treasured his approach and concern for our family.

• • •

At last our tiny bundle arrived. We discovered for the first time that we had been blessed with a healthy baby boy. Being genuinely surprised with the baby's gender isn't easy these days with all the available technology. We managed to remain in the dark, with constant reminders to curious technicians: "We don't want to know!"

Before we were married, we knew we would name our first boy John Houston, after his great-grandpa, grandpa, and me. Plus, we liked the sound of it. A mere hour into Houston's young life, I began one of many little family traditions—giving the baby his or her first bath. I learned a little bit about each of our six children in the process. Amid the splashing, I discovered the snugglers, the water-haters, the squirmers, and the screamers. I discovered that each baby is completely unique from the start. I prized that insight.

Houston turned out to be the perfect first baby for a young couple. He slept throughout the night from his opening evening on the planet in his Salt Lake maternity ward. Remarkably, he never wavered from that pattern. He was easygoing. He didn't squawk with the clumsy handling of his first bath and has never changed his spots. At age twenty-four, Houston still doesn't make waves.

After a day or two of bonding, the time to leave the hospital arrived. Mother and child were wheeled down the exit ramp by a complete witch—literally. It was Halloween, and the attending nurse sported a ghoulish costume, warts and all, to capture the spirit.

It was all fun and games until we arrived back at the condo and closed the door behind us. Suddenly the weight of the world descended upon our shoulders. With no witches or goblins to help, we were alone with Houston for the first time, wondering, *Where is the manual? What do we do now? Can we learn as we go, as we had when siding the house?* These questions were answered over time, but the pace and focus of our lives would never be the same.

The cavalry arrived the next day in the form of Nada's mom, Matilda. She was a gift from God! She could handle anything and probably had with her thirteen children. Nothing surprised or rattled her. Jaundice, crying, or projectile vomiting all seemed to be old hat. Mostly she provided reassurance and a sense of calm. From the moment she arrived, we stopped tiptoeing as though we were carrying nitroglycerin. We confidently scooped, tugged, hustled, and bustled like normal. We just included Houston . . . and his stroller, car seat, and diaper bag. The knowledge Nada's mom passed on to us in a few short weeks was a college education in itself.

• • •

FATHERHOOD

In order, our children (Houston, Michael, David, Lindsay, Laura, and Samuel), arrived over the next fourteen years. Michael was born with the umbilical cord wrapped around his neck. This was a major concern, forcing Nada to bed rest and to remain constantly on her side for the last two months of her pregnancy. David was born with chronic ear infections and seemed to never sleep. Lindsay appeared hand first, prompting Dr. Rasmussen to suggest the baby was going to be a girl. His reasoning? She was already asking for the credit card. Laura arrived in the late morning. I noticed an unusually bright star over the Wasatch Mountains, east of the hospital, and named it Laura's Star. Samuel offered one of the biggest challenges. At full term, he was still upright in the womb. He needed to turn. I tried daily to nudge him gently, as recommended, but he balked at any gymnastics. Finally, with the help of ultrasound imaging, our doctor discovered his foot was stuck. Carefully—and quite painfully for Nada—he dislodged the foot, and Samuel flipped like a veteran gymnast. They strapped down Nada's belly to keep him in that position. He was born before the sun rose the next morning. Nada would often say, "It's all worth it once the child's born."

Nada had some of that Alaskan wilderness toughness. She endured without whining. She showed a lot of class in the process. In the end, the baby's safe arrival always made the ordeal of pregnancy and childbirth quickly fade into the background. Nada felt that the real labor began when we took the baby home.

• • •

We began our new life as a family, trying to incorporate our responsibilities as parents into our hectic NBA lifestyle. We decided to bring our children along most places, diaper bag and all. I know we probably missed out on some fun times as a couple because we were intentionally strapped down. But when the avalanche of memories flood back, I wouldn't make any trades. The memories of times spent throwing footballs in the basement, taking first bike rides, and sword fighting with wrapping paper tubes are irreplaceable. Even the trying times with the children brought rewards that we treasure. Nada and I learned a lot about our children and ourselves, having our own brand of fun in the process.

As the years rolled past, we were often asked, "How do you survive having such a large family?" I would always defer to the wisdom of my mother-in-law, Matilda. When asked how she did it with a family of thirteen, she would predictably reply, "It was before car seats and child abuse." I tell any inquirers that we just try to keep plowing forward. I guess you just get it done—there is no manual. Just as anything else, if you want good results, you have to put in the time.

As the family grew, new challenges appeared. Nada and I quickly became outnumbered when our third child, David, was born. The plot thickened when back-to-back girls arrived, changing the game plan. It wasn't until Samuel came five years after our youngest daughter that we felt the most stretched. He wasn't the problem. Balancing the needs of an infant and a high school freshman with just about everything in between *was*! Still, we enjoyed trying to meet the challenges of parenting.

Reflections

Raising a family of six children has been an adventure. Fatherhood is an incredible gift. Nada and I stumbled along with good intentions and humility. We arrived at a hybrid style of sorts in terms of raising the kids. We rejected some traditional methods and embraced others.

We often joked about our traditional roles, with me as the

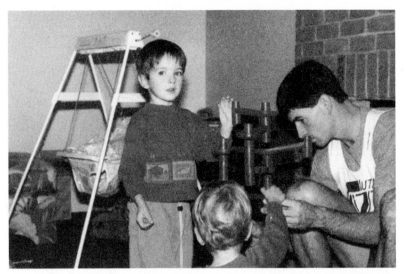

Hands-on dad, circa 1993. Left to right: Houston, Michael, and John.

breadwinner and Nada as the homemaker. We did cross over as necessary. I cooked, cleaned, got up with the children, and took care of them when they were sick—but only sparingly. Nada would occasionally take out the garbage, mow the lawn, and work outside the home. We both pitched in where we could without overly defined roles. Common sense dictated much of this division of labor. Nada was a better cook, and I'm pretty sure she couldn't guard Isiah Thomas (not that I could).

We took on the challenge of parenting together from the beginning. A cornerstone of that teamwork was our decision that Nada would stay home with the children and I would go to work. Our decision in this regard was made considerably easier by my occupation, but I am certain we would have accepted almost any economic hardship to keep her at home. It was that important to us.

Nada and I also found ourselves faced with a far more serious issue during her last pregnancy with Samuel. At age thirty-nine, she was bumped up into a higher risk category for birth defects.

Nada and new addition David.

As a result, we were asked if we wanted an amniocentesis procedure to determine if any defects existed in the baby; the purpose of the test is to allow parents time to terminate the pregnancy if serious defects exist. For us, it was a rhetorical question they were required to ask because they already knew our answer. We would accept the baby as it came. No test was necessary.

I have given the issue of the rights of an unborn child a great deal of thought over the course of many years. My upbringing was a valuable guide. Simply stated, I believe that an unborn baby has the right to life. This is not a regurgitation of my religious or family upbringing. Nor are my thoughts connected to any political party or philosophy. For me, the logic is simple—no one should be able to dictate whether an innocent child, literally with his or her whole life ahead of them, should live or die. I'm convinced the fetus, once the cells start dividing, is a developing human being. No amount of definitional massaging is going to change its DNA to something else. In this country we recognize that everyone is endowed by the Creator with certain inalienable rights. Preeminent among these is the right to life itself.

Women should certainly have the right to choose what they

do with their own bodies. They have fought and sacrificed for those and other freedoms that haven't been granted historically. They should expect nothing less, and we should tolerate nothing less. However, once conception occurs there is a third person whose rights must also be considered. The mother is responsible for that life. Her rights don't trump those of her child. I believe the vulnerable young life inside of every mother merits the same protections we guarantee to everyone in this great land of ours.

History will most likely judge us harshly for allowing the practice of abortion to exist on our watch. Having said that, it is important to note that shoveling blame or generating guilt is not my objective. I condemn no one. Unfortunately, abortion is legal and accepted by a large portion of our country's population. That is the culture we live in. Accepting this as a fixed and final practice, however, denies the positive forces in our history. We have faced many moral scourges and found a way within our democratic process to become a better society, a better place to live. We have confronted and, to a large extent, conquered ugly realities such as slavery, segregation, and gender discrimination. We should celebrate the fact that a great nation, like a great team, sticks up for its weakest members. In this case, the unborn need a voice. They deserve the same chance all of us received or we wouldn't be here to argue the point.

• • •

Nada and I were blessed six times with the gift of new life. Each of the children was unique and beautiful in his or her own fashion. Each arrival brought adaptation and change to our lives as well as the other children's. They were bumped to different rooms and seats at the dinner table. Through it all, Nada made the largest sacrifices and lifestyle changes to become a mother of

six. She possesses countless talents that remain anonymous outside of our home because she values motherhood above all else.
For my part, the routines that I had deemed so vital rightfully
became secondary to my responsibilities as a father, but they
did continue. I took my pregame naps usually curled up with
a baby. Game day departure times suffered with emergency diaper changes that often required a wardrobe change. No longer
could I spend all day thinking about the game as activities with
the kids abounded. Helping with homework also crept into my
pregame routine. These changes were good; they offered a different perspective. Basketball wasn't the most important thing in the
world. That realization, ironically, helped me play more relaxed
and, in turn, play better. Many more changes would greet me as I
blended my career as a member of the Jazz with my young, growing family's needs. As I have already indicated, the foundations
given to me by my parents have proved invaluable. I enjoy being
a dad. Being a good parent, however, is a challenge. I haven't always succeeded. But meeting that obligation is far more important to me than being a good basketball player ever was. Along
with Nada and our children, I will keep working at making the
family better tomorrow than it was today.

CHAPTER 12

A Gilded Opportunity: Salt Lake City and the Utah Jazz

Nada and I were adjusting to life with our first son as my fourth season approached. After a few games, I had worked my way into the starting lineup, a position I would hold for the next fifteen years. Our team was discovering some solid chemistry under the unorthodox but wise leadership of Coach Frank Layden. He cleverly mingled a large dose of humor with his instructions on the finer aspects of the game and deeper lessons in life. We had found a mixture of young and seasoned players who were working well together. Thurl Bailey, Mark Eaton, Darrell Griffith, Bobby Hansen, Marcus Iavaroni, Karl Malone, and I had earned Coach's confidence and a lion's share of the minutes. There was no revolving door with the Jazz organization, which gave us time to develop as a group. As a result, we were becoming a good team.

It struck me then how lucky I was to be in Salt Lake playing with the Jazz. Top to bottom, I was around great people. My success would be completely intertwined and often dependent upon them and the opportunities they provided. Even now with the benefit of hindsight, I can't conceive of a better situation than the one that actually unfolded for me in Utah.

The opportunity began with the city and its people. Salt Lake City, nestled against the Wasatch Mountains, is clean, safe, and beautiful. It was here, in my home away from home, that I continued growing into manhood while raising my family in an extraordinary environment. I loved having what I considered the best job in the world while enjoying the abundance of healthy activities that Utah had to offer.

Largely thought of as the "Mormon State," Utah didn't fit some commonly held stereotypes. For one, the notion that Salt Lake City is overwhelmingly Mormon is simply false. Actually, the city is somewhat diverse with a substantial Catholic minority.

Although more diverse than I originally thought, church and state do coexist closely. Salt Lake serves as both the Utah capital and as the headquarters of the Mormon Church. The state capitol building overlooks the expansive Salt Lake valley and Temple Square just a short way down State Street. There, at the coordinates of (0,0) on the city grid system, the magnificent Mormon temple stands beside the Tabernacle, home of the world-renowned choir, in the precise center of the city. Temple Square and surrounding buildings serve as the Mecca or global center for LDS faithful around the world.

I didn't have any trouble adjusting to life in this larger city. I felt invited and welcomed at all kinds of functions without feeling pressured into converting. My only real beef with the land of Zion came during the NCAA playoffs one spring when *all* the television stations preempted the Final Four games in favor of the LDS general conference. Everyone missed some great games. There must have been some sports fans high up in the church who disliked missing the NCAA Finals, especially when the

Running Utes were involved. By the time the Final Four rolled around the next year, the scheduling conflict was resolved and didn't happen again. I was happy with the decision.

The Mormons are an active, mission-oriented congregation with a focus on conversion. However, I was never asked if I wanted to be blessed or baptized into the church, and never once was I put in an uncomfortable situation. We had a few laughs each preseason when Jazz physical therapist Moe Forsyth would dip me into the pool to test my body fat and playfully suggest that I had just been baptized into the Mormon Church. I became friends, in some cases close friends, with many of the Mormon faithful. Most of these friendships were a result of our mutual association with the Jazz. Jazz owner Larry Miller was a member of the LDS Church, as were many of the people who worked for him in all of his businesses. These people, all of a different faith than me, not only made my opportunity with the Jazz possible, they enhanced and enriched the experience.

• • •

The unique atmosphere within the Jazz organization began at the top with our first owner, Sam Battistone. Sam made the risky and courageous decision to move the team from New Orleans to Utah. They traveled with the baggage of a huge debt load, bearing what I heard was over 15 percent interest. The team struggled in many ways, mostly financial. As each challenge unfolded and added to the burden of the next, the outlook became more bleak. At one point Sam sold a first-round draft choice (who turned out to be Dominique Wilkins) for the bargain price of one million dollars in order to meet his payroll obligations.

Mr. Battistone silently bore the brunt of all the team's troubles. He was always visible, sitting in the front row of the

Delta Center with his wife, Nan, and their beautiful children. Sam showed class at all times. For years he held on and endured the financial losses with grace until he could find a way to keep the Jazz in Utah permanently.

During the worst of these times, he flirted with the idea of moving the team to Las Vegas. In fact, the Jazz played a number of regular season games there my rookie season and in years prior, perhaps testing the water or laying the groundwork for a possible move. One particularly momentous basketball accomplishment occurred in one of them. To the delight of a large crowd of predominately Lakers' fans, Kareem Abdul-Jabbar broke the all-time NBA scoring record against the Jazz at Vegas's Thomas and Mack Center, our home away from home. The team was nearly shipped to Las Vegas for good as a sale to business magnate Adnan Khashoggi loomed. The deal was virtually completed when the league denied the transaction at the final hour. Adnan refused to participate with investigators on his other business dealings overseas, so thankfully, the transport never left the Salt Palace parking lot.[1]

Mr. Battistone continued to hold on as proposed deals continued to fall through. Then, rescue arrived in the form of Larry H. Miller.[2] Although he rode in like a warrior with a rough-and-tumble manner, Larry was much more than his veneer suggested. His frayed, competitive edges belied his extraordinary native intelligence. He possessed the depth of knowledge and understanding of a man who had worked his way up through the trenches while cataloging information along the way. When I dealt with Larry in a business setting, as I would do many times over the upcoming years, I always walked away feeling as though I had crossed swords with a pirate. He had street savvy, business experience, and a battle-tested background. He also calculated numbers in his head quicker than I could punch them into a calculator.

Larry had made it through high school only by the skin of his teeth. He walked away from college after little more than a month. This left him with some unfinished edges. He wound up taking a job for a Toyota store in the parts department. Something obviously clicked for him behind the counter, which piqued his interest and intellect. Amazingly, he organized the department and committed the entire parts book to memory to aid his efficiency. Needless to say, he advanced quickly through the ranks until he owned his first auto dealership, a Toyota store. Over time, with hard work and a proven formula for success, he began to purchase other stores. Ultimately he became one of the largest automobile dealers in Utah, and then expanded throughout the western region of the US, including Spokane.

• • •

Larry used the fruits of his success to buy a half interest in the Utah Jazz for $8 million, helping Mr. Battistone to relieve some of his burdensome debt load. Approximately a year later, he bought the other half of the franchise for a reported $14 million. His purchase of the team appeared to be the best thing for all parties. The Jazz became securely ensconced in Salt Lake with an owner who was determined to make the franchise work in that location. With the purchase, Mr. Battistone and his family finally vacated his owner's office and the financial stress that had gone with it. He and his family still sat in their familiar front row seats when they attended home games following the team's sale. Sam has since moved on to other successful enterprises, which include Dreams Inc., a large sports memorabilia company. His work adorns the offices of people in high places around the globe.

His presence can also be found in institutions, such as Hall of Fame venues, for all sports.

The Jazz simply could not have taken root in Utah without Sam. He brought the team to Salt Lake. His instincts about people enabled him to make hires that would ultimately prove foundational to the Jazz's success. He laid the groundwork and then brought in Larry Miller to complete his vision. As things turned out, their passion for the same dream—a successful and lasting Jazz franchise in Salt Lake City—was mutual and infectious.

From the moment Larry came on board, things changed. Our reserved, sharply dressed, and extraordinarily pleasant owner had given way to a maniac in tennis shoes. Similar to his point guard, Larry Miller was cursed by the fashion world. Sporting sand-knit stretch pants and a polo shirt, he occasionally donned his own Jazz jersey. Fitting snugly over his roundish frame, with the number nine and the name Miller on the back, he would actually take the court with the team for warm-ups. Our strange new comrade brought new meaning to the notion of active participation. He would hustle after rebounds, hand us the ball, and drop into his best defensive stance. Poking, prodding, bumping, and even trash-talking, he tried to ready us for battle. It quickly became apparent that this owner was going to be seen, felt, and heard. His involvement didn't end on the court. After one particularly uninspired effort and loss, Larry stormed into the Salt Palace locker room huffing and puffing like a rhino. His fury was spread evenly among the players, coaches, and trainers as his eyes met each of ours. He offered us some rather stark evaluations, delivered in particularly indelicate language—a thorough dressing down that left us with a clear understanding of how he felt about losing. He then blew out just as he had blown in. Coach added no postgame

Michael Stockton and Larry Miller in one of Larry's prized Cobras.

remarks that day. Nothing more needed to be said. There was a new sheriff in town, and he was in sharp contrast to the old one.

Considering this first impression, I was fortunate to receive the blessing of actually getting to know Larry Miller closely over the next two decades. Our relationship expanded to include many aspects of life. I learned to value and respect him more every day. As I so often had with my father, I began to seek his counsel as well as his conversation. I felt that he grew to trust my input and thoughts in many areas, inside and outside basketball. Over time our relationship evolved into a friendship that didn't need duct tape and bailing wire. We both could endure insults and compliments without ill will, and we didn't need to baby the relationship. Mostly we could trust each other. Having a boss as a friend is not always wise. Fortunately, it worked for us. Neither of us felt uneasy without the natural barriers that usually exist between the roles.

Over the years I watched how Larry treated his employees. He made it his business to know a little bit about each of his numerous workers. Getting to know them by more than their name was a priority. Striking up conversations with all employees within the organization without regard to their station was part of his method of operation. He made saying thank you a trademark. Larry treated people well even after he succeeded. I used to joke with him when he would take me out driving in his Shelby Cobra on mountain roads or at his race track: "It's good to be the king!" The beauty of Larry was that he shared the blessings he had with others. He was a good king.

• • •

NBA players normally didn't cross paths often with the "suit and tie guys" in the front office. We knew they were there and important to the organization, but we seldom saw them. We rubbed elbows on a regular basis, however, with our public relations staff. Dave Allred, Kim Turner, Dave Wilson, and Patti Balli were among the department's most gracious (and thick-skinned) personnel.

As part of the NBA collective bargaining agreement, players were contractually required to make up to twelve annual appearances on behalf of the team. Although many organizations throughout the league essentially ignored this provision, the Jazz held our feet to the fire. The players bucked mightily at the inconvenience. Unfazed by our protests, the PR staff called, reminded, prodded, and dragged us, sometimes grudgingly, to every event. Imagine trying to track down and escort a bunch of young, wealthy athletes somewhere they don't want to go. The Jazz staff was consistently up to the challenge.

I could grouse with the best of them. Somehow they managed to ignore my and everyone else's resistance with a tireless sense of humor. All of our complaints weren't completely unfounded. One night I was scheduled for an hour-long autograph session at a local mall. I signed for two hours but eventually had to leave.

Walking past a line of many people who had been waiting for at least that long created more ill will than it was worth. Ultimately, the staff and the players combined to work most of the kinks out of the system to make the appearances easier and better for everyone.

Some of the more difficult but inspiring appearances were the annual Christmas visits to the Shriner's Hospitals for Children and the Primary Children's Medical Center in Salt Lake. These visits usually occurred after long Eastern road swings when we were tired and convinced we needed a break. The visits took us into less than happy and often tragic circumstances when we wanted to focus only on the holidays. Invariably, we found the gift of the Christmas spirit where we hadn't planned on looking—in the eyes and hearts of the parents and children we met during these visits.

Shepherded by our staff, I learned that some of the most rewarding things we do can seem deceptively difficult before we do them. Walking into a room full of somber, concerned parents and loved ones looking after a child with steel bolts and brackets coming out of his/her skull is an example of something that would be much easier to avoid. I often found it hard to find words of any kind when I entered a child's room under these conditions. Then, a Jazz ball would pop out from the staff's goodie bag and eyes would light up around the room. The parents would begin to relax and share their stories while gently nudging their child to warm to us and the newly autographed basketballs. Smiles all around usually resulted. We always left each room with greater gifts than we had brought.

The efforts of the PR department often made it possible for us to be the type of people we wanted to be but couldn't without a little nudge. Putting others first is hard, especially when it feels as though you have no time and are being tugged in every direction. In the end, I enjoyed almost every appearance. I'm so grateful to the Jazz front office for insisting.

• • •

Spearheading the front office was Judy Adams. She was known simply as Judy. No other title was required. She was the hub of the Jazz wheel. Everything crossed her desk. Successful businesses of all types seem to have their own version of Judy, although I doubt any could be more valuable than ours. She became as indispensable as a friend to me and my family as she was to the organization as a key employee. She was also the bridge between the office and the basketball side of the operation.

The sweats and sneakers bunch were a lot more comfortable in the training room than they were in the front office. The argument could be made that the trainers knew the players better than their own mothers did. If I ever wanted to know something about a player, I'd ask their trainer. They wouldn't tell me, of course, but they'd know.

Don "Sparky" (Magic Fingers) Sparks was just that kind of trainer. He occupied the head seat in Jazz sick bay for most of my early years. He had moved with the team from New Orleans, where he had worked with legendary Hall of Famer "Pistol Pete" Maravich.

Don defies adequate description. His Southern accent was distinctively delivered with his unmistakable high-pitched twang. Just like little lambs, we all *knew* his voice: "Five o'clock bus, me-en. Git-cher own bags ta-morra." He was old school. His methods, though often a bit unorthodox, usually worked like a charm. One time we arrived at our hotel in Portland to find none of our rooms cleaned and ready. He said, "Fine. I'll sleep rat-cheer in the lobby." Lying flat on his back in the lobby, he looked like a dead man. Guests walking by stopped for astounded double takes. Our rooms were quickly cleaned—and they were ready early the next time we rolled into town.

Sparky was on call twenty-four hours a day, seven days a week when we were on the road. He was in charge of every non-basketball detail. As if that weren't enough, he also sat next to Jerry on the bench. He kept track of fouls and gave advice on health issues. He could give Coach the skinny on whether someone was really hurt or "sufferin' from a bruised ov-ry," as he liked to put it. He had quite a sense of humor.

One time he took things a step too far. In the final minute of a tight game with the Washington Bullets, he provided perhaps the first-ever instant replay in the NBA. He disagreed with a call on the floor. Reaching over his right shoulder to where Hot Rod Hundley and Ron Boone were announcing the game to viewers back home, he grabbed their monitor, turned the screen towards the ref, and pointed with a smile. His helpfulness was rewarded with a technical foul. Those two shots and possession of the ball for the Bullets nearly cost us the game. Fortunately for Sparky, we prevailed. He would have felt terrible if the outcome had gone against us. We tried our darnedest to avoid letting that happen. He was one of us, part of the team. We were going to make every effort not to disappoint him. Sparky seldom let us down either.

He took his loyalty to extraordinary lengths. Once when the life of one of his ex-players seemed to hang in the balance, he took it upon himself to stage a drug house rescue in Atlanta. He paid for his own flight and braved what had to have been frightening circumstances to drag one of his own to safety. No one could have taken better care of us than Don Sparks.

Two injuries cemented our friendship early in my career. I

tried to stay out of the training room in those early days because I was always afraid they would cut me if I got hurt. By year four, I couldn't avoid sick bay. My first trip for treatment involved a pulled hamstring prior to an exhibition game in Louisiana.[3]

Sparky and I saw a lot of each other while he nursed my leg. His most memorable treatment occurred before our next exhibition game at Weber State in Ogden, Utah. I had no intention of missing any games, exhibition or otherwise. I was ready and willing to do whatever he said in order to play.[4] After a few treatments, I was convinced that I was ready to go. All I had to do was persuade Sparky. That task appeared simple as the old fox immediately feigned agreement with my assessment. "Sure, Johnny. I'll jist massage'er a litta bit at shoot aroun'." Knowing full well what would happen, he gave this trusting soul an *extra-deep tissue massage*. By the time the game rolled around, I was so sore I didn't *want* to play. I didn't even want to *walk*. The massage did, however, give me time to heal. I never suffered a recurrence. Unconventional as he was, Don generally got the results he wanted for his players.

The second injury that strengthened our bond of friendship involved a severely sprained ankle in the Minneapolis Metrodome. We were engaged in a pretty good tussle with the expansion Timberwolves when I landed on the edge of someone's foot. Normally a sprain meant a short hobble back to the visitor's locker room to snug up a tape job and return to play. It's a little different hike in the dome. The court is barely within walking distance from the locker room for a healthy player. Sparky and I still laugh about the trek we took that day to tape my ankle. After leaving the court, I limped and hopped at least forty yards to descend into one of the baseball dugouts. From there we entered a maze of corridors that began with what seemed like a towering,

Clementine (Frei) Stockton, John's mother,
in nursing school, circa 1955.

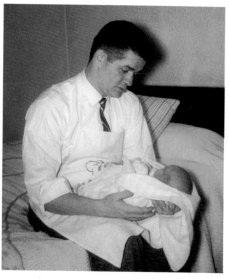

Jack Stockton in his bar apron from
work, with baby John, 1962.

John as a toddler.

Stockton siblings, left to right: Stacey,
Leanne, John, and Steve.

The Stockton family, circa 1969.
Front row, left to right: Clemy, Leanne,
and Jack. Back row, left to right:
John, Steve, and Stacey.

John, fifth grade, 1972.

Steve Stockton's grade school basketball team. Coach Linebarger is back
row, right. John is front row, second from left; Steve is back row, far left.

St. Al's 6th–7th grade championship basketball team. Coach
Pickett is in the back, and John is center front, no. 14.

John, seventh grade, checking into a game at Gonzaga University.
Coach Pickett is giving John instructions as Tim Mahoney looks on.

Gini and Coach Kerry Pickett, circa 1978.

John's high school senior photo, 1980.

John playing for the Gonzaga Bulldogs, Gonzaga University, circa 1983.

John played four seasons at his hometown Gonzaga University, finishing his career as the school's all-time leader in assists (554) and the sixth-leading scorer (1,340 points).

Press conference on NBA Draft day, 1984.

John and Nada's wedding, 1986.

PHOTO BY ANDREW D. BERNSTEIN/NBAE/GETTY IMAGES

After playing behind Rickey Green, Utah's incumbent starting point guard, his first
three seasons, John earned the starting job in 1986 and never let it go.

John on his first Father's Day
with Houston, 1987, Spokane,
Washington.

John and Houston vacuuming
together in their Salt Lake
apartment, 1988.

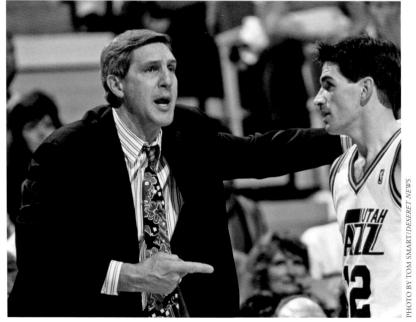

John listens to Coach Jerry Sloan.

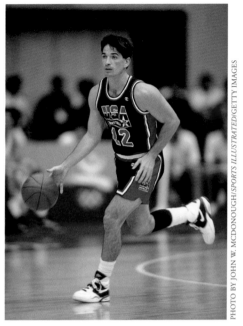

Coach Kerry Pickett and his wife, Gini, with John at the John Stockton School of Basketball, 1990.

John playing in the 1992 Summer Games in Barcelona, Spain.

The 1992 USA Men's Basketball "Dream Team." Front row, left to right: David Fischer (team physician), Scottie Pippen, Christian Laettner, Patrick Ewing, head coach Chuck Daly, David Robinson, Karl Malone, Charles Barkley; back row, left to right: assistant coach Mike Krzyzewski, assistant coach Lenny Wilkens, Michael Jordan, Larry Bird, Earvin "Magic" Johnson, Chris Mullin, Clyde Drexler, John Stockton, assistant coach P. J. Carlesimo, Ed Lacerte (trainer).

John and Karl Malone hold up the All-Star MVP trophy
after playing for the West team, which won the 43rd
NBA All-Star game, 135–130, in Salt Lake City.

The 1996 USA Men's Basketball Team wins the gold. Left to right: Charles Barkley, Grant
Hill, Anfernee Hardaway, David Robinson, Scottie Pippen, Mitch Richmond, Reggie Miller,
Karl Malone, John Stockton, Shaquille O'Neal, Gary Payton, and Hakeem Olajuwon.

"The Shot" that sent the Jazz to their first NBA Finals in 1997 with a game- and series-winning three-pointer against the Houston Rockets.

Karl Malone hugs teammates Jeff Hornacek (no. 14) and
John Stockton as Greg Foster (left) joins in the celebration after
the Jazz beat the Rockets 103–100 in Game 6 of the
Western Conference Finals May 29, 1997, in Houston.

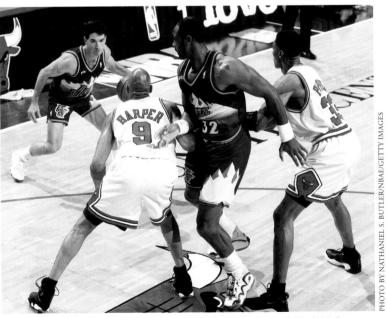

Utah's success flowed from the partnership of John and Karl Malone.
Behind the lethal pick-and-roll duo, the Jazz were a perennial playoff
team that reached the NBA Finals twice, in 1997 and 1998.

John driving solo in Larry Miller's Cobra.

Larry Miller congratulates John Stockton on his 10,000th NBA assist during a game on October 10, 2002, against the Celtics in Salt Lake City, Utah.

John, surrounded by his wife, Nada, and children, pulls a string to unveil his retired jersey in the Delta Center, November 22, 2004, in Salt Lake City, Utah.

John's jersey is unveiled on November 22, 2004, in Salt Lake City, Utah.

In addition to retiring his jersey in November 2004, the Jazz erected a statue, *Threading the Needle*, in his honor outside their arena.

John Stockton and Karl Malone's families at the retirement of Karl's Jazz jersey in 2006. The Stockton family, left to right: Houston, Michael, Nada, Lindsay, John, David, Samuel, Laura. The Malone family, left to right: Cheryl, Karl, Kay, Kylee, Daryl, Kadee, Karl Jr., Karlee.

The Stockton family and famed UCLA basketball coach John Wooden at an awards ceremony for Coach Wooden's Paralysis Project of America. Coach Wooden once said of John, "He's the only pro I would pay to watch play."

John Doleva, President and CEO of the Basketball Hall of Fame,
Michael Jordan, David Robinson, Jerry Sloan, John Stockton, and
C. Vivian Stringer at the Basketball Hall of Fame, 2009.

Frank Layden, John, and Jerry Sloan, 2010.

John thanks the crowd during the ceremony to
retire his jersey, November 22, 2004.

sixty-step ascent that ended with a winding series of halls that finally connected with the visitor's locker room. In that distance I stubbornly turned around four times, convinced my ankle felt better and that I could still play. After trying and failing to go more than about two or three steps each time with Sparky comically mimicking my turns like a synchronized swimmer, I finally accepted my fate and surrendered to the ice bucket. I missed the rest of that contest and the next two regular season games. These were my only absences up to that point in my career. In the days that followed, Sparky prescribed ice, stimulation, microcurrent, and acupuncture to get me back on the floor. The one thing that was most effective was Sparky's hands-on therapy. It far surpassed the gadgets. This was a serious sprain with substantial bleeding that "Magic Fingers" reversed in short order. I was back on the floor in less than four days.

Sparky was ably assisted in the training room by Terry "T. C." Clark, who doubled as our equipment manager. T. C. hailed from the Sunshine State and sported more of a "Flo-i-da" accent. He was much younger than Sparky. Over time T. C. became my primary trainer. He and I saw a lot of each other after Coach Sloan threatened to fine me if I didn't tape my ankles. I wasn't sure if Jerry was serious, but I thought the prudent measure was to get taped. T. C. and I became good friends through many rolls of tape. T. C. was kind of an ornery version of Radar O'Reilly from the famous TV series *M*A*S*H*, without the small-town innocence. He had buddies everywhere and could get things done in a flash. He had to be efficient and he was. He seemed to have every conceivable detail covered, either on his list or in his bag. T. C. worked the system and took great care of us. He gave me my first pair of short trunks, and I didn't argue; they were just like everyone else's at the time. These shorts became somewhat of a trademark for me as basketball "trousers" became the norm. The truth of the matter is I simply wore what T. C. gave me. I was glad to have a uniform. A couple years before I retired, he finally asked me if I wanted to lengthen my shorts a little. I agreed to an extra inch—not wanting to rock the athletic apparel industry! We all counted on T. C., and he didn't disappoint.

The trainers worked with a top-notch medical team that essentially donated their time and considerable talents. Russ Shields, Lyle Mason, Michael Lowe, and Craig Buhler were an eclectic but interesting group of practitioners. They provided their services for little or no compensation, considering what they did. Each of these men took turns going beyond the line of duty to take care of me over the course of my career. From serious health issues and surgery to minor upkeep and daily care, their significant talents were put to good use. They also infused medical kits full of personality to the mix. Jazz players missed very few games due to injury—a credit to the entire medical staff.

Over time the doc that I spent the most time with ended up being our team chiropractor, Craig Buhler. Initially, I was less than open to the idea of him even touching me with his somewhat unorthodox treatment methods. Later, after watching and experiencing some incredible healing, I gained complete confidence in him, and our association widened.

I became both a believer in and a student of his methods. Using pain as a warning light and muscle testing as the body's tool for communication, he was able to eliminate pain and increase function for almost all chronic and acute injuries without the use of drugs. Under his care, sprained ankles stabilized and became pain-free in days, not weeks or months. Tendonitis went away with only a few treatments. It's not an overstatement to say that Dr. Buhler was largely responsible for me enjoying

John, early in his career, guarding Magic Johnson.

a durability and longevity that few players have come close to matching.

Hot Rod Hundley, the longtime radio and TV voice of the Jazz, also didn't miss many games. In my opinion, he was the best announcer in the league. Hot Rod used his distinctive raspy voice and unique ability to describe the action on the court; he employed a style that was all his own. Listening to Hot Rod describe the action, listeners could vividly imagine Thurl "Big T" Bailey getting off a "cork-screw jumper" from the corner or "The Mailman" throwing down a "thunder dunk!" A listener might even find himself outside the arena, watching the "Golden Griff" launch a shot "from the parking lot." And exceptional plays always received Hot Rod's signature endorsement: "You gotta love it, baby." Hot Rod was fun to listen to, and his audience

John, Houston, and Hot Rod Hundley.

always knew the score. His ability to describe the action and paint a unique word picture made him one of a kind. For years, he shared the Jazz fans' love for their team while delivering a remarkably neutral view of the action on the hardwood.

Sitting beside Hots and forming a dynamic duo was Ron Boone. "Booner," a former NBA player and ABA star, was well respected and loved around Salt Lake. He had played much of his career with the Utah Stars and amassed an impressive record of 1,041 consecutive games played. The feat isn't officially recognized because it spanned the two leagues; the number does, however, offer some insight into the type of competitor he was. These two announcers were an indispensable part of our team. Whether at home or on the road, they did their job fabulously and were smart enough to know where not to tread. Though both were tremendous professional athletes in their own right, the duo never tried to coach us. In my early years, Frank Layden capably filled those shoes.

A GILDED OPPORTUNITY

A product of New York disciplined parochial schools, Frank Layden used coaching as a tool to make his players better people. He didn't shy away from that responsibility. He embraced the roles of coach, teacher, and parent and took the accompanying obligations seriously. With his gravelly voice and direct approach, we could tell he cared about us, even when he was barking at us. Most of the comments I remember from Coach Layden had more to do with how to be a good person than how to become a good basketball player, although the two roles often ran together. I frequently recall his sage advice to me at our first meeting: "Don't change who you are now that you've 'arrived.'"

While visiting Spokane after his retirement, Coach revealed a lot about himself on the golf course. As our round grew long, he got tired of watching me slice the ball all over the course. Finally, he rasped, "Don't keep making the same mistake over and over again. Change something!" A leopard can't change his spots—he was a born coach.

His one-liners—too numerous to count—that should be long-forgotten still resonate as I think back on them. I will always carry his deeper lessons with me. He often made the point that we were role models, which he termed "examples to young athletes and young people. Whether you accept it or not, that is what you are. Accept it and do it well." He urged us further, "Don't sweat the small stuff—the stuff you have no control over. There are plenty of big important things that you do have control over that you should concentrate on doing well."

Coach was hysterically funny yet serious about his work. He told jokes often as a method of making a larger point about a game or life. He frequently spoke in public with a distinctive style. People would roll in the aisles at his self-deprecating deliveries such as "I have to hurry; they feed me every fifteen minutes,"

179

a reference to his ample girth. Coach also had a special ability to use humor to relieve tension. One time when we were watching film from a previous game, the camera zoomed in on Coach's popped shirt button, which had exposed his belly. Because we were coming off a couple of losses, the tension in the room was palpable. Nobody wanted to show a reaction of any kind. From the back of the room, Frank bellowed, "I need a sign that says, 'Space Available.'" We all busted our seams laughing. By the way, we won the game that night.

Dealing with Coach wasn't always a humorous experience. Sometimes we needed to fasten our seat belts when riding with him. He could lambaste a player with the best of them. One game against the Celtics in Provo makes the point. Larry Bird had stuck us pretty good in the first half. In the locker room, Frank broke loose with any and all issues he had been storing up for just such an opportunity. Pacing with his arms crossed and glaring into the eyes of one man after the other, his voice deepened. As the gravel boiled up from the gut, he used his finest New York accent while pointing at three or four guys with fresh contracts, "What are you making—$200,000; $600,000? How about you? $800,000?" He paused. "Well, what do you think Larry Bird is worth, then? 10 million, 50 million?" This story didn't have a happy ending as the second half was more of the same. We lost to the mighty Celtics.

His tirades weren't always limited to the team. Following a Jazz victory in Madison Square Garden, he had a classic New York argument just outside our locker room with a belligerent Big Apple guy wearing a big cowboy hat. With words flying and fingers jabbing, the heated exchange ended with Coach needling the urban cowboy: "What'd you do, find that hat?"

Whether in practice or in the game, Coach insisted on common courtesy. He preached, "You don't need to tie or untie your shoes when I'm talking." Coach jumped on me one time for clipping a fingernail during his pregame talk. He said that he almost got hit by a shard whizzing by! His point was to be ready well before any meeting, practice, or game. Coach expected us to be focused on what he was saying and the game that was about to begin. Being ready also meant that everyone had the same gear on, all the way down to the same socks. He didn't allow individuals to wear extra clothing that might say, "Look at me." We were a team. Shoes were different, of course, as they were provided by different shoe companies. Regardless of the brand, however, they were to be laced tightly and our jerseys had to be tucked in prior to the pregame meeting. Tucking a shirt in can take some guys a half an hour when they check into a game. His system eliminated all the stalling nonsense.

Frank Layden also excelled at coaching and motivating. During the playoffs of my fourth season, he really shined. After dispatching the Trail Blazers, we matched up against one of the greatest Laker teams of all time. The contest was a mismatch, but we didn't know it. Following a disappointing loss in game four, which gave the home-court advantage back to the Lakers, Frank called about six of us into his office. He told us to ignore what the press said. "Don't you give up now. We are going to get these guys down there and win this. Stay with me!"

With the difficult playoff psychology and a young team, he convinced us we would succeed. At that moment we would have run through a wall for Coach. We lost game five by two points as a pair of unfortunate plays helped the Lakers escape with a pivotal victory. But we won game six by twenty-eight, demonstrating that we were for real. As it turned out, the champs got off the mat to win game seven by eleven. We weren't able to complete the job at that point, but we were coming! We had put quite a scare into the champs, put ourselves on the map, and come away with an even deeper belief in ourselves and in our coach.

Coach Layden built the team from an underachieving group of players into a legitimate contender. In 1983, the year before I was drafted, the Jazz experienced their first winning season. They had won the Midwest Division Championship. That group broke the ice, allowing future teams to build upon their success. This is perhaps the hardest step in all of sports—changing a losing environment into a winning atmosphere. Within a few years, we were challenging for a title. Frank Layden was pointing us toward the future—a very bright one.

Shortly after the start of the following season, a large cloud fell upon our team. Frank resigned his post as head coach while retaining his role as general manager. Unaccustomed to change within the Jazz organization, I was shocked by the announcement. Coach must have felt he was losing a little of his zeal after so many years of success. Long after his retirement he told me, "You have to absolutely love what you are doing or you will become a slave to it." That sentiment must have been building for a while before his decision to retire. Coach stepped out of the limelight humbly and enjoyed more time with his wife and friend, Barbara. "You quickly become much like yesterday's newspaper," he playfully noted years later in describing his departure. Maybe so, but in his case, that issue is worth saving to read over and over again.

• • •

The NBA waits for no one. There was no time for lingering sentiment. We had games to play as Frank clearly understood. That is exactly what our new skipper and former assistant, Jerry Sloan, directed us to do. This marked the beginning of the longest uninterrupted tenure of any head coach in the history of the league.[5] Jerry's advance left a vacancy at assistant coach that needed to be filled. An old friend fit the bill perfectly.

In an amazing twist of fate, two buddies would be reunited. Coach Phil Johnson was a young assistant to Dick Motta of the Chicago Bulls in the early '70s when the Bulls had a fiery young guard named Jerry Sloan. For the next forty years, their lives were intertwined with the game of basketball.[6] In 1988, Phil rejoined the Jazz coaching staff, this time as Jerry's assistant.

I had some real concerns about my future without Coach Layden. Frustratingly, just as I had earned his confidence, he hung up his clipboard. I had no idea how Coach Sloan viewed me as a player. Jerry was more intense and a lot less fun than Frank. And when Phil came on board, he always appeared grumpy, so I had doubts about his assessment of my game as well. At least those were my thoughts in the beginning. I decided to heed the words that Frank had etched in my mind: "Don't sweat the things you can't control. Just go out and play."

As it turned out, my worries were unfounded. Our new head coach and his longtime friend came to have an incredibly positive impact on my career and life. In addition to being top-drawer mentors and teachers, they were terrific men. My respect and admiration for Jerry and Phil grew over the years. There is a lot more to the story of our friendship than our association on the basketball court. I enjoy and value their company and counsel to this day.

Coach Sloan, far from being the unfettered madman he is sometimes thought to be in NBA lore, is a thoughtful but hard-nosed country boy who has been around the block a few times. Behind his country "skookum" façade lay strength and wisdom—the kind attained only from overcoming meager and humble beginnings. He got his training in the school of hard knocks and keenly remembered the lessons along the way. Walking to school ten miles seemed normal to Jerry. This is not the tall tale of an old-timer, as I've seen the route myself. The distance is accurate, and there are no shortcuts. The house in which he grew up no longer stands. The woods have gobbled up all remnants of the old homesite. But Jerry remains connected to the rural setting and rich soil he sprang from in southern Illinois. Every year he spends some time off recharging his batteries on his farm in the Land of Lincoln.

Coach has keen, alert eyes that miss nothing. He doesn't always let you know what he sees either. When he does, you squirm a little, wondering what else he knows. Pulling the wool over his eyes is next to impossible. He sees through malarkey with piercing looks and knowing smiles. While listening, Jerry will often look into his hand or at his desk, fiddling with one thing or another, while he considers the right words to call you on your particular brand of baloney.

Coach Sloan is quick to point out that he learned a lot from Coach Layden. Knowing who deserves credit for what is difficult. I'm certain neither cares. Like Frank, Jerry eliminates the small stuff that could cause problems. We all wore the same uniforms and sweats to practices, and no jewelry made an appearance on the court. This ensured no one dressed in a way that would call individual attention away from the team. If we wanted to stand out, he would suggest we do it with our play. He didn't believe in fines, even though he had threatened me with one over the ankle taping incident. Jerry wanted to treat us like men. Our job, in return, was to act like men. Be on time and abide by team rules without being monitored. He knew the value of operating like a team. This included checking on each other. "Don't sit on the bus joking about a teammate being late. Call him early or go get him yourself, so he isn't late," he would preach.

Jerry has a burning passion for the game of basketball, especially the NBA. That love is genuine; he couldn't fake it if he wanted to. Coach remained one of the finest ambassadors of the NBA and the game of basketball until his retirement in 2011. He continually stood up for what he thought was right and wrong with the game. He was often misunderstood by fans and people within the NBA, including officials, because he didn't waver from the principles he held. I didn't always agree with Jerry but I never had to question his sincerity. He coached to win and had our best interest at heart. I shared many great experiences with him in addition to our years together with the Jazz. These memories include the '96 Olympics and the visits with my family to his farm in Illinois.

In the years before teams traveled on chartered airplanes, Jerry could be found after most road games standing sentry in the hotel lobby bar—always in full view of the entrance. I'm sure this vantage point helped him keep tabs on his team. "I can set my watch by you," he'd tell me as I strolled in after dinner. I think he liked the consistency of my habits. In later years I felt more comfortable sitting down to talk with Coach when I came back to the hotel. If we didn't have a game the next night, I might have a beer, but I mostly stuck to water, the nectar of the gods. I seldom drink anything else.

We would talk about all sorts of things: kids, sports, player personalities, and current events. Sometimes he'd tell stories about the old days. I loved listening to those. Hot Rod might pop in and offer a couple of doozies as well. These times were a lot of fun. Often a crew of players would join the circle—Mark, Karl,

Jeff, Thurl, or our big redhead, Adam Keefe. Those were the best times. It was camaraderie at its finest.

Parked next to Jerry during these gab sessions on the road was Coach Johnson. Usually after spending time with Jerry, I would belly up to the bar next to Phil. We mostly talked hoops, although the topics could be as far ranging as our taste in literature to why I stunk that night. Sometimes he offered his insights on the competition—what he saw about players, their talents, and their strengths and weaknesses. Phil was a library of knowledge that I not only enjoyed but benefitted from greatly.

We all covered a lot of basketball in those casual conversations with the coaches. Separated from the heat of battle by a couple of hours, we could cover ground inaccessible during the game. Things that frustrated us about their coaching or vice versa could be unearthed in this removed and more relaxed atmosphere. The discussions were never hostile; they were open and sometimes animated. Feathers didn't get ruffled as real and important sentiments were aired. Serious issues or specific details about someone's play were fair game. A motivational challenge or two might be thrown out: "You won't be able to guard that guy!" or "This team won't let you get away with that!" These informal exchanges made us better players and them better coaches. We could see each other's perspective. I'm nostalgic about those evenings as they remain on my highlight reel.

Phil and I grew to share some interests off the court as well. His wife, Ann, was a speed-reader. She could digest a large book in a day. Ann would suggest only the best for Phil to read. He passed along her suggestions to me but more important helped me to begin a long relationship with nonfiction works. His love of reading was contagious—a gift I had not expected to receive from him. In short order, I was hooked. He started me with

John playing with Phil Johnson's bobcat as John's children watch.

shorter reads, books such as *Endurance*,[7] which chronicled Ernest Shackleton's adventures in Antarctica. Later he led me into much larger challenges, such as *Undaunted Courage*,[8] which depicts the journey of Lewis and Clark, and many more interesting and exciting literary adventures. I often exchanged these books with my dad and Coach Pickett back home for their best choices as well, which included *Truman*,[9] and *Freedom from Fear*.[10] I really enjoy nonfiction books. Seeing what other people went through and understanding their decisions from a time so different from our own is enlightening. They remind me to avoid being judgmental. Unless I've walked in someone's shoes, in their time, I don't think I can fully appreciate the challenges they faced.

Phil also shared a love of animals in the wild, resulting in Ann adopting a rather unique pet—a full-grown bobcat. The massive feline was injured in a trap and was convalescing in the Johnson home. As curious as that cat, I visited often and usually brought my family with me. On one occasion we caught a glimpse of the extraordinary speed and strength of their pet. Cuddled up next to me on their couch was my two-year-old daughter Lindsay. Clad in a bright Little Red Riding Hood coat, she captured the attention of the bobcat the moment we entered the house. Noticing the feline's interest, I assumed a huddled, protective position, never taking my eyes off the cat that was watching Lindsay from about fifteen feet away. In a flash the bobcat appeared on my shoulder above Lindsay. The animal had moved so quickly I didn't have time to flinch. Fortunately, the giant kitty was just curious, but the situation offered real insight into the nature of animals in the wild.

Phil and Ann went a step further when they discovered my family's enthusiasm for the wild kingdom. They introduced me to Doug and Lynne Seus. Doug is the friend and trainer of Bart the Bear, a thirteen-hundred pound grizzly of television and movie fame. They invited us to his home near Heber, Utah, to meet Bart and a dozen wolf cubs he was training for the movie *Julie of the Wolves*. I loaded up the minivan and headed into the mountains for a family field trip. Watching Doug tussle with Bart and hold his own explained why Doug had almost ripped my arm off while shaking hands to say hello. He let me feed one of the smaller bears, while my son David befriended a wolf cub ironically named "Old Man." My intention that day was to see the animals, to be able to say "We did that," then hurry home as is my nature. I didn't want to impose on the Seuses. After a spell, I slowly tried to maneuver our crew toward the car ride home. Lynne wouldn't hear of it. She insisted, beyond politely, that we sit outside, enjoy some homemade lemonade, cheese, and crackers, and take in the beautiful scenery. The day turned out to be remarkably enjoyable, despite requiring me to function outside of my normal comfort zone. I seldom sit still, particularly with strangers. But from the moment I sat down with them, an unfamiliar sense of peace came over me. The beautiful scenery and the company of such nice people overwhelmed me. After just a few short hours, I felt as though the Seuses were lifelong friends. The day and the company were both exceptional.

Doug and Lynne are rare and special people. They pioneered Vital Ground,[11] an organization dedicated to preserving and restoring habitats for grizzly bears. In doing so, they have protected and preserved wild spaces for other animals and mankind as well. The Seuses' philosophy has proven irresistible for me. They have provided opportunities to help protect the world in which we live. I am grateful to have them and their work in my life.

On the ride home, I was left thinking about how circles of friends filled with good people develop. Quality individuals introduce members of their circle to other quality people and a new circle begins. This reminded me that all of our coaches, Frank, Jerry, Phil, Gordon Chiesa, Kenny Natt, and Scott Layden, were all good, well-rounded people. Each would have been successful at any career they might have chosen.

•   •   •

Having quality coaches and mature players makes a lot of things possible. You can collaborate with a common purpose. You can also become friends. We enjoyed each other's friendship without sacrificing professionalism. The coaches didn't try to make decisions for us on the court, and we didn't try to coach for them. We shared a common trust that I valued.

In the end, the quality of my experience with the Jazz rested heavily on the strength of the bond I shared with my teammates. Teammates, the good ones, are like brothers. In some ways they are even closer. Locker rooms and team buses are sanctuaries where conversations that are not intended for all ears can be openly aired. Some of the best times I've ever had have taken place inside a locker room or on a bus in a close-knit group. Each man pokes a little fun, pops off, and tests boundaries in a group banter that usually leaves everyone chuckling. I loved these exchanges with my band of brothers.

When you walk out of a locker room onto that 94' by 50' rectangle, your teammates and coaches are the only people you can count on for the next couple of hours. The bond only strengthens in the rigors of an NBA game. Athletic competition at that level demands reliance on one another, unlike anywhere else I have seen. I'm thankful to have enjoyed this pure competitive experience for nearly two decades. It made going to work and the endless preparation worthwhile.

I'm afraid the beauty of this competitive experience is gradually being chipped away by the forces of progress, which seem always at the gate with new promotional glitz and technology. Cameras and microphones are everywhere, invading even our most private domains. The Internet, with its omnipresent tweets and Facebook postings, is about to take the encroachment to a level that no one could have possibly anticipated only a few years ago. I devoted a large portion of my life trying to win basketball games. The so-called "showtime" of it all didn't interest me in the least. I have always felt that the game itself was and is the whole show. I recognize that the public's interest and enthusiasm are at the core of all success in professional sports. Reasonable and effective marketing, including access to athletes and sensible use of technology, is obviously necessary. Still, excess is dangerous and easy. I know it adversely affected me.

I have never liked having a camera or a microphone in a team huddle. There is no doubt that these intrusions affect the free exchange between coaches and players. I know I went mum as the league mandated access to our huddle. The watchful eye kept me from offering input to our team because our keys to success didn't need to be shared with other teams over the airwaves. In addition, keeping comments fit for a dual purpose is an impossible challenge. Those appropriate for teammates in the heat of battle aren't necessarily suitable for a television audience. It's difficult to maintain responsibility as a role model and be an unfiltered contributor during a game. I would like to videotape a courtroom lawyer, a CEO, or a lawmaker, for example, when they don't intend their words for public consumption. Certain information is and always will be intended to be private. Stick a camera at someone's dinner table and observe the effect. Some will play to the camera, some will say nothing, but everyone's behavior will be altered.

• • •

People are obviously curious about athletes and their lifestyles. I was often asked, "Which one of your teammates is your best friend?" My response typically began with an explanation: "It's not like high school or college where you hang out with your teammates most of your free time." Still, for most players, outside of their families, teammates are their closest friends for eight months of the year. Just as in any large family, certain members connect with some more than others.

Early on I spent a considerable amount of time with Mark Eaton and Thurl Bailey. Either they couldn't shake me, or they enjoyed my company. Another teammate who put up with me during my formative years was Marcus Iavaroni. He was a bright guy who had graduated from the University of Virginia in sports psychology. Marc brought toughness and championship experience to our team. He and I sat together for most plane rides and shared many great in-flight conversations. I was generally the beneficiary of his insights and experience. One particularly important conversation with Marc comes to mind. The topic was officials and the discussion spawned a change in my attitude. I had confessed to Marc that I felt a few referees "killed me" and a few others weren't giving me any breaks. Drawing on his education, he suggested that maybe I was contributing to the problem with the belief that a given official didn't like me. He added that my body language probably betrayed these sentiments. He was convinced that this acted as a self-fulfilling prophecy.

I wasn't convinced immediately but decided to try the strategy. With a little self-talk, I changed my thoughts—nothing more. I told myself before each game, "This referee is a professional and a good one. He has nothing against me." (Sometimes conceding even that much took some serious mental energy.) Amazingly, it seemed to work. I certainly sensed a positive difference in the way I saw the game being called. Perhaps my new mind-set merely changed my focus to the things I had control of, mainly my play. I still had rough outings with the men in stripes, but, all and all, Marcus's approach was helpful.

What drew me to Marcus in the beginning was that he knew how to win. He had won the World Championship with Dr. J and the Sixers in '83. What sold me on the man was his willingness to sacrifice himself, to play underappreciated roles without demanding credit. He did whatever was needed for us to succeed. Sometimes that meant giving up an important foul. In a huge playoff series against Portland one year, he set two mammoth screens that changed the entire tone and psychology of the series. The fouls shortened his time on the court, but they were the key to us moving on to the next round. He was instrumental in our victory without being a star on the stat sheet.

Marcus's attitude extended to practice. Coach Sloan was angry with the team one morning at our Westminster College practice site. Referring to Karl, Jerry asked, "Won't anybody get up and guard this guy?" Two minutes later Iavaroni was walking past Coach to the training room holding a broken and bloodied nose with his hands. On the way out, he calmly offered a jab to Coach in his best Long Island accent: "Is that close enough for you, Jerry?"

Even though they played the same position and each took a few lumps in practice, Marc wanted to help The Mailman become a star as quickly as possible. In the process he quickly became a fan himself. Karl was a physical load! When Karl got the ball in a game, Marcus would yell to the guy trying to guard him, "Torcha chamba!" ("Torture chamber!") because he knew firsthand how miserable it was to try to guard him. In short order, The Mailman became the best power forward in the game. Marcus helped him do that, and we all built a friendship in the process.

Explaining how these special friendships take root, grow, and develop within a team is as hard as explaining the phenomenon in life. Through plane-ride conversations, common interests, and similar philosophies, friendships are sometimes born. Occasionally, friendships grow even when interests, backgrounds, and basic philosophies differ.

This was the nature of my friendship with Karl Malone. I had an incomparable opportunity to play with Karl and, if it's possible, an even better one to get to know him as a man. Despite his physical blessings, Karl had no fast track or easy road to success. His father died when he was young. His wonderful mother,

Shirley, raised Karl and his many siblings in a humble house next to their store and fishing pond. No other structure could be found within miles. Karl was proud of his home and his heritage. He spoke with an unembarrassed Louisiana accent when he talked about his "sissers and mom at the catfee-ish pon'."

Extremely bright, Karl was much like Coach Sloan. His eyes picked up everything. Quick in a battle of wits, he holds his own with the best, and he has a remarkable memory. He files things he learns away for future reference. Karl often surprised me by the things he had observed or learned. Generous to a fault, he shared his good fortune with others. Family, friends, and complete strangers witnessed and benefitted from his willingness to give. Two hundred percent tips or hundred dollar bills for a needy soul asking for some "fragments" (loose change) were common.

He also handled sticky situations well. Once on an airplane, an older man greeted Karl with, "Hey, there, boy!" I watched as his immediate angry impulse gently cooled as he recognized the man meant no offense. "Hello, there, sir!" Karl responded without a trace of resentment as he took his seat. Later, I asked him about his congenial response. He told me he felt that overreacting would have made an awkward situation worse. He didn't want to contribute to any stereotypical notions about black people, the Utah Jazz, or professional athletes. I was impressed, as usual, with his great judgment. His restraint showed tact and wisdom. Lashing out at the man would only have made a bad impression in the eyes of everyone on the plane—Karl understood that.

I once saw him tested in a more humorous way in the Salt Lake airport. While waiting for our luggage at the carousel, a lady mistook Karl for a skycap and summoned him to carry her luggage. Without fuss or hesitation, Karl said, "Why, sure, ma'am." He snatched the bags and followed the lady to her car full of Jazz fans staring out the windows in total disbelief. Karl loaded the bags into the trunk, refused the tip, and said, "Have a nice day." He took pleasure in his own kind act and the irony of the whole situation.

. . .

Working with the Jazz was an adventure of a lifetime. I shared the experience with some great people. Most of us shared a love of hard work and humble beginnings that we carried with pride. Together, the owners, coaches, staff, and players accomplished some incredible feats, and we helped each other reach our dreams. I lived a golden opportunity.

CHAPTER 13

The Olympics, 1992: The Team of My Dreams

*"An Olympic medal is the greatest achievement
and honor that can be received by an athlete. I would swap
any World Title to have won gold at the Olympics."*[1]

—JEFF FENECH, AUSTRALIAN OLYMPIC BOXER, 1984

In 1991, following a playoff loss to Portland, my young family and I found our way back home to Spokane to enjoy the summer. We had had a nice season and playoff run but hadn't been able to get over the hump in the Western Conference Finals against a terrific Blazer team led by Clyde Drexler. I wasn't quite ready for the off-season as I felt we had left some unfinished business in Portland's Memorial Coliseum. I was resigned to make the best of this early exit with some overdue adjustments to my off-season conditioning program. Coach Sloan had convinced me that recovery was more important at that stage in my career than playing every day. Following his advice, I didn't play in the Spokane Summer League with my brother, Steve. I also took a sabbatical from daily "ratball" games and retired from the Jack and Dan's softball team. This soothed Dad's annual irritation about me risking injury on the diamond.

Nada and I spent most of that welcomed free time at the lake with the boys, which now included David, who joined the family in June. Not much of a sunbather, I filled my days with physical activity of all kinds—mountain man labor such as cutting, splitting, and stacking firewood gave way to waterskiing whenever the elements provided smooth water. When the wind kicked up, I'd mountain bike, run, or try my hand at windsurfing, an exhausting wrestling match on a fun-house platform. The boys tagged along in nearly every activity and quickly learned to keep up. They could even balance on my windsurfer, riding double with me after I gained some competence myself. To stay sharp I lifted weights "Rocky" style, without fancy equipment, and shot hoops in the driveway around cars and pinecones.

These uncluttered times created some of our best family experiences and memories. Spur-of-the-moment discovery missions, games, and activities of our own creation filled each day. We searched for animal tracks and hunted elusive frogs. Playing catch with a football while jumping off the dock was a family favorite. Reenacting the formation of Lake Missoula and the Great Flood on the sandy beach gave the geologically inclined an artistic outlet. Campfires often capped off the day's events as stars close enough to touch filled the night sky. S'more-encrusted faces listened intently to scary stories, legendary tall tales, and adventure books that I would read by the miner's light attached to my head. One by one the boys would fade off to sleep in the fresh night air. This warranted a piggyback or shoulder ride to bed. Nada and I would linger by the fire catching up on the day as falling stars and northern lights replaced the fire and the full day as both burned to a close.

When we weren't at the lake, we spent most of our time at home or at Mom and Dad's. I was still refurbishing the house bit by bit. It was while at home that summer, on an otherwise unremarkable day, that the phone rang. As usual no one showed the slightest inclination to pick up. Somehow, before the patience of the caller evaporated, I found myself with the receiver to my ear.

ASSISTED

"John, this is Rod Thorn of the NBA."

This can't be good, I thought. Rod usually called to discuss on-court situations that might involve fines.[2] I had called his office only once, years earlier, to discuss my first technical foul. I told him, "Yes, I did swear at the official, but I used it as an adverb!" He chuckled, as he hadn't heard that one before, and dismissed the fine. I never went to the well again and accepted my future punishments as they came.[3]

This time Mr. Thorn bore only good news. "Congratulations. You have been selected to play for the United States in the 1992 Summer Olympic Games in Barcelona." I was speechless. After a pause I heard, "Are you interested?" I could only muster a stunned question: "Are you serious?" Like an excited kid, I had already mouthed the invite to Nada. I had heard that they might use NBA players for the Olympics but immediately dismissed the rumor and had never entertained the notion that they might select me. I thought my Olympic ship had sailed without me in 1984. As Mr. Thorn confirmed that he was indeed serious, it was all I could do to restrain myself. I calmly responded that I'd have to discuss it with Larry, Coach Sloan, and, of course, Nada. He assured me that the Jazz people were already on board. I didn't doubt him for a moment but still felt obligated to ask them personally. I told him I would call him back immediately. Since Nada had sidled up to eavesdrop on the conversation and was already doing back-flips across the living room, I was pretty sure she was good to go! I quickly called Larry and Coach Sloan, and each confirmed his enthusiastic support for my Olympic participation. I could almost see their smiles over the phone line. Nervous that he might change his mind, I couldn't call Mr. Thorn back fast enough. I blurted out my acceptance the moment I heard his voice.

I am often surprised by my reaction to hearing momentous

news of any kind. This day was no exception. I was so stunned that a quiet reserve came over me. Like a duck appearing calm on the surface while paddling like crazy under water, my mind was racing with the implications of my selection. I explored the magnitude and meaning of being chosen for our Olympic team. After all these years, I was going to represent my country and get a chance to fulfill my long-lost dream. Even in this excited state I recognized the selection carried with it a heavy responsibility. Representing my nation and its dreams couldn't be taken lightly.

Deep in these thoughts, I hadn't yet fully absorbed the names of my soon-to-be-teammates. The roster read like a *Who's Who* of basketball: Magic Johnson, Larry Bird, Michael Jordan, Karl Malone, Patrick Ewing, David Robinson, Chris Mullin, Scottie Pippen, Clyde Drexler, Charles Barkley, and a college player to be named later. Ultimately, this open spot was filled by Christian Laettner, a senior at Duke. I was going to the Olympics with possibly the greatest basketball team ever assembled.

The '91–'92 NBA season began with a noticeably different flavor. My selection to the Olympic team had somewhat validated me as a high-level player but had also placed a large target on my back. I felt that a few opponents wanted to prove I didn't belong on the squad. Whether I imagined their intentions or not, I was equally determined to prove that I did. This extra emotion and intensity added to the drama of every game. The most pronounced of these situations involved Isiah Thomas.

Isiah had raised the bar for me at the AAU National Championships during my high school years. His play at that tournament established a new benchmark that I aspired to. His standard of excellence through college and the NBA was one I believed many players, both big and small, tried to achieve. According to reports, he felt snubbed at being passed over in the US Olympic selection process. Isiah was a great player—a champion at every level at which he had played. He had a great case for his selection, but that was beyond my control. Being a fellow small point guard, the focus of the obvious comparison fell squarely upon me and *my* selection to the team.

This leap of logic certainly made for interesting games versus Detroit that season. These were always tough battles under normal circumstances, but the games that season were played with an even higher degree of intensity. Both Piston contests felt as though they had a personal dimension from the start. From the opening tip of the first game at the Palace in Auburn Hills, I perceived that Isiah was trying to score a hundred points. He settled for about forty and the win. The contest was a heck of a game. The hardest part for me was avoiding a personal duel. I knew we couldn't win if I tried to outscore him. We had to stick to our game plan if we had any chance on their home floor. In the end, we fell short. I actually played well and felt especially good about sidestepping the one-on-one affair. I was proud of my teammates for responding well under the circumstances as well. They knew what was going on yet stayed focused.

The rematch in Salt Lake that season was something I looked forward to and dreaded at the same time. I loved the challenge but hated the focused attention. As play began in the Delta Center, Isiah started in a similar fashion as he had in the earlier game in Auburn Hills. This time, however, we were handling the Pistons pretty well. Unfortunately, a nasty situation arose. Isiah had driven hard to the hoop, and Karl had correctly come over to help. Mid-drive, Isiah repositioned the ball to create space for his shot. Moving the ball while in the air is a common technique among the great players, and Karl reacted to his fake while attempting to block the shot. Hanging in the air, Karl's arm made solid contact with Isiah's forehead, splitting his brow. All of the hype and tension of the past months came to a boil. Unfortunately, Darrell Walker came off the Detroit bench and threw a haymaker at Karl while Karl's back was turned, and a melee broke out on the court, which quickly degraded into an ugly scene.

No Piston could or would believe Karl's foul was an accident. The foul itself probably wasn't all that severe. Hard plays at the rim are common and understood. After getting clotheslined once myself without a call, I was told by an official, "You shouldn't go down there!" In this case I certainly saw no intent to injure; contact is a part of the game. The play could just as easily have ended in a bucket or a blocked shot. The league reviewed the tape using slow-motion technology and disagreed. I suppose the possibility exists that the NBA made their ruling simply to keep the peace. In any event, Karl was suspended for a game and fined.

The Piston's "bad-boy" image had some substance. They often placed themselves in controversial situations. I was aware of this firsthand, because I had received stitches on a couple of separate occasions at the hands of their big men. Once, while running back on defense, an elbow "found" my eyebrow. (No suspensions were levied against the Pistons if any readers are keeping score.) It's all part of the game—no grudges but good stories.

Still, after the dust settled, something pretty cool happened. Isiah found my dad's phone number and called him. He apologized for the comments coming from his camp and said he had nothing but respect for me. Isiah explained that he felt he deserved to be on the team *with* me, not instead of me. Dad relayed that story to me some time—years—later. This was a remarkable gesture on Isiah's part that I will always remember and appreciate. He certainly didn't have to make the call. His effort meant a lot to Dad and me.

ASSISTED

• • •

As a result of the USA's commitment to the Olympics, that season ushered in a whole new experience for me—drug testing. Each Olympic player had to be above suspicion to ensure we remained beyond reproach. I learned more about drugs that season than in all of my prior years combined. I never thought I would have to know anything about masking agents, banned substances, false positives, or anything else related to drugs. There are lots of ways to fail a drug test, even if you are innocent. Your hands can come in contact with drugs by simply touching tainted money, for instance. Being around people who smoke drugs can also cause a positive (failed) result. Over-the-counter medicines, such as allergy medications, cold remedies, and even vitamin supplements may contain banned substances. I'm not a fan of blanket drug testing—one false positive could ruin a career or an otherwise innocent life forever. I had never used an illegal drug, but I didn't want to risk testing to prove my innocence. Nevertheless, the Olympic policy was unavoidable and enforced.

I suspect experts in narcotics know how to mask usage or handling. We didn't. So we had to learn what innocent habits or actions could potentially come back to haunt us. I was told in one practice test, actually in the '96 Olympics, that our thinnest and least suspicious player tested positive (almost humorously) for steroids. It resulted from a cream applied to his scalp for a rash. Another member of the team, I heard, tested positive for a different banned substance after taking a cold remedy tablet. We couldn't have that happen at the Olympics. If I wanted to participate on the Olympic team, submitting to the testing policy was unavoidable. USA Basketball[4] was taking no chances. There was no room for error.

THE OLYMPICS, 1992

•   •   •

In 1988 the US had suffered its first loss in the Olympics since the infamous triple "do-over" fiasco to the Russians in 1972.[5] An athletic and talented group of college players coached by John Thompson had fallen victim to a group of NBA veterans and European professionals.[6] Soviet players such as Sarunas Marciulionis and Arvydas Sabonis had seen everything in their expansive professional careers. They were unaffected by the pressure style employed by the young US college team. That loss changed the direction of American basketball forever. A decision was made to send our professionals to compete with their professionals. Enter the "Dream Team."

In Olympic play only the host team and the previous gold medal champions automatically qualify for the next Olympic Games. Because of our defeat in 1988, we were in the rare position in '92 of having to earn a spot at the games. The qualifying event, the Tournament of the Americas, was originally slated for a Latin American venue on a date that made it difficult for NBA players to attend.

USA Basketball had some decisions to make. They could send a surrogate, such as a quality group of college players, to try and qualify. That qualifying team could then step aside for the Dream Team at the Olympics. Another possibility included purchasing the rights to the tournament and playing on US soil at a more suitable time. USA Basketball chose the buyout option. The Tournament of the Americas would be played in Portland, Oregon, a month before the Olympics.

The team opened training camp in La Jolla, California, a week before the qualifying tournament. Practices were long, and the American players quickly grew familiar with each other. We were all used to a week of training camp before the NBA season began, so we were comfortable with the format. Following our first practice, we were feeling pretty good about ourselves when a group of college stars entered the gym for an unannounced scrimmage. Feeling a little too confident about our "Dream" lineup, we chuckled at the intense game faces donned by our younger college opponents as play began. M. J. smugly offered a preliminary warning, "Welcome to the NBA, boys!"

In a few short minutes, the smiles were wiped off our faces as the motivated and intense group of college stars pounded us. Looking back, they had quite a squad themselves with Grant Hill, Bobby Hurley, Chris Webber, and Allan Houston, just to name a few. The scrimmage provided a defining moment for our team as we all realized that nothing less than our best effort would do.

The next day we exacted a measure of revenge on the young squad. They took the pounding that day. We welcomed them to the NBA for real this time. I don't think they realize to this day how dramatically they helped us to become a better team in the process. Because of our loss to the kids, we discarded the "cools" and put on our game faces. As a result, practices became legendary for their intensity.

By the time we arrived in Portland, we were well honed for battle under the leadership of Chuck Daly, Lenny Wilkens, Duke University coach Mike Krzyzewski, and Seton Hall coach P. J. Carlesimo. True to the nature of the personalities on the team, the practices continued at the highest level of intensity. Intersquad games were often heated, building to some dramatic crescendos. Individual matchups that would have been advertised for weeks in advance during the regular season materialized routinely in a flash. With a short blast from Coach's whistle, a quick lineup change would invariably give rise to other classic duels. For the players, these high-profile matchups became commonplace.

An ordinary practice card might feature Jordan head-to-head with Clyde Drexler, or "Sir Charles" versus The Mailman. Deep in the paint, The Admiral (David Robinson) and Patrick Ewing would wage a battle of the big guns, while Mullin and Bird tussled from extremely long range. Another sudden whistle might send Scottie onto Clyde, while M. J. and Magic locked horns. Meanwhile, Karl might slide down to do battle in the trenches. Personally, I spent a lot of time trying to contain Magic Johnson. Breaks from this impossible assignment usually pitted me against M. J. or his sidekick, Scotty Pippin.

Those practice scrimmages were as challenging and as much fun as any game we encountered in the tournament. As a unit we took advantage of our collective talents, the very same abilities we dreaded during the NBA season when our Olympic teammates were our opponents. Strangely enough, with a set of such great scorers as these, it was our defensive prowess, combined speed, length, and a remarkable group basketball IQ that made that Olympic team so formidable.

I was struck by how well the team played together, with pinpoint passing and instantaneous reads. Out of the gate the offense had timing, floor balance, and rhythm that few of us had ever experienced. These players had reached the level where they could play together purely on instinct—on defense, too! It was basketball heaven!

• • •

The outcomes of the qualifying games were somewhat predictable. Lopsided scores were the expectation as we entered our pool play game versus Canada. Suddenly, and unpleasantly for me, fate intervened. While sliding over to help stop penetration, I banged legs with teammate Michael Jordan. His knee struck me on the outside of my lower leg. As contact goes, the collision seemed minor; the damage resembled a charley horse. However, when the ball was inbounded to me, I found my leg wouldn't work properly. The injury didn't hurt badly, but when I tried to run, my leg felt as though two broken ends of a bone were grating against each other. For the first time in my life, I asked to come out of a game.

X-rays revealed a fracture of my right fibula, the nonweight-bearing bone that allows the foot to change directions. The doctors didn't feel that this kind of break required a cast, but the fracture would take six to eight weeks to heal. The Olympics would be over in about seven. I had gone from basketball heaven to a place far below that. My spirits sank as many negative thoughts swirled within my head. The injury dredged up memories of my feelings in Bloomington after I was cut from the 1984 Olympic team.

Chuck Daly approached me as I tried to choke down my meal that night and bluntly announced, "We're going to have to replace you. We'll talk tomorrow." Just when I thought I couldn't feel any worse—I did!

My old buddy, The Mailman, raced to my room when he heard the news and did his best to keep me from jumping out the window (figuratively, of course). Charles Barkley also stopped by to lift my spirits. His visit was an unexpected and much appreciated gesture.

I saw Charles perform a lot of special actions with people that summer. I was surprised and amazed at how positively he responded to absolute strangers. He would stop at seemingly any time to talk with anyone as we walked down the street. The more downtrodden they appeared, the more time Charles had for

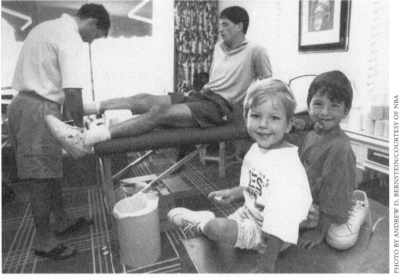

PHOTO BY ANDREW D. BERNSTEIN/COURTESY OF NBA

*Ed Lacerte works on John, 1992, with Michael
and Houston looking on.*

them. I learned that summer what a unique and genuine man Sir Charles is.

By the time I met with Coach the next morning, I had been buoyed by several players on the squad. The central theme of their support was, "We've got your back. Do not let anyone take you off this team." Again, these gestures were greatly appreciated.

My face-to-face with Coach Daly the next morning began with him stating, "We can't go into this thing shorthanded!" From my perspective, no one was going to come close to beating this squad under any circumstances. So I responded, "Coach, this team could play with any five guys and win easily," but quickly added, "I will be back anyway." Those were the last words on the subject. I never received a call, or maybe I just didn't answer the phone. In the end, I wasn't replaced.

• • •

ASSISTED

The wheels of recovery were already in motion. Ed Lacerte, our trainer, who wintered in the same capacity for the Boston Celtics, had already acquired a flotation suit for me to continue my workouts. With our first aquatic efforts that morning, we began a campaign to recovery. This nicely coincided with the beginning of a friendship as we would see a lot of each other for a while. Ed ran me weightless through a reasonably ruthless workout in the water. He then presented me with a T-shirt decorated with a caricature of me paddling in my suit emblazoned with the words, "NO PAIN, NO SPAIN!"

Along with Dr. Dave Fischer, the team orthopedic surgeon for the Minnesota Timberwolves, Ed had acquired a bone stimulator to help promote the healing of my fibula. This was an electronic device that I wore on my hip and attached to a padded metal halo that ringed the injury site. The contraption supposedly created a magnetic or electrical current that promoted bone healing. The directions called for its use seven hours per day. Results beyond that time period were inconclusive, according to the manual. With the idea that if one is good then two must be better, I asked if lengthening my exposure would be harmful. When they said no, I bought extra batteries and wore the halo almost all day and all night thereafter.

Sad and more than a little embarrassed, I watched the rest of the qualifying tournament from the sideline. I hobbled dutifully out for introductions and gift exchanges with our opponents each night. The gifts usually consisted of a pennant or a small flag and a pin as a representation of that player's nation. These were traditionally exchanged in a pregame ceremony that consisted of two opposing battle lines. In our case, the lines often collapsed quickly and prematurely in the excitement to meet, take photos, and get autographs from the likes of Larry, Magic, and Michael.

The break in formation disrupted the clean, quick exchange, delaying many start times.

One evening, lined up in this pregame formation prior to our contest against Puerto Rico, I looked across the floor and saw my Jazz teammate, Jose Ortiz, "Piculin," as he was called by his countrymen. Before the exchanges I got his attention and pointed at him, mouthing the words, "You better come over to me. Don't leave me hanging," with accompanying body language as if I was ready to fight. After an initial puzzled look, he put it all together and chuckled. We had a nice laugh during our gift exchange in relative obscurity as the remainder of the Puerto Rican squad scrambled toward our marquee players. We parted with a quiet, "See you in Barcelona."

As expected, the Dream Team qualified for the Olympics by winning the Tournament of the Americas. Through the experience we gained respect for the Latin players. We hadn't been exposed often to their style of play as few had found their way to the NBA yet, but it would only be a matter of time.

· · ·

The team enjoyed a brief hiatus—about a month—prior to another training camp in Monte Carlo immediately before the Olympics. I think everyone returned home for the break. Upon my arrival in Spokane, I took my new flotation suit down to Gonzaga, where Steve Delong continued advancing my pool workouts. Gini Pickett, who had become a successful local triathlete at the time, often joined me in the water. I also lifted weights. Steve carried and handed me the dumbbells so that I wouldn't reinjure myself. I hated being waited on like that, but Steve never really cared about how I felt. Results took precedence over my feelings. He knew he couldn't make the bone heal more quickly, but he was going to guarantee the rest of me would be ready the moment the injury was mended. We even shot baskets on an actual-sized pool hoop to maintain a little touch.

My only break from these workouts was a trip to Salt Lake City to see Craig Buhler and have him work his magic. I was leaving no stone unturned. With the Olympics around the corner, it was going to be close, but if everything went perfectly, I might recover in time.

As things unfolded, I almost didn't make the trip to Barcelona, but not because of my broken leg. The team was scheduled to reunite in New Jersey before flying to Monte Carlo. I nearly missed the plane out of Spokane. I'm sure I would have without the intervention of the United Airlines gate agent who held the flight. How do you almost miss a flight . . . *to the Olympics?* The short answer is to travel with a wife and children. In this particular instance, Nada was on the phone at home with her sister hashing out some, no doubt, vital details until thirty minutes before the flight while the rest of us waited in the stuffed minivan parked in the driveway. We were lucky they delayed the departure! The aircraft door closed immediately behind us and we taxied out the moment we reached our seats.

From Newark we rode in style on the MGM Grand's private airplane. The jet was truly grand, with every available amenity. The Lakers used this plane during the season. At the time, only some of the teams in the NBA had moved from commercial airline travel to private charter. Detroit and Portland were among the first to commit full-time to the practice and reap the rewards, with the best records in the league and numerous trips to the finals. The enormous benefits of chartering were surpassed only by the enormous costs. This was a hard pill to swallow for the smaller-market teams. The expense even gagged the big boys a bit. The Jazz didn't make that jump for a while, but when they did, the move was beneficial and necessary. It leveled the playing field and gave us a chance to vie for the title. Not having to go through the hassles of commercial travel also prolonged many of our individual careers, at least mine.

• • •

The flight to Barcelona was a treat for everyone. All of the families got to know each other en route. Clyde Drexler seemed like the Pied Piper for a while as he played flash card games with almost every child on the flight. Our son Michael was reluctant at first. At three years old, he hadn't quite forgiven Clyde for poking his dad in the eye in one of our recent playoff games and told him so. Clyde handled the situation well and they became "buds." We all took turns entertaining the packs of kids who spent the flight migrating throughout the cabin.

Before we could set foot in Barcelona, we were sentenced to the isolation of another training camp. This time we had to endure Monte Carlo. We accepted our fate without a whimper. The city had a nice facility connected to an Olympic-sized stadium. It became the site of some additional legendary scrimmages. I had the best seat in the house this time around, pedaling a stationary bike on the sideline while waiting for my leg to heal. I marveled at the talent on the floor and the players' abilities to mesh. At some point during each practice, Ed Lacerte and I would hit the stadium track for brisk walks. We both hoped to progress to an easy jog, but my leg wasn't quite willing to cooperate.

I combined work and play in the historic port city as my workouts continued in the hotel swimming pool. For the time being, this was my training camp. I was joined poolside by my own dream team: Nada and the boys. I taught Michael how to swim in

Broken leg rehab, 1992.

that hotel pool using Houston and his fearless approach to water as an aid. A photo of the three of us underwater, eyes wide open and smiling, appeared in the pages of *Sports Illustrated* that year.

With Ed never far off, the family took to the Mediterranean. The gorgeous coastline of Monaco and the fabled ocean became our playground. With a nod from Ed one afternoon, we rented jet skis and took to the sea with boys clinging to us like baby monkeys. We returned to the beach, which proved to be rather European! We were shocked at first by the views and decided that many sights are better left . . . covered.

We took a breathtaking side trip one afternoon to an ancient mountain village in France called Èze. The town, which seemed to cling impossibly to the edge of the mountain, hasn't changed much in several centuries. Everyone wondered how the people could have lived and built in such a place. We traveled to Èze that day with the president of USA Basketball, Dave Gavitt, and his wife, Julie, along with his right-hand man, Tom McGrath, and his wife, also named Julie.

I learned on the trip that the Dream Team almost didn't happen, and that I was one of the reasons the experiment had gone forward. I certainly knew that I wasn't the big draw on this squad, so the words caught me by surprise. Apparently, working with

PHOTO BY ANDREW D. BERNSTEIN/COURTESY OF NBA

Houston, John, and Michael enjoy some time off in the pool after rehab.

such high-profile athletes created unimaginable stirrings behind the scenes. Once the pros lined up, so did endorsements from all corners of the globe. This was a huge financial boon for USA Basketball as corporate giants helped fund much of their program. The downside proved to be entangling contracts, especially in the shoe and apparel industry. Nike, Converse, Adidas, and LA Gear understandably wanted "their" players to remain visibly connected to their logos. Negotiations nearly reached an impasse.

I had heard early that summer that the Nike players were opting out of the Olympics, which was completely unacceptable to me. The Olympic opportunity was far too great to pass up for any squabble. Jumping the gun a little, I immediately called my Nike representative and firmly asked them to "take me out of my contract. I am not opting out of the Olympics." My rep calmly explained that wouldn't be necessary and assured me that I would be able to play. Following that phone conversation, I called Dave Gavitt, whom I hadn't met at the time. I told him about my

*Homes built into the mountainside in Èze, France, near
the US team's training facility in Monaco.*

discussion with Nike and confirmed I was playing. I made it clear
that nothing would get in the way of my participation.

On our tour of Èze, Dave and Tom told me that my timely
call went a long way toward saving the concept and reality of the
Dream Team. The call had actually interrupted their discussion
about disbanding the team and returning to using college players.
The contractual conflicts had become seemingly insurmountable.
Dave said that following my call to him, he told Tom that he
thought they could get it done with the professionals after all. My
unconditional commitment to play apparently provided the shot
in the arm they had needed. Dave never looked back as he, Tom,
and USA Basketball created history.

After all the preparations, we finally reached the promised
land: Barcelona, Spain. Our first duty was to join the athletes at
the Olympic Village to collect our required credentials. Dangling
from a lanyard around our necks, IDs allowed us access to

everyone and every place that we needed to be. Every participant, no matter how famous, was required to wear the official tags. The moment we exited the bus, however, it was immediately apparent that we weren't like the other athletes. By then we already knew that our accommodations would be different, which separated us in more ways than one from our Olympic comrades.

The check-in process demonstrated why that decision was made. There, even the world's finest athletes and coaches stopped what they were doing to take note of the Dream Team. Olympic officials, staff, and security personnel forgot themselves and their posts as they rushed to get a closer look. Spontaneous cheers erupted: "Maa-yeeek! Yor-dan! Laa-ree!" for Magic, Jordan, and Larry Bird. These three superstars and a few others had attained a Beatles-like status worldwide. The scene played out surreally—like living inside the celluloid footage from a '60s Beatles' deplaning in New York City.

USA Basketball and the NBA could not have anticipated the extent of the reaction but had long since made the decision to house the team away from the village in a hotel they could protect with enhanced security. A large force stood sentinel around the clock, watching over the Dream Team. Choppers circled overhead while snipers, perched nearly invisibly on neighboring rooftops, scanned the crowded streets for signs of trouble. Along with this, a vigilant SWAT team lay in wait while Secret Service types mingled with the crowds, forming a presumably impenetrable network. Whenever we traveled, a heavily armed motorcade packing visible automatic weapons on the back of two-man motorcycles aided the choppers with our escort.

The rooms of our four-star hotel were very small, unlike their American counterparts. Ours was nearly filled wall-to-wall by a queen-sized bed. In fact, we moved furniture into the hallway to

The Stocktons in Monte Carlo, Monaco. Left to right:
David, Nada, Michael, John, and Houston.

make room for a playpen that doubled as a crib for David and an inflatable mattress that Houston and Michael shared with our babysitter, Cara Tangaro.[7] Once everyone was up and showered, the mattress and playpen had to be stowed in the bathroom to make ample floor space to move around.

What we lacked in space we made up for in excitement. One night while the rest of our family slept, Nada washed some clothes by hand in the sink. She had brought along some rope to fashion a clothesline just in case. With square footage at a premium, she crawled over the air mattress, across the bed, over a stack of luggage, and through a window to reach an adjoining roof. The handy flat surface was walled by towering buildings on all sides. As she was tying her clothesline, an armed SWAT team suddenly descended upon her and her laundry out of the

Nada hanging laundry at the hotel in Barcelona, which precipitated an unexpected encounter with the SWAT team.

darkness in full force like ninja warriors. They scared the wits out of Nada but, fortunately, were disarmed quickly by the Batman undies draped across the makeshift clothesline. We found out later that the Drexlers, in the room next door, had reported noises on the roof, precipitating the all-out raid.

• • •

Barcelona is a huge city with millions of people. As in all big cities, traffic was a common problem made worse by the Olympics. Standard travel time from our hotel to the basketball venue easily exceeded an hour. But we covered the distance in about twenty minutes with the benefit of a police escort with blaring sirens. Streets cleared like a scene from *Dick Tracy* as we zoomed by the obediently sidelined vehicles.

One night as we rolled towards our game with Puerto Rico, I looked at the cars and buses that had been scrunched together on the side of the road to accommodate us. One of them was the Puerto Rican team bus. I happened to catch the eyes of my buddy

Jose Ortiz as he observed the spectacle from his seat on their side-lined transport. I simply couldn't disguise my amusement. His look of absolute surprise as he recognized the irony of the situation was priceless.

To say our team was spoiled by these escorts would be an understatement. On one occasion, as we were returning from watching some track and field events, we became ensnarled in a normal Barcelona traffic jam. Only part of our team was traveling by bus, so we didn't warrant a full escort. Spotting a subway entrance and being completely comfortable with my anonymity, I exited the bus in favor of the trains with my family, which included my seventy-year-old mother-in-law, in tow. Several players and their guests followed suit amid polite objection from our protective staff. This detour was a memorable coup. It saved us about forty minutes in traffic but took four years off the life of NBA security chief Horace Balmer. He really gave us an earful when the nearly empty bus finally returned. Horace and his team were remarkably efficient throughout the Olympics and for the entire year prior to the games. They had actually been on alert and preparing for that length of time. We all slept well because they hadn't.

The reality was that when I wasn't in the company of the team, I didn't need much security. That's why I knew I could safely take the subway and walk every night on Barcelona's famous La Rambla. The ancient street, divided by a broad, land-scaped boulevard, was populated by seemingly thousands of pedestrians at all hours. The people-watching opportunity was extraordinary. For me, it provided an exciting and entertaining training ground for my therapeutic strolls. La Rambla stretches a couple miles from the bustling square of Placa de Catalunya to the harbor, where a monument to Christopher Columbus stands at the very spot from which he departed in search of the New World in 1492. It occurred to me on one of my walks as I stood before his statue that I had completed a full circle.

I was never recognized while attending events or walking the streets of Barcelona. NBA Entertainment caught wind of this phenomenon and offered me a new video camera to demonstrate my obscurity. I accepted the offer and retraced my worn steps down La Rambla, taping the faces of oncoming tourists as I passed. Nada and kids accompanied me as a hidden camera followed from the wings to catch all of the action. As expected, no one showed a hint of recognition. Finally, I greeted one woman wearing a Dream Team T-shirt sporting the faces of all twelve players. The lady was an American and still showed no signs of recognition. I asked her questions about the Dream Team, such as, "Who are your favorite players?" "Have you met any of them?" She responded that she had seen Charles Barkley but hadn't actually met him while she proudly pointed to his smiling image on her shirt. Houston and Michael couldn't take it anymore. They pointed at my picture and blurted, "Daddy!" With the cat out of the bag, I felt obliged to autograph the shirt to make up for the *Candid Camera* routine. The rustle of excitement as the camera crew closed in opened a Pandora's box as additional fans then gathered to request an autograph. The kicker was that most of them still had no idea who I was even after reading the legible signature. They were merely playing follow the leader. The autograph world remains an oddity to me.

USA Basketball scoured the countryside to acquire tickets to other Olympic events for the players and their families. They went beyond the call of duty. Everyone in my group attended as many events as possible. We marveled at the ability of all the Olympic athletes in their various sports. My overall experience was dramatically enhanced by the opportunity to witness the Olympic spectacle as a fan as well as a participant.

On the hardwood, the Dream Team steamrolled through the opposing corps in pool play with only one minor incident. Sir Charles slugged a player from Angola after he had warned him repeatedly to quit whatever it was that he was doing. The stir caused only a few raised eyebrows along media row as neither the victim nor the Angolan squad matched up well from a size perspective. Charles looked like a bully, and the team ribbed him pretty hard after the game, but that was the extent of the fuss. In any event, his knightly charm diffused the situation and everyone moved on no worse for wear.

Meanwhile, my late-night walks with Nada on La Rambla and pregame test runs had yet to foster any confidence that my leg would work properly. I could move straight ahead but changing directions still eluded me. This kept me securely on the bench, where Magic joined me while nursing a sore hamstring. His contagious enthusiasm and thoughtful insights on the game lightened the weight of my injured reserve blues. Between high fives and fist pumps we exchanged viewpoints on individual players and the psychology of the game itself that I found profoundly interesting.

As the medal round approached, Magic had healed, and I was getting the sense that my body might cooperate enough to provide me with a chance to play. Coach Daly left the matter solely up to me. "When you are ready, let me know," he told me in a businesslike fashion. I suited up for the first game but couldn't quite pull the trigger after putting myself through some paces on the practice court prior to the match. I still worried that my leg would snap (or at least crackle) if I truly engaged it.

Before the next contest, the semifinal, I could feel a noticeable difference. Almost six weeks to the day from the injury in

Portland, the snapping sensation left. For the first time since the collision, I was gaining a degree of confidence about being able to play, though I had no illusions about moving or cutting quickly. I was nowhere near normal but felt as though I could move well enough to contribute. In the NBA, playing with an injury is commonplace. Players learn to adapt around sore ankles, pulled muscles, and even occasional bone breaks. I was at the point where I felt I could manage the injury, compete, and contribute.

Reconnecting with basketball heaven wasn't a difficult assignment. As Coach Layden used to say, "Passers always have a ride home from the gym." Play continued seamlessly when I was inserted into the games. I focused on contributing without disrupting. Surprisingly, I scored with some ease as good shots were abundant with a potent lineup always on the floor. My passing was nothing to write home about—mostly making routine entry passes. Nothing I did resembled the free-flowing environment I had experienced with this team prior to my injury. Defensively, I played it safe but sound. I simply held the ground in front of my man and tried to maintain good help position. After six weeks of not practicing or playing, the full flavor of the chemistry and fluidity I had enjoyed with these guys before was hard to reacquire.

Although I didn't set the world on fire on the court, the honor of being a part of basketball history was something special. The Dream Team would change basketball around the world forever. The bar had been reset, much as Jesse Owens had done some fifty years earlier in the long jump. A new level of enthusiasm for the game infused players from around the globe as our team breezed into the gold medal game.

From a competitive level, the championship game was as unremarkable as it was spectacular from a performance standpoint. With all hands on board, focused, and driven, the outcome was never in question. I witnessed some of the finest play I had ever seen. It really was a sight to behold as the fans were treated to the extraordinary play of these immensely talented men who had truly become a dream *team*.

I played more and more comfortably in the championship as my leg made another significant improvement. With barely a limp, I cherished every moment on the floor. As the clock wound down to zero, the ball found its way into my hands. I hadn't premeditated it, but as I stood there with history in my grasp, I was struck with the idea to hold onto it. As I dribbled down the court in the final ticks, our Croatian opponents began yelling at me. I was thinking they were going to foul so that they might capture the prize. Through their broken English, I was surprised to hear, "No shoot! No shoot!" Their actual motive was to preserve the score so they could claim the moral victory of having lost to the Dream Team by the fewest number of points. I obliged but protected the ball until the horn sounded. I tucked the treasure under my arm, just as I had with my red, white, and blue ABA ball years earlier, trying to keep it away from Steve and his friends. I had the game ball!

All that remained was the celebration, and we were late for the party. By the time we neared the locker room, Lithuania had already been toasting their bronze medal—their first as an independent nation. They greeted us with boisterous cheers. Many of them hugged and kissed Charles. I think the affection embarrassed him, but it created a real belly laugh for the rest of us. Next, we gathered ourselves in the locker room. All there was time for was getting dressed for the medal ceremony. But the awards presentation would involve a little more than I expected.

The long-awaited ceremony was to be broadcast around the globe. The Olympic pictures and videos would be reproduced and used for years. For a brief moment, as the business of the real world set in, the previous controversy involving logos and apparel resurfaced. Contractually sensitive about being seen wearing another company's logo, some quick-thinking players enthusiastically draped the Stars and Stripes over their shoulders to hide any trademarks. I think they would have worn the flag in any case.

As the team approached the presentation platform, my heart skipped a beat. There I stood beside my friend and teammate Karl Malone. It was nice to share the moment with him.[8] I looked at my teammates, grown men smiling like little kids. As the medals were draped around our necks one by one, my thoughts traveled back to Spokane and the many people there who had participated in my journey. I gulped as I imagined what they might be feeling. From their familiar seats in the living room on Superior Street, where my Olympic dreams began, I pictured Mom and Dad tuned in and privately wrestling with their emotions. Finally, I peered through the bright lights to wave at Nada and the kids, all crying with a mixture of joy and exhaustion as they proudly waved their American flags.

We stood at attention as the American flag was raised and the national anthem began. I had always imagined singing the anthem out loud, but the words deserted me when the time actually came. I could only stare at the flag with my lips quivering while avoiding direct eye contact with friends and teammates, knowing that would open the floodgates. The whole building joined in one final, rousing cheer for the three teams on the podium as our Olympic experience came to a close.

The euphoria subsided as scores of photographs with teammates, coaches, and basketball personnel were taken. It had been a long summer, and everyone was anxious to get home. My family and I returned that night to the hotel only to pack up and prepare

The "gold medal" Stockton family.
Left to right: Nada, David, Houston, John, Michael.

to leave. One of the highlights of the whole trip, for me, was draping the medal on Nada and the boys. Clearly it meant a lot to each of them—but to some more than others. Houston, at four, handled the medal almost reverently, seemingly understanding some of the deeper meaning behind the gold pendant. As he passed the medal on to Michael, Houston seemed to understand that his little brother wouldn't be quite so careful. He tried to coach him on a little delicacy. The advice went unheeded. Michael immediately began twirling the ribbon that held the medal around his finger. Before anyone could react, he shot it toward a steel cabinet handle. The medal-on-metal collision put a nick in both. The object of my dreams had been damaged only minutes from the podium. After a nervous pause as everyone waited for my reaction, we all exhaled together. At three and a half, Michael obviously didn't mean to damage the medal, and he had provided me with a story I would tell for years. The nick has come to represent the best of Olympic memories. We draped the damaged goods over one-year-old David and snapped some pictures so he could some-day feel included.

• • •

That night the team boarded the MGM Grand jet for a quiet but happy flight back to US soil. Most of us parted ways on the East Coast but some enjoyed the added benefit of staying on the chartered flight to Portland, Oregon. The plane was going to be used for an upcoming Nike trip, so we merely hitched a ride to the Rose City. From Portland the family and I caught a shuttle back to Spokane. As I finished the last leg of the journey, I considered the magnitude of the experience. I wondered if the 1992 USA Olympic basketball team would actually change the world of basketball as David Stern had suggested. I know playing for my country made for a summer I will never forget.

CHAPTER 14

The Olympics, 1996: A Second Selection

*"The most important thing in the Olympic Games
is not winning but taking part; the essential thing in life
is not conquering but fighting well."*[1]

—PIERRE DE COUBERTIN, FOUNDER OF
THE MODERN OLYMPIC GAMES

There will never be another Dream Team. Just as the excitement of your first bicycle or your child's first steps, the experience will always be one of a kind. The enthusiasm for the first NBA players to represent America in the Olympics will likely remain unparalleled. It may never again happen that eleven future Hall of Famers will combine their talents on one Olympic team. So, in 1996, when the international basketball community came together to compete in the Olympics, I knew the Dream Team experience couldn't possibly be repeated.

The differences became apparent early on with the selection process itself. With Bird and Magic long retired and Jordan electing to forgo the opportunity to play in his third Olympics, the lineup would have a different face altogether. There had been so much discussion in the media and around the league over the course of the NBA season that I wasn't shocked this time by my invitation. I was prepared to accept on the spot. I don't know that I could ever turn down an invitation to play in the Olympics.

Both the team and coaching selections were more widely anticipated than in 1992. Lenny Wilkens, the only man that I am aware of to be inducted into the Naismith Hall of Fame as a player, coach, and member of a team, capably took the helm.[2] Coach Sloan was selected to assist him along with college legends Bobby Cremins of Georgia Tech and Clem Haskins of the University of Minnesota.

I was genuinely happy to see our Jazz skipper recognized for his coaching excellence. Although he resists attention and credit with the tenacity of a bulldog, Jerry deserved this honor. His appointment as an assistant should have put him next in line for the head coaching spot in the 2000 Olympics, if the selection precedent had been followed. Coach's balanced temperament—combining intensity with understanding and common sense—would have made him a perfect choice. He somehow makes players want to compete as a team. His expertise was undeniable as he coached the Jazz to the best record in the NBA for two of the next four years. Sadly, he was overlooked when it came time to select a head coach for the Y2K Olympics.

The '96 Olympic training camp began in Chicago in June of that year. The process of getting to know each other went as quickly but not quite as smoothly as it had in 1992. Even before the first dribble, I found myself in a nervous pickle. As we all stretched in a circle and talked, eager to get started, my knee locked in a bent position. I couldn't straighten my leg. Trying to keep my predicament "on the QT" as the group continued, I whispered to my partner, Karl Malone, "Quick, pull my foot out. My knee is locked!" The puzzled look and shocked expression on his face made it clear he had no intention of assuming any physical therapist duties, even for his old pal. With Karl declining to treat me, I was forced to call upon our licensed trainer, Ron Culp, the trainer for the Portland Trail Blazers, who I had met over a decade earlier, before I was even drafted into the league. In a whisper I pleaded that he skip the evaluation phase and quickly and quietly help me. Despite his initial surprise and reluctance, he rolled up his sleeves and went to work, gently extending my leg. With no one the wiser, and with the three of us enjoying a collective sigh of relief, practice resumed.

Not having to qualify in the Tournament of the Americas, USA Basketball needed to find some method that would allow us to prepare for the Olympics. The Olympic committee settled upon a form of barnstorming. Before packed houses at selected sites, we traveled to develop and sharpen our competitive edge.

The first stop on the tour pitted us against a group of college stars in Detroit. As in 1992, the collegiate team was loaded with terrific players. We probably again underestimated them and overestimated ourselves. Tim Duncan, Brevin Knight, and company probably should have beaten us that night. In front of a standing-room-only crowd, on national television, with a large piece of humble pie awaiting, our team came together at the finish and eked out a victory.

Oddly, one of the highlights of this barnstorming tour became our police escort. Some of the coaches and players had developed a rapport with the men in blue from their respective NBA hometowns. These relationships spawned a competition between police departments. Grant Hill in Detroit, Charles Barkley in Phoenix, Karl in Salt Lake, Reggie Miller in Indianapolis, and Lenny Wilkens in Cleveland all fanned the fires of a friendly escort competition.

Police drill teams from each city tried to top the others' performance. At breakneck speeds amid blaring sirens, motorcycle officers would treat our bus to a show of handstands and acrobatic maneuvers I wouldn't risk on a mat with a safety harness. It was all very entertaining, and we looked forward to their performances at every stop.

Despite the inevitable and unfavorable comparisons with the Dream Team, our '96 squad was plenty talented and laden with showstoppers. The Barcelona holdovers of Malone, Robinson, Pippen, Barkley, and I were reinforced by such formidable players as Shaquille O'Neal, Hakeem Olajuwon, Reggie Miller, Grant Hill, Mitch Richmond, and Gary Payton. Glen "Big Dog" Robinson was an original selection who was replaced by Gary. I never learned why, but Glen's only participation, as far as I could tell, was in some early photographs. Still, with these new players aboard, the team retained much of the rock-star status that characterized the '92 squad.

The mania was revealed in a frightening situation following an exhibition game in Indianapolis. As we were leaving the court, fans who were pressing hard against a guard railing to reach us overwhelmed the barrier. A mass of humanity crashed to the floor. Some fell from as high as ten feet. The few players still lingering nearby jumped into the fray to assist those in distress. In a matter of moments, however, we were pulled out of the scene by security. They didn't leave any room for argument as they ushered us abruptly to our locker room.

When I phoned home that night, I was shocked that no one had heard about the near-tragic incident. That was unusual because my family usually knew all the NBA news before I did. I hoped that was an indication that no one was seriously hurt.

• • •

We arrived in Atlanta as the clear favorite. Again, for security reasons, the decision had long been made that the team and their families would be housed away from the Olympic Village. As a result, we were placed at the Omni Hotel in downtown Atlanta. The Georgia Dome, only about a block away, would have been a fast, easy walk, but security concerns once again prevailed. An armed escort led our bus through a maze of streets ("around our backside to get to our elbow," as Coach Sloan might have muttered) while delivering us to the ramp at the arena for each game. We understood the intent behind taking these circuitous routes and maintained our focus on our mission.

As the games began, something about the competitive atmosphere was seriously different. The faces across the court at introductions weren't smiling and excited. Instead, they were hungry and intense. Their eyes conveyed a will to win and a belief in their chances. They were no longer looking for autographs. Foreign players had flooded into the NBA since '92. This time we faced other NBA stars, not uniformed fans from abroad. I remember thinking that David Stern's comments about the Dream Team changing the face of basketball forever had been insightful.

Since few NBA superstars at the time declined invitations to play, we still had a talent advantage, especially in the big and tall department. Supporting this claim were lopsided scores similar to '92. The margins, however, didn't reflect the difficulty factor. The victories were hard-won, but the greater challenge added to the excitement.

• • •

Not all of the excitement took place on the court at the Georgia Dome. Once again, USA Basketball went to monumental lengths to provide tickets to other Olympic competitions. Just as the families of other basketball players, our family signed up daily for a limited number of seats. We witnessed the beauty, grace, power, and speed of the track and field events at

John competing in the 1996 Summer Games in Atlanta, Georgia.

close range. The competitors looked as peaceful as someone reading a book while motoring down the track at ridiculous speeds. Seeing Carl Lewis or Michael Johnson round the final turn and attack the homestretch was an experience never to be forgotten. My family and I were thrilled spectators among thousands packed into the Olympic Stadium watching these remarkable athletes perform.

My family and I were eager to see everything the Olympics had to offer, so we requested tickets constantly. The group had changed quite a bit since the last time around. The boys had grown, we had added Lindsay, and Laura was on the way. On occasion the demand was so overwhelming that we sometimes had to settle for lesser-attended events such as boxing, swimming,

John meeting members of the US women's gymnastics team, 1996 Olympics.

and men's gymnastics. We took advantage of every opportunity, usually on short notice, and sprinted off to the distant venues.

I soon learned what I'd been missing. I was floored by these athletes' talents and what they had trained their bodies to do. Even though these competitors were fellow Olympians, I didn't fully appreciate the preparation necessary to achieve this degree of excellence. I was so impressed I couldn't quit talking about what I had seen. I have since become a fan of almost all Olympic events. Each discipline is filled with extraordinary athletes competing fiercely for the highest honor in their sports.

As in '92, we met many fellow Olympians, assorted actors, dignitaries, and other sports professionals. They normally came by our practice sessions or met us in our dining area at the hotel. The US women's gymnastics team was among the first to visit and the only ones to do so on the team bus. The contrast between

232

the petite and the large was remarkable. But tucked inside those tiny athletic frames were huge hearts as they became the first American women's gymnastics team to win a gold medal.

A special highlight for me was the opportunity to volley with US table tennis champion Jim Butler. The exchange was deflating for someone who previously fancied himself a pretty fair hand behind a paddle. Jim toyed with me to the point of actually maintaining the volley by directing shots off of my paddle. I stood helplessly as he rifled spike after spike off the frozen rubber surface held defensively in front of me.

I also had the distinct pleasure of riding atop the famous Budweiser Clydesdale wagon. Having been around the King of Beers all of my life, I got a particular kick out of this experience. I learned that each horse has a different responsibility, much like each member of a basketball team. Most obvious from my vantage point on the driver's seat were the duties of the extra-large duo at the back of the team. In order to round a corner, the front pair simply walk around the turn. As anchors, the back pair must throw their massive derrières into a side shuffle away from the turn to maintain the line of the beer wagon. Without this well-practiced maneuver, the beer would get bounced to a froth, with the wheels going over the curbs.

One of the neatest experiences I had was being introduced to Muhammad Ali. Watching as he captured the hearts of all the kids (ours included), as well as the adults crowded around him was touching. To this day "The Champ" maintains an infectious charm and charisma that attracts people decades after his reign. He smiled graciously for countless photos with admirers young and old. I was pleased to see that he had come away uninjured from a scary situation at the opening ceremonies.

These ceremonies had begun for us with another example of

PHOTO BY ANDREW D. BERNSTEIN/COURTESY OF NBA

Members of the 1996 USA Men's Olympic Basketball Team meet "The Champ," Muhammad Ali. Front row, left to right: Reggie Miller, John Stockton. Back row, left to right: Scottie Pippen, Muhammad Ali, Karl Malone.

security measures pushing the limits. We were sequestered with the US women's basketball team in a suite at Fulton County Stadium. We were not allowed to join the main body of US athletes. This hideout strategy almost backfired and nearly delayed the US contingent's entry into Olympic Stadium. At the last moment, someone busted into the room with the command for us to hustle down and funnel into the procession with the other US athletes in the sea of red-trimmed white hats atop snappy blue blazers. We managed to slide in smoothly.

I'm glad we didn't miss the opening ceremony. It was moving and spectacular. The roar of the crowd in that packed stadium was deafening, and the magnitude of the moment took my breath away. I felt small among the multitudes, and yet my chest puffed out at the same time. It was a thrilling experience to mingle with the various athletes from so many nations in that happy procession.

We all cheered as Muhammad Ali was announced and he prepared to light the Olympic torch to mark the beginning of the Games. As he angled the torch to perform his duties, the wind redirected the flames in the direction of his outstretched arm. An audible and collective gasp was heard throughout the stadium. From a distance, the flame appeared frighteningly close to burning the champ. Fortunately, the fire didn't "lay a glove" on the man who always boasted he "floated like a butterfly," and he escaped without injury.

There was a second brush with tragedy during the games. Late one evening, as we finally tucked ourselves into bed, an explosion rocked the Olympic community. The tremendous boom shook our hotel to its foundation. The vibration reverberated up through each floor of the sturdy structure. We could actually hear the rumbling coming towards us. Our immediate concern was for the kids. Wide-eyed thoughts of an earthquake gave way after a few moments to the possibility that a truck might have struck the base of the building. I never considered the possibility of a bomb. No alarms sounded and no evacuation instructions came. We called the busy switchboard to gather some information. The operator assured us that whatever had happened wasn't in the hotel, and we began to allow ourselves to believe that we weren't in serious danger.

What had actually occurred wouldn't be clear for some time. A peek out the window indicated that the boom hadn't originated in our hotel. Directly across the street was Olympic Park, where our kids played each day and where I had ridden the Budweiser wagon. In many ways it was the center of Olympic activity. On this night, panicked people by the thousands were sprinting desperately away from the park in our direction. Our anxiety began to give way to curiosity. We wondered what had happened across from our concrete fortress. We later learned that a pipe bomb had been detonated in the park just a couple hundred yards from the hotel entrance. The thought was scary and sobering. Not knowing who had detonated the bomb and why made matters worse. Some of my teammates went as far as sending their families home for the rest of the games. We decided to stay put. We felt safe with USA Basketball and NBA security.

On the court I felt as though I earned my keep more fully this time. I participated in all practices and games as well as a few spirited postpractice competitions. I loved shooting competitively with Reggie Miller following practices. Attempting to match shots and wage verbal warfare with Reggie was no easy chore, but it was a lot of fun.

I thoroughly enjoyed our basketball games in Atlanta. On a couple of nights, we "played in a tuxedo," as Coach Sloan liked to say. The lopsided scores kept us from having to roll up our sleeves and get dirty. The festive "black tie" atmosphere was unexpectedly interrupted for me, however, following our semifinal victory. We had easily dispatched Australia, and we were enjoying some lighter moments in the locker room afterwards when I meandered to the bathroom. Little did I know how much distress that casual act would cost me.

After coaches Wilkens and Sloan arrived and completed their postgame remarks, I received a tap on the shoulder. "John, will you come with me for a moment?" the voice said. I had been randomly selected for drug testing. I never thought they would choose me in a thousand years, but they did.

The drug testing agents escorted me to a special Olympic testing area to provide a specimen. Unfortunately, I had just relieved myself and the well was dry. The testers didn't care. They had all night. For an hour and a half, they waited while I downed water and sports drinks one after the other to assist in the process. My temporary incarceration provided ample time to contemplate what was at stake. I thought of all the ways I could fail the test. I became uptight as I considered the consequences of a false-positive result. The truth was that I had never touched an illegal drug of any kind in my whole life and had followed every precaution that the NBA and USA Basketball provided, yet here I was at the mercy of a handful of lab technicians. The outcome at this point was out of my control, and I wasn't at all comfortable.

All the haunting contingencies I had learned about resurfaced. Could someone have put something into our water or our food that day? Perhaps I had innocently touched some tainted money or inadvertently inhaled some contaminated secondhand smoke. A positive result would unalterably damage my reputation and tarnish my life, my family, and USA Basketball forever—with the ease and simplicity of one test. I understood why they have to test, but the process, quite honestly, was daunting. One contact, any error in testing, or a single inexplicable outcome, and my world would have come crashing down around me.

Under duress, I finally delivered. As I should have expected, none of my fears came to pass. I rejoined the team late for dinner amid jokes and laughter about my inability to produce. I was relieved in more ways than one.

My most significant contribution on the court came in the gold-medal game. The team was struggling against the inspired Yugoslavians. Nobody sensed any pending doom, but the game remained relatively tight well into the second half. Lenny gave me the nod, and I eagerly took the court.

Point guards can, and probably should, judge their impact

mostly by the scoreboard. The components of playing well at this position aren't always found on the stat sheet. One such skill is locating the hot hand on the floor. In this case David Robinson fit the bill. We ran the familiar pick and roll often with David finishing effectively. The whole team found a nice offensive rhythm in the process. Shots began falling from all over the court. A united defensive front delivered the final blow. Disrupting their flow, we capitalized off of steals, blocked shots, and misses. We blew the game open—at least that is how I remember it!

At one point during that stretch, the man I was guarding knocked down a couple of threes while I was playing help defense. Scottie Pippen hollered out from the bench, "John, stay at home." I smiled and snapped back, "This seems to be working!" The difference in the score should have been enough proof. I felt that he, of all people, should have understood. He might have been one of the best help defenders to have ever played. Still, it made for an amusing exchange. Coach Wilkens quickly settled the playful disagreement by siding with Pip. "Stay home," he instructed me with his trademark smirk.

With the game out of reach and time winding down, Lenny called me aside and said, "Get the game ball." I already had the leather sphere in my sights but was sure something would keep me from grabbing it this go-around. Incredibly, the ball found its way into my hands as the buzzer sounded. No one tried to foul or persuade me not to shoot as the Croatians had four years earlier. I exited the court with the championship game ball under my arm . . . again! Both basketballs remain on display in the concourse of the Delta Center, now called the EnergySolutions Arena. I wanted people to be able to enjoy these mementos.

The gold medal ceremony lacked the outward affection of the 1992 Games—that is, nobody kissed or hugged Charles. Even so, the ceremony was emotionally charged. There I was, once again, standing on the podium, shoulder to shoulder with Karl, both of us peering down together at Coach Sloan, our friend and mentor. One by one my teammates bent forward to receive their gold medals, many of them for the first time. Sharing something such as an Olympic championship with new teammates is surprisingly touching. As the American flag was raised, the recording of the anthem was drowned out by the singing of tens of thousands reveling in the moment. The strength of their collective voices was powerful and inspiring. The song ended with a resounding cheer. We all joined in. At age thirty-four, I knew that my Olympic opportunities had more than likely come to an end. I probably would not even be considered in four years, and I wasn't taking this experience for granted.

Everyone was almost giddy as we took photo after photo of teammates sporting their gold medals! I particularly enjoyed draping my medal over Jerry Sloan's neck. Inconceivably, coaches don't receive medals at the Olympics, so sharing mine with him had special meaning. Jerry, Karl, and I commemorated another experience together with a group photo that still means a lot to each of us.

By day's end, most of my family had donned the golden treasure at least once. This time around nobody twirled, slung, or damaged it in any way. Seeing the faces of everyone who wore the medal was a reward of its own. The magical pendant means a lot to people. It is hard not to be emotionally touched when you witness its impact.

Many years after the Games the gold medals retain their allure. I often take them with me when I speak at schools or gatherings. Children and adults alike never seem to tire of seeing and holding an Olympic Gold. Their sparkling eyes and reverent handling suggest that the medallions' appeal will continue to linger. The glow seems to be equally intense for the avid fan or the casual observer.

I hold the honor of having played on two USA Olympic Basketball teams. Although nothing can surpass the first experience with the Dream Team, winning the Olympic Championship on US soil had its own special significance. Future teams will struggle by comparison.

Clearly the luster of NBA players participating has begun to fade. More players now decline the invitation to participate, opting to rest their injuries from the long, arduous NBA season. Still, my hope is that future players will recognize the high honor of being selected to participate and accept the responsibility to play. I'm fairly certain they will never regret sacrificing a summer for their country. I guarantee the best players from Argentina to Zimbabwe will play hurt, crippled, or broken for the chance to represent their nations. I expect nothing less from our players.

The rest of the basketball world had made enormous strides since 1992. Driving this progress has been not only the increased exposure to basketball as it is played in the United States but also a growing national pride in other nations. Foreign players seem to live for the opportunity to knock off the United States. I personally don't believe this should ever happen. The United States is home to the best basketball players in the world. Defeating a US team should be a tall order unless we are forced to compete with less than our best and most highly motivated players. When America puts its best foot forward, no nation is better.

Practicing as a unit for an extended time would be the surest insurance policy for continuing success, but time is scarce particularly for the stars who vie for the NBA title each year. Convincing

The Stockton children at Christmastime. Front row, left to right: Laura, Samuel, Lindsay. Back row, left to right: Houston, Michael, David.

the best players to participate and finding the right mix will be a difficult task. The selection process will be a crucial challenge.

Both of my Olympic experiences were among the greatest of my life and remain some of my family's best memories. They were all they were cracked up to be and more. As a participant and a fan, I enjoyed the finest spectacle in all of sports with my family, friends, and supporters. My dreams had come true.

CHAPTER 15

Walking with an Unfamiliar Shadow

F*ame* is defined by Webster's dictionary as the state of being widely known or enjoying popular acclaim. In the world of my youth, that described Dad. I heard stories about his deeds from people as I grew up. Apparently he provided jobs when he didn't need the help or advanced loans when no one else would. In the neighborhood sandlot, fame meant only one thing—athletic success. For kids growing up in my era, that meant making the winning basket, catching a touchdown pass, or being the victorious quarterback. Those were the feats that led to recognition. We figured out that no one came to watch anyone excel on a math test. All young kids enjoy being noticed, praised, and appreciated in a distinctive way. For most of us, me included, that translated to seeking attention through sports.

I tasted fame in nibbles during high school with my success in basketball. When I woke up for school after a game, Dad might comment, "You got some ink." In local sports, "getting ink" was almost always good. Where I grew up, reporters seldom ripped anyone. The articles were pleasant to read and fueled a desire to excel and improve. Friends at school or neighbors might comment, "Hey, nice game! I read about you this morning. Good job!" That was the depth and breadth of the hoopla.

This more or less continued throughout college. I was only asked for an autograph once as a Bulldog. Caught off guard, I wasn't flattered by the request. I was embarrassed. Awkwardly I signed and secretly prayed that no one had seen me do it. During my last year in college, my name occasionally appeared in some of the national publications, but such notice effected no change in my lifestyle. Nobody in my circle of awareness treated me differently because of this distant notoriety. There were few negatives from the exposure up to that point in my life.

Fame's larger shadow crept up on me as a professional. Despite having been a first-round draft pick, I had very little sense of elevated recognition. As the years passed and I gradually earned a spot in the Jazz's starting lineup, I began to experience exposure at the NBA level. Like most aspects of my new world, I learned to adjust but was uncomfortable with the leap from the beginning.

• • •

Most folks consider fame in a much larger context than their neighborhood. In today's world with the Internet and all of its various applications for instant communication, fame or infamy can grow like a wildfire. Still, television remains as one of the primary means of creating and identifying "the famous." Television, as no other electronic tool, arguably manufactures and multiplies this phenomenon. When you are seen on TV, the seeds of fame are planted. If you are seen repeatedly, you *are* famous. I started to become aware of television's magic reality when I joined the Utah Jazz. We drew almost 17,000 fans each game, but it was through regional and local television that the greater Salt Lake community became aware of me. Through sheer numbers, which the medium provided, more people *knew* me than I ever thought possible. As the spotlight found me more often, a larger-than-life silhouette came to exist. The final straw was my selection to the 1992 Olympics as a member of the Dream Team. It was then that I officially crossed the Rubicon, the proverbial point of no return, and left obscurity behind for good.

Even with this steady increase in recognition, life off the court remained manageable and enjoyable. Salt Lake City is a robust community but was dwarfed in terms of media coverage by cities such as New York and Chicago. Fan access to me at that time was generally limited to games, occasional interviews, and Jazz appearances. Twenty-four-hour sports talk shows, behind the scenes specials, and their generational cousins, Facebook and Twitter, either didn't exist or hadn't arrived in the Wasatch Mountains. My life was pretty simple. All I had to do was play basketball and make a few required appearances.

Exposure, though still pretty minimal, presented my family and me with new challenges, especially as the shadow of fame lengthened. Being by choice basically a private person, getting over these hurdles wasn't always easy. I understood that the financial rewards of the NBA were based upon the sustained interest of fans—the more the better. This created the necessity for tradeoffs between interaction with the public and the maintenance of a private life uncomplicated by fame. This is how the Stockton clan tried to come to terms with being a public family.

Searching for Solutions

As I came to be acquainted with fame outside of my neighborhood, I no longer sought it. In my early days with the Jazz, convinced I wasn't long for the NBA, I tried making a couple of commercials for a few extra bucks, but the experiences proved awkward. To make matters worse, I was recognized more on the streets for being in the ads than I was for playing ball. Going forward I decided to be quite a bit more selective when I put myself out for employment on the airwaves.

Frank Layden always graveled, "If you want [to make] money and receive awards and recognition . . . then win!" He was right. As our team continued to succeed, opportunities and accolades followed. The door to the public cracked open for all of us as a result, inviting intrusion into previously private areas of daily life. It always surprised me how quickly this could mushroom out of control—for me, at least. I came to be seen, fondly, as the boy next door by some fans, and it wasn't at all uncommon for uninvited strangers to show up at my house. Once, a school bus full of kids armed with pens and pads arrived with no warning whatsoever. On many occasions fans or autograph seekers would pull up a chair at a restaurant and intrude on a family conversation. I even had private time interrupted in the restroom with a tap on the shoulder or a knock on the stall door. It doesn't take many bad apples to develop a distaste for the pie. I needed some boundaries. The rules I came up with were not rigid guidelines burned into stone tablets. They were more like evolving adjustments with trial and a lot of error.

I tried to pattern these boundaries after the common courtesy and good manners I had learned by observing the Golden Rule—by treating people, even those in the limelight, the way we would like to be treated. That might require some thought. It may seem as though asking for an autograph would be flattering to any celebrity. For some this may be true but certainly not anywhere or at any time. For me, there had to be parameters, especially for those who didn't seem to appreciate that I was trying to lead a reasonably normal life. People who haven't "walked in these shoes" may not understand the absolute need for these courtesies. Thankfully, most do—most of the time.

As I wrestled with various approaches myself, I marveled at Coach Sloan and Charles Barkley for the way they comfortably mingled with the public. They were genuinely friendly with strangers and seemed to welcome the inevitable interaction that came with the territory. I also remember to this day watching Jack Nicklaus at a golf exhibition in Spokane when I was about sixteen. He walked down the path between holes as his adoring fans jostled for just a glance. I lined up for a picture but forgot to wind my camera. Noticing my dilemma, Mr. Nicklaus paused, waited, and smiled into the lens as I recovered to snap the picture. Even at that age I realized what grace he possessed and how comfortable he was in his skin. At times I have tried to emulate his actions with varied and limited success. Everyone is different. I tried to do my best in these situations but never felt as though I got it quite right.

Ripple Effects

Overall, I think the biggest drawback to being a public figure is the potential impact that status has on family and loved ones. When anyone has the public in their life, they welcome them into the lives of their loved ones as well. As my exposure grew, Dad was approached ever more frequently at the Tav to get something signed, first for a friend, then for friends of friends, and so on. Mom always seemed glad to help without regard to the implications. My brother and sisters became intermediaries for their circles of friends as well. Everyone wanted to please and to avoid being rude. What didn't seem at first like a big deal gradually added pressure to all of my most important relationships.

Coach Pickett strategizing with Michael Stockton,
Hoopfest, Spokane, 1997.

It finally came to a boil with one of Spokane's biggest and best events, a three-on-three basketball tournament known as Hoopfest.[1] Some of the event leaders felt I would be a good poster boy. I was looking for a more normal and private existence in my hometown, so I declined. One of the event board members at the time felt I "had a duty" to accept and applied some nasty pressure, mostly on my Dad. My brother also took some heat as I was out of reach in Salt Lake City.

Eventually Steve called and asked me to reconsider for Dad's sake, adding that a lot of bad things were being said about me. I snapped back that I didn't care what people thought of me. His common-sense response brought a terrific perspective that I have never forgotten. "I care," he forcefully reminded me. The truth was, I also cared, but knew I couldn't control their comments. Steve made me realize that, like it or not, I couldn't insulate my loved ones. They would feel the repercussions of my actions, good or bad.

Sometimes what happened had little to do with anything I did. One night as a newlywed, I escorted Nada to her first Meet the Jazz party, a huge PR event kicking off each season. Media and fans alike pushed and shoved for position around the players. In the rush Nada was shoved aside and hit on the head with a news camera. That was unacceptable and would get old very quickly.

I made a point from then on to insist, in one way or another, on manners from media and fans whenever we crossed paths.

• • •

As children arrived, bringing a new wrinkle into the fame equation, we had to adopt new rules for our family. Nada and I wanted to include the kids in almost everything. It wasn't healthy or feasible for us to heavily shield them or to hide out in any way. They needed to learn to be comfortable and to deal with people in all situations. We couldn't do that by keeping them in the shadows outside the reach of my fame. On the other hand, Nada and I also didn't want to immerse them so totally in the exposure that they would begin to feel famous themselves. We didn't want them to feel as though they were entitled or as though they owned every place we were visiting. In this world, that was a huge challenge.

Our purpose was to have the kids get more than a toe in the water without throwing them into the deep end. We talked a great deal about what the kids saw and experienced and tried to provide some sage guidance. Still, life was different for them. When people recognized me, they would often make kind gestures such as offering us the privilege of cutting into lines in a theatre or grocery store or free ice cream cones. We felt it was in our children's best interests to decline most of these offers. We wanted to make it clear that they weren't "America's guests" with special privileges. We also insisted that they had to remain polite and courteous, even if the comments weren't so cordial. These are hard lines to walk for adults, let alone for children. Our kids were often left wondering why they didn't get to have the free ice cream cones.

With family in mind, I set some personal boundaries and guidelines for my public role. For one, home was simply off-limits. There, I was a husband, father, neighbor, and friend. I didn't accept fan mail or public attention of any kind at my house. It wasn't solely a comfort issue; it was also a safety issue. I received numerous suspicious packages and letters that had to be picked up by the police. Some were truly worrisome while others wound up being benign, though that wasn't always obvious.

A case in point is a box of pistachios that I received from a prison inmate. The suspicious package was somehow delivered to our doorstep without postage or markings. We took no chances. I had learned that lesson in my rookie season when the infamous Mormon murders took place in Salt Lake City.[2] Explosives disguised as parcels killed several people in a high profile case that shook the community. These homicides etched a healthy respect for odd mailings, which I retain to this day.

I preferred not to do autographs, photos, or give talks when my children were present unless they had joined me at an appearance designated for that purpose. There, they had to understand and conform to the rules of the event. My kids had to realize that this was part of my job.

It's hard to explain this to someone who has never faced these dilemmas, and I was often criticized by people who just wanted

David, Michael, and Houston cheering on their
dad in the NBA playoffs, circa 1992.

a moment of my time but who were politely turned away. "Who does he think he is?" or "What harm would it do to sign one autograph or take one picture?" were the criticisms I heard. But it wasn't just *that* one moment but *all the other moments* that we were dealing with.

I also consciously avoided discussions about basketball or my career whenever our children were with me. I didn't want my kids rolling their eyes by the time they were teenagers every time they heard my name mentioned. I wanted to prevent overexposure and its many potentially harmful effects.

To accomplish this, Nada and I kept our summers wide open. We really tried not to plan or schedule anything, including "once in a lifetime" opportunities, such as all-expenses-paid cruises and golfing trips that seemed to pop up each summer for NBA players. Many of these offers were tempting, but we opted for the lake with the kids. Time is precious.

The autograph world would continue to present many opportunities to pass or fail over the years. In the right time and place, a simple signature can be such a positive exchange. Signing a worn-out ball or a torn piece of scrap paper for a young child because that was all they had felt right, with both of us leaving with a smile on our faces. Autographing twenty collector cards or photos that someone just happened to have with them wasn't as warm and fuzzy. Many people thought that I didn't give out autographs. The truth is that I have signed tens of thousands. But I have to admit, there aren't many appropriate times and places that work very well for me. Starting a precedent in any public area can create more problems than it is worth.

Tussling with legitimate public access versus unacceptable intrusion can be a fine line, to say the least. Sometimes I was intentionally harsh in handling people I felt were, effectively, stalkers. They were easy to spot. Autograph seekers of all ages and sizes showed up at all hours at our hotels in every town on our schedule. Collectors saw nothing wrong with following a cab to a restaurant. Young kids were used as front men for collectors. It was often tough to figure out who the good guys were.

I bungled many of these situations. I'm almost too embarrassed to count. One particular incident sticks in my head to this day. I was waiting for Nada in my car outside a new sandwich shop we wanted to try. Slumped in my seat to avoid recognition, I spotted a young boy about twelve years old riding his bike. Somehow he recognized me as he buzzed behind the car. I was attuned to this type of behavior and instantly recognized the signs.

Back and forth he rode as inconspicuously as possible trying to confirm I was who he thought I was. I tensed in my seat as he triggered an angry "being stalked" feeling inside of me. He innocently and excitedly approached my window to say hello, only to be greeted by an unfriendly bark. I rudely shooed him away. My words weren't bad, but my tone was. He put his head down and rode off. After a moment I realized what I had done. I started the car and drove around the neighborhood in the direction he had gone to apologize and sign something if he still wanted it. No luck. I couldn't find him and have to live with being a creep. Hopefully, the young man proved to be a little more mature than me and doesn't hold a grudge against someone he once admired. A small cue had put me on edge. It wouldn't be the last time. I struggled continually with the demands of being famous, probably more so as I grew older. I admitted this problem to Coach John Wooden one time in a conversation over the phone. His sage and simple advice, "Just be better tomorrow," continues to help me in a lot of ways.

My self-improvement efforts were tested more often than I would have hoped. On one occasion, while watching my two oldest boys' football games, a seemingly nice man approached me and started talking. Houston's team kicked off on field one, while Michael's squad received on field two. With two games going on at once, I swiveled like a turret to keep track of the action on both fields. The man and I enjoyed a nice conversation until shortly after halftime. Out of nowhere the topic suddenly changed. He wanted me to go over to meet his family and sign autographs. I thought he was joking. "During the games?" I asked, then politely declined. Immediately he erupted into a tirade of profanity, all of it directed at me at high volume. It aroused the attention of two police officers who patrolled the games just in case parents got out of hand. I was more than a little glad they happened to be there as they directed him out of the park. I was forced to keep an eye on him thereafter. It only takes one.

Probably the most troubling part of that incident was that I was trying to enjoy one of my favorite activities—watching my kids play sports. There I was, just as every other parent, watching closely for a block, a catch, or a tackle to hang my hat on—a play that makes the day. My oldest son, Houston, happened to catch his first touchdown pass that day—a desperation heave from his best friend, Luke Hristou, accompanied by his uncharacteristic end-zone dance that remains a memorable highlight. Luckily, I didn't miss the moment, but I could have if the guy had had his way.

Reflections

Trying to become comfortable with the many effects of NBA fame was and is a continuing challenge for me. Still, fame, whether seen as a gift or a burden, comes with responsibilities and obligations that can't be dodged. I always understood that to a point, but don't think I fully understood the opportunities in these responsibilities. Larry Miller opened my eyes.

He was a card-carrying workaholic who ran many businesses including the Utah Jazz. Over the course of his lifetime, he never forgot his humble beginnings or the work ethic that vaulted him to his successful station in life. He continued to toil long hours after he had attained success but always seemed to find time for others. You might say he manufactured time to help people. He wouldn't ask often, and almost never insisted, but wanted me to do more for people outside the game. One time he asked me to visit a very sick child about an hour and a half drive from Salt Lake. I knew by the request that I was going, so I jokingly responded, "If you'll go with me." The next morning he pulled up to my house and honked the horn. Visiting the child was a special time. I felt as though our visit made a difference.

Besides making time to do the right thing, fame carries another inherent responsibility: conducting yourself so that any young people who look up to you don't see a fool. Coach Layden made this perfectly clear to me and my teammates in my rookie season. "Like it or not, you are role models—act like it!"

In the early '90s, Charles Barkley countered that notion in a controversial Nike advertisement where he proclaimed, "I am not a role model!" His declaration created quite a stir. I believe he intended to deliver the message that he was a warrior on the court, a competitor. Charles wasn't trying to be a nice person when he played. He went to battle to win. It was just an ad. My response when I heard the criticism was simple. He knows he's a role model and from my point of view a good one. We are all role models but secondary ones.

Parents should be the primary examples to their children. If the weight of being this type of role model to all children falls on professional athletes, both the parents and the child are probably going to feel let down in the end. The private lives of professional athletes, when open to scrutiny, can certainly fall short of perfection. The same can be said of anybody in any profession. Being a good role model is hard, especially for parents and guardians—we only have control over the examples we set.

My brother has a great perspective on being in the spotlight. I heard an interview he did once for a TV station in Salt Lake. He was asked if it bothered him to watch his little brother succeed and become famous. His response was as revealing as it was honest. In short, he said that he was proud of me but wouldn't want to trade my life for his. He knew it would be fun to play in the NBA but wasn't sure about the rest of it.

Handling all the aspects of fame wasn't a skill I grew up with. I didn't know any famous people as a kid on Superior Street. Perhaps they would have been the wrong ones to ask anyway. Oddly enough, at the end of the day, my humbler roots provided the best roadmap.

Though it may have taken me awhile, with the help of people such as Larry Miller and many others, I have come to realize that fame and wealth have provided me with opportunities that very few people get. Among these has been the chance to be a better man than I might have been without the challenges and opportunities that both presented.

• • •

I loved playing basketball, and the rewards were beyond my wildest expectations. Fame, however, was a companion that kept me outside my comfort zone. It's really that simple. These days that discomfort remains quiet most of the time, only spiking with things such as my Hall of Fame induction. These unimaginable honors do keep me on my toes and remind me to stay humble and appreciate the normalcy I have reacquired. A humorous moment during my induction occurred that reconfirmed that if I kept my feet on the ground a fall wouldn't be too painful. As I entered Symphony Hall on a red carpet to receive one of basketball's highest honors, a man started shouting and carrying on: "Yeah, you're the greatest . . . !" Embarrassed by his zeal, I just smiled and kept walking. As I got closer to the gauntlet of enthusiastic fans, the admirer took it up a notch. I braced myself as we nearly brushed shoulders. While he continued gushing praise, his final offering, "Yeah, Big Baby!" shed a little light on the moment.

To my surprise, walking right behind me was Glen "Big Baby" Davis, a rising young star with the Boston Celtics at the time. It brought me down a notch as I realized the exuberant man had no idea who I was and didn't care. Humility is never far away and always ready to slap you in the face.

When I quietly and abruptly announced my retirement in 2003, Larry insisted upon a retirement party. He wasn't going to take no for an answer. Larry felt that I owed it to the fans, and he was right. Nada agreed; she felt it was the appropriate venue to say thank you. Still, I balked at a public tribute. I wanted out of the spotlight, not back into it—no more suffocating attention, just a quiet ride into the sunset. I was wrong. The gathering turned out to be a very special evening for me and for my family.

CHAPTER 16

Championship Rings and Some Underappreciated Things

For nineteen years my teammates and I toiled in pursuit of an elusive championship ring. That's a long time. It's also a lot of games. We suffered through a lot of heartache along the way as each season ended in failure, only inches from the summit. I take great satisfaction in knowing we didn't leave anything on the trail behind us. Between all of the agony of the defeat came unparalleled exhilaration and unforgettable experiences. The memorable good times far outweighed the disappointments.

As much as it might sound like a cliché, I value my journeys to the NBA Finals despite the outcomes. I believe that most winners treasure their journey as highly as their victory. Getting beamed up to the crest of Mount Everest would be a sterile accomplishment for any competitor without the challenge of the step-by-step climb to the top.

We lost consecutive NBA Championships to the Chicago Bulls in 1997 and 1998. The losses don't diminish the value I place on playing in the finals. Both opportunities were among the greatest thrills of my lifetime. I would have rather lost a hundred times on that stage than not to have competed there at all.

It was that special. I hold the greatest respect for those who have reached the pinnacle to be crowned champions—because I know how hard it is to accomplish.

What could possibly make such a maddeningly frustrating journey so special? Camaraderie and community are the cornerstones. We certainly had both in Salt Lake. Competition—pulling our oars together, often to exhaustion, game after game, year after year, against equally determined opponents also binds these memories. Still, I believe that small and unpublicized daily preparation and effort lie squarely at the center of why those treks hold such intrinsic value. We all believed the commitment was worth it despite the risk that we might come up empty—nineteen times in my case.

I became ever more certain that the will to win wasn't as important as the will to prepare to win, as the saying goes. I learned along the way with my teammates under the guidance of Larry Miller, Frank Layden, and Jerry Sloan about becoming a champion without winning a championship. I learned that all victories didn't show up in the standings. Trying every day to win practice drills such as wind sprints or shooting matches when nobody is watching is in some ways the essence of becoming a professional. These habits become contagious, and everyone inches closer to a common dream. Maybe that's why I loved practice so much. There I could lose without that embarrassed, split-in-my-pants feeling I got whenever we lost a game. In practice you can always try again. This attitude created a culture of winning for the Utah Jazz and forged an unforgettable bond between each of us on the team.

Fortunately, my teams succeeded far more than we failed. The Utah Jazz made the playoffs every year I played. We never experienced a losing season. The Jazz boasts one of the longest, if not the longest, consecutive playoff streaks in the history of the league. These and many other consistent markers of success are a testament to the excellence of the Jazz organization and the never-quit mind-set of the players and coaches who represent the team.

Assaults on the summit of any professional sport begin long before the championship series or contest. Often they are years in the making. The preparation process can be quite slow, requiring adjustments to accommodate the changing nature of the game.

Things such as rule changes may seem insignificant but can actually tip the scales of success dramatically for any given team.[1] They can also affect the very nature and direction of the game of basketball. I'm convinced that, unfortunately, the general direction of rule changes for a long time has been to carve out greater space for the individual athlete while curbing the impact of team play. This narrows the opportunities to participate. In general, only "cookie cutter" athletic prodigies get serious looks. In my opinion, tinkering with the game to distort the natural balance between team and individual play is counterproductive.

•   •   •

Our thrust towards an NBA Championship probably began in earnest in 1988. You never really know where you stand until truly tested by the best. The Lakers fit that billing. A seven-game playoff series loss to the "Showtime" squad proved to be a first step up a long staircase. Though still a little wet behind the ears, we thought we were contenders. Coach Layden persuaded us to believe in ourselves when the rest of the basketball world didn't. Our close loss to the best and the way it unfolded gave validation to our dream of reaching the championship.

We stole an early victory at the Forum and that gave them

John battles Michael Jordan as Karl Malone sets the pick.

something to think about. After they had tied the series in Salt Lake, we took the floor in L.A. for the pivotal fifth game against the likes of Magic, Kareem, Worthy, Rambis, and Scott. A win would have put our young and hungry team in the driver's seat with game six at home. Naïvely or not, we thought we had more than a fighting chance. We were pushing the champs to the brink of elimination.

As the clock wound down in that fifth game, we had the ball out of bounds on the sideline in front of our bench with the score tied. We planned to take the last shot knowing we would either win or go to overtime. Things didn't go according to plan. We turned the ball over on the inbounds play. In-bounding the ball at midcourt was more difficult in those days because we couldn't use the backcourt as players can under today's rules. On the next play, Magic drove down the lane. I slid over to help and deflected the ball down to his knee. He managed to recover enough to kick it to my man, Michael Cooper, who sank the winning shot at the buzzer. After crushing the Lakers at home by twenty-eight in game six, we ultimately lost game seven on their court—but we were far from defeated in any psychological sense. We took home lessons that would help us in our future quests for the championship.

Even before the Lakers series ended, our constant search for the right combination of players within the NBA's ever-changing environment continued without interruption. A large part of the foundation was already in place in the form of a stable organization and first-rate coaching staff. We also had a cornerstone by the name of Karl Malone. Many of my teammates, past and present, contributed to shaping, molding, and nudging Karl into becoming the anchor that good teams must have to be successful. He became both an immovable object and an irresistible force who carried the load for the Jazz for nearly two decades. Karl brought national attention and credibility to the organization. He made me better; he made all of us better.

Roughly a decade passed between that disappointing Lakers series and our first opportunity to play in a championship. The process of finding the appropriate pieces to the championship puzzle continued in the intervening years. We all became painfully aware that this climb involved no magical leaps, only well-considered decisions and perseverance. Personnel decisions made by the club tended to be some of the more painful aspects of our ascent. Finding the right combinations can be difficult and saddening. We hadn't done a lot of trades during my tenure. The traditional stability of the Jazz made me uncomfortable with any change.

Regrettably, one of the most memorable swaps the team

completed included my friend Thurl Bailey. Big T broke the news to me himself. I was heartbroken. Thurl had taken me under his wing my rookie season, and we had become family in the years that followed. It was hard to accept that he was leaving.[2] Easing the pain, the team acquired Tyrone Corbin, who became a great addition to the squad. In the years that followed, Tyrone and I also formed a friendship, though things were never quite the same without Thurl—the price of moving in a new direction, I suppose.

• • •

Another aspect of building upward for any organization is the financial and business side of the equation. A franchise must be able to secure the services of the key players they are counting on to form the nucleus of an upward-bound team. This is difficult, especially for the small market teams such as the Jazz. The difficulty of meeting market prices was a huge obstacle that the Jazz managed to overcome. Karl, as you might expect, was always the largest challenge. He deserved and demanded a salary at or near the top of the league. Karl and the Jazz collaborated for the better part of two decades to keep him in Salt Lake. This loyalty is a tribute to both Karl and to the organization.

The rules and techniques of negotiations are interesting, especially if you are not directly involved. Gamesmanship can heat up both sides of the bargaining table as each massages the same evidence to gain an advantage. Each player's worth is determined relative to others at his position throughout the league. Often this is like comparing apples to oranges. Many circumstances enter into the discussion. For example, does the team win or lose? What are the player's stats? Does he score most of the points while his team consistently loses? This exercise seemingly can, and usually does, go on forever. Reaching an agreement is not an easy process.

For some, a determining factor in negotiations can be the team's ability to pay—what are the organization's financial constraints? What are their plans for signing others to make the team better? Does this question even concern some players? Many are ready and willing to leave in a heartbeat for only the promise of greener pastures. For a few, the desire to remain with their team can override the irresistibility of the almighty dollar. In the end, negotiations are important to the players and the organizations. The best strategists generally gain the advantage.

Then there was my own unusual negotiation style. Though not exciting or newsworthy, my evolution in the process was interesting. I learned a lot about perceived value and emotional attachments. Like a stray cat fed at the back porch, I was attached. I couldn't think of anything much worse than breaking into a new team. I loved my teammates and coaches. Salt Lake had become my home away from home. They were going to have to rip my jersey off to get rid of me. I suspect the club knew this. Offers through my agent, Jim White, remained persistently low, with minimal guarantees. In one of the first renegotiations of my career, I felt outgunned, mostly by my own emotions. I didn't feel as though the Jazz took either Jim or me seriously, so I decided to part ways with a very good man who took good care of me in the time we worked together.

I hired David Falk as my agent to handle my contract talks that season. He was the highest profile representative in the business and exceptional at his job. His creative mind, understanding of the NBA's financial rules, and dogged persistence kept GMs around the league on their toes. David would find new angles and open old wounds to achieve maximum leverage for his clients. I was proof of his prowess. The day I informed the Jazz of his hire, all contract years currently on the table became guaranteed. I obviously felt good about my choice. As the season progressed, however, the talks stalled, and I began to have my doubts.

I started to hear comments in the media that supposedly came from me or my camp, which certainly didn't reflect my sentiments. As the impasse continued, I began to hear about the things I was *demanding* and was surprised to learn that I might be going elsewhere. Since this was as far from my intention as possible, I realized that some leverage was being applied. This was a reasonable tool, and I understood the tactic, but I never felt comfortable with any threat of leaving. The truth is, I didn't have any other place I wanted to go.

As the All-Star break loomed, I grew more uneasy with the lack of progress in these negotiations. We seemed no closer to a deal than we were on day one of the process. The mid-February break offered a nice chance to recharge the batteries and prepare for the playoff push. It also seemed like the perfect time to conclude negotiations. I wanted all contract concerns for next season put to bed before we returned. The biggest problem I had with the process was that I simply wasn't comfortable having someone else speaking for me. I respect honorable people who say what they mean and mean what they say, and I wanted to be able to include myself in that group.

I decided to call Larry Miller. I was yet to establish any relationship with him other than dodging his tenacious defense in pregame warm-ups. "Can we meet?" I asked. He agreed, and we sat down in his office at his Chevrolet dealership. We spent some time getting to know each other before I asked, "Why are we stalled?" Without blaming anyone, he let me into his head for the first time as he explained his position. Then he handed me a piece of paper and said, "Write down what you think you are worth, and I will write down what I think you are worth." After some thought and some scribbles, we exchanged papers. They both revealed the same number. The contract negotiations immediately came to a successful close.

Could I have made more money and perks by sticking with Mr. Falk? I think so, but there was a real chance that I wouldn't have been playing for the Jazz or at minimum would have lost some goodwill. For me, the gains wouldn't have been worth the losses. The deal felt right. I knew it was fair, albeit not the maximum I could have exacted. That was never my goal.

The signing of that deal began a wonderful relationship with Larry Miller that I would treasure professionally and personally in the years to come. All subsequent negotiations between us went off in a similar fashion; mutual trust was the key element. In fact, in one of our last contract talks, we didn't even discuss money. I told him, "You pay me what you think is fair and I will sign it." It was that simple. Larry confessed later that my comments added significant pressure to his side of the bargaining process.

My final contract broke the mold in two regards. Larry offered me a deal that would have made me the highest paid point guard in the league. He was proud of it. I wasn't sure I warranted that consideration but was grateful. I countered his offer with a substantially lower one. Both of us, I think, were showing the appreciation we had gained for each other. Funny how straightforward the negotiations can be when trust is the essence of a relationship.

Before we completed possibly the oddest negotiation in NBA history, I threw in still another wrinkle. Standard player contracts usually contain provisions limiting off-court activities. They are mostly reasonable considering the team's investment. Exclusions for things such as skydiving, whitewater rafting, mountain climbing, and a litany of other physical activities are usually included. The prohibitions extended to summer basketball, softball, or waterskiing. With six growing children, I was uncomfortable with the thought that my contract would become void if I played catch or mountain biked with my kids and got hurt. When I told Larry, he laughed and responded, "You go write your own provisions." I took pen in hand and composed a paragraph with as much legalese as I could muster: "Heretofore and notwithstanding the provisions cited in Chapter 2 . . . athlete may participate in all activities with his kids, including baseball, basketball, and the like . . . and so on and so forth." Larry accepted it with a chuckle and sent it to the league verbatim. They also accepted the wording. The whole process was as fun as it was educational.

• • •

Contract negotiations, ongoing signings, and trade maneuverings slowly started locking the pieces together for a championship run. Unfortunately, the moving target can be elusive as players get old, injured, retire, or move on to greener pastures. You can't preserve a currently perfect piece to fit into a later puzzle. The process can be confounding. The Jazz had to do it the hard way. Because of continual success, the Jazz never had a lottery pick in franchise history.[3] The team was built on the skillful selection of later draft choices. Two such choices were in the second round. Both were key additions, demonstrating how perceptive and talented the Jazz selection group was.

Bryon Russell was enormously talented but made the team primarily through his effort on the defensive end. I remember well his first training camp. Bryon arrived in great condition. He outworked all of his competitors. The roster at the time was full with guaranteed contracts, so the club had to eat one in order to sign Bryon. He must have made quite an impression on the coaches to prompt that action. Many prospective players don't make a team because of their potentially negative impact on group chemistry. Bryon's upbeat personality greatly enhanced his value to the team. He became a starter and enjoyed a long and successful career.

Shandon Anderson was also a second-round selection but came to camp with space available, so the team didn't have to boot anyone this time. He fit the Jazz perfectly. He improved our athleticism and speed while adding a clever knack for many elements in the game including getting open for layups and defending. Unlike many players who don't make it in the NBA, these two men focused on defense first. They could both score but didn't shoot every time they touched the ball to prove it.

Free agency and outright trades are another way to build or add to a team. Utah, just as teams in most small markets, suffers from a disadvantage in this arena. Lack of cash is one obvious reason because TV revenue is less in a smaller market. Another less conspicuous factor is that fewer opportunities exist for lucrative endorsements for the same reason. In terms of perception, these cities are often seen as dull in comparison to the bright lights of N.Y. or L.A. Nestled in Salt Lake, the home of the LDS Church, the Jazz, for instance, can appear less than "jazzy" to some. The prospect of living in a squeaky-clean community with limited night life and minimal diversity can stigmatize a team and a city in terms of free-agency attractiveness.

Larry Miller must have had a remarkable understanding of these prejudices. His feel for people as well as for the financial and organizational complexities of big business allowed the Jazz opportunities in this small market that might have passed them by with another owner.

With all of these challenges, the Jazz did a remarkable job assembling a team that was ready for a run at the championship. Three times in five years we made it to the conference finals without reaching the big dance. We kept knocking on a door that refused to open. We rapped harder in 1997.

We faced an old nemesis in the Houston Rockets in the '97 Western Conference Finals. They had beaten us there in 1994 and in the first round of the playoffs in '95 on their way to the title with newly acquired Clyde Drexler from the Trail Blazers. Clyde and company had also escorted us out of the playoffs on a couple of occasions while he was in Portland. In addition, the Rockets had added another large arrow to an already full quiver in the person of Sir Charles Barkley. As a result, we had a few obstacles to overcome, which made the series more than a little interesting.

We held serve at home, winning the first two games. In game two, however, Charles took exception to my legal back screen. Attempting to make a statement, he unapologetically picked me up and threw me on my back, anything but a knightly move. No reprimand was levied.

The next morning I couldn't stand up, having suffered a level-two back sprain. When we arrived in Houston for game three, Mike Shimensky, our trainer who took over after Sparky, was committed to pulling out all the stops to have me ready. Craig Buhler was already on the trip, and Mike called in biomechanics expert Greg Roskopf to assist "Buhls" to try and pull off a tall healing order. Greg, like Buhler, had helped solve numerous physical ailments for me over the years.

Their combined results were magical. Stooped over in my

hotel room, I needed nothing less than magic. For nearly eight hours over two days, they activated core muscles in my legs, pelvis, and spine. Their methods weren't exactly pain free, but the results were. When they finished, I had absolutely no pain and a full range of motion. This was achieved without the use of painkillers or other drugs. I went into the game at 300 percent. I received a fair amount of credit for toughness, but the truth was that the pain was gone, solely a result of the combined efforts of my imported healing team.

Their feat didn't immediately yield dividends on the court, however, as we lost both contests in Houston. The second of those games ended with a miraculous three-pointer by another old nemesis, Eddie Johnson, who had treated us in a similarly rude fashion when he was with the Suns. He struck again that night as he and his teammates circled the court in a victory celebration. In Eddie's postgame remarks, the speechless gunslinger deemed the shot and the ensuing party as "surreal!"

We held serve again at home in game five, but Mr. Johnson's shot had provided a new air of confidence for the already secure Rockets. That buzzer-beater created a ripple of doubt that lapped at our fringes. From the media's perspective, there were now some questions as to whether or not we could actually win a seven-game series against these Rockets.

Still, we were up three games to two when we flew back to Houston and certainly didn't want to extend the series to a seventh game. Our chances to put them away looked bleak as we trailed in game six by sixteen points late in the fourth period. As strange as it may sound, sixteen points is a tenuous lead with half a quarter to play in an NBA game. The shot clock, the three-point line, the continuation rule, and stopped time after made baskets all contribute to more exciting and numerous comebacks than expected. We had lost twice in deciding games in our recent playoff history, once to Eddie Johnson and the Phoenix Suns and appropriately to these same Rockets. So, we hadn't lost confidence since we knew firsthand their lead could evaporate in a hurry.

The mood and momentum of the game did, in fact, shift suddenly. Greg Ostertag, our often-maligned young center, began blocking or affecting every shot. That was one of his strengths. He was big and long with a feel for altering shots. Greg gave us a boost offensively and the Rockets lost their edge. Our defense swarmed, resulting in a frenzy of late-game fast breaks. We were closing hard as the finish line approached.

With only a few ticks left on the clock and the score tied, we had the ball out of bounds on the sideline in our half-court. We ran the same play that had deserted us versus the Lakers nine years earlier. Experience made us better at executing the play this time around. Karl set a mammoth screen that provided our opportunity. I read and reacted to the defense correctly. With Clyde and a host of Rockets awaiting the curl, I popped instead. Outside the design of the play, but within the list of possible options, the ball found my hands on time and on target. Our collective read of the defense had resulted in a long three-point opportunity staring straight down the barrel. It was a driveway shot I had practiced a thousand times on Superior Street. We only needed a point, but I knew the "3" was our best chance with Olajuwon looming near the basket. I had forward momentum, so I knew I could accommodate the range. My only thought as the ball snapped into my grasp was to follow through! Fortunately, I stepped into the most perfect jump shot of my career. As if it were a movie scene, all sound ceased to exist as the ball rotated in slow motion toward the hoop. I knew it was in but that assumption had failed me before. Many times on game-deciding shots I had felt confident, only to watch the ball rim out. I waited this time before allowing even a ray of hope to creep into my mind. We almost heard the net ripple as the ball swished without brushing the iron. The rest really was surreal, if the word means what I think it does—dreamlike. Eddie was right. Witnessing the ball tickle that twine when it meant so much was indeed surreal.

To say it was the biggest win in Jazz history would be a gross understatement. I have heard people talk about where they were when "The Shot" happened. Jazz fans hold the memory with a reverence normally reserved for things such as landing a man on the moon. They speak nostalgically of an eruption of noise audible throughout the Salt Lake Valley as jubilant Utahans ran out of their homes in celebration. Nada and the kids were not an exception. They grabbed pots, pans, and spoons and ran out into the street, clanking to their hearts' content with the rest of the Salt Lake community. No doubt they were also dancing to the same tune in the hometowns of Coach Sloan, "Horny," The Mailman, and myself in Illinois, Louisiana, and Washington. The celebration sites were at least as numerous as the members of our team and staff. I know from my own scouts at home that much of Spokane celebrated long into the night with Jack and Dan's serving as the epicenter of the party.

On the court, it was bedlam. We shared a special elation that night on the enemy's turf. I was lost in the moment as we jumped around in a pile circled by our own arms. "We did it!" were the only words I could muster from within that clench. The team had finally hurdled the last barrier to the championship. In the process we slayed a couple of dragons and exorcised some demons. With all of that going on, I was still too caught up in the euphoria to speak. In the crowded postgame interview room, the only thing I could come up with in answer to the flurry of questions was the ridiculously concise description of "Neat."

On the bus ride to the airport, I sat motionless and said essentially nothing until teammate Adam Keefe came over and excitedly shook me. "Get up and yell, cheer, do something!" he jokingly demanded. Nothing I could have said or done would have done justice to how good I felt. I did allow myself a short illegal call home to Nada and the kids from the bus. I was only able to listen to my family's excitement. Quietly, I remained seated as the bus moved along. I was so deeply immersed in our victory that I couldn't honor Adam's demand. That was okay as part of me and perhaps part of everyone had already moved on to the finals. We retired to our own thoughts. I'm not exactly sure what my thoughts were after everyone settled in for the ride. It was my first bus ride in thirteen years as a player headed to the NBA Championship series. I scanned the bus and my teammates onboard. The twelve-man roster of that '96–'97 team really was a sum greater than the total of its parts. They were a unique group; everyone seemed to genuinely like each other. Most teams learn to get along—getting along came naturally to us.

Adam did a lot more than urge me to celebrate big victories. He had become one of my all-time favorite teammates and a close friend. He did, however, possess a couple of amusingly contradictory traits that always seemed to leave me scratching my head. Strangely, he could answer every question on almost any crossword puzzle but couldn't complete any of them. Being part of the "spell-check generation," he'd leave off one letter or add another, effectively sabotaging each exercise.

Athletically he resembled a heavy-legged plodder with unearthly white legs but could really leave the floor. Actually Adam brought a lot to the Jazz table. He stayed prepared and into the game every night—whether on or off the floor. When Adam was on the bench, his insightful comments and unfailing enthusiasm could be counted on. He was a major contributor who fit our team like a glove. He ran like a deer, wasn't afraid to get his hands dirty, and was also quite the character.

A curious moment during one ordinary game demonstrates how he could stir the pot with the best of them. In that particular contest, I had spent the majority of my time driving to the basket. It wasn't lonely in there as the defense aggressively swarmed. I managed to unload the ball to Adam for a couple of layups while being tugged, grabbed, knocked down, and landed on. During a time-out he nonchalantly pulled me aside and very seriously but very politely offered some unsolicited advice. He held his hands up at chest level and said, "I like passes here. If you can just adjust them a little, it will help." He had cast his line, and I took the bait.

Are you serious? I remember thinking and responded defensively, "I am lucky any of those passes even got near you." He never cracked a smile and hustled back out to the court. Karl heard the entire exchange and couldn't restrain himself from laughing out loud.

Seated not too far from Adam on that bus was Jeff Hornacek. The magnitude of his contribution to the team cannot be overstated. It is not an exaggeration to say that we wouldn't have been on that victory bus ride without him. He also filled a seat in a cozy carpool with Adam, Greg Foster, and me.

"Horny" had come to the Jazz in a late season trade just before the 1994 deadline. Larry Miller called me immediately after the trading period had expired and matter of factly asked, "How would you like to play with Jeff Hornacek?" I thought it was a trick question under the circumstances but answered seriously

Teammates and friends. Jeff Hornacek, Karl Malone, and John.

nonetheless, "I would love it!" Larry responded with the happy news, "We just traded for him."

Jeff was a godsend. The day of his arrival marked a step forward for the Jazz organization. Personally, I hadn't enjoyed playing against Jeff. He was one of those rawboned guys with talent and mental toughness to burn. He routinely killed us when he played for the Suns. Now that he was on our side, things had changed. We won something like ten games in a row immediately upon his arrival. At some point we recorded one of the longest consecutive road winning streaks in league history at fifteen games.[4] We started winning consistently on the road, something that historically had eluded us.

Hornacek was a phenomenal shooter, both open and under duress. But more important, he was a complete basketball player.

His shooting range carried over to his "D." He somehow managed to effectively guard both the big, powerful guards and the "jets." His incredibly active hands baffled the biggest offensive stars with his ability to deflect passes, shots, and dribbles. Jeff's mind never rested. As an artist with a pencil, he would draw plays on his hand while calculating in his head the shooting percentage of any player in the lineup. Jeff knew how everyone on the floor was performing. This helped greatly during games. He offered accurate statistical tidbits, such as, "Let that guy shoot; he is one for nine right now," or, "Find Antoine; he's six for six."

The Iowa State walk-on performed like an all-star nearly every night all while dragging his leg around. He had come to the Jazz on a wounded knee and had limped around for years while continuing to succeed. Hobbling one night versus Golden State, with his shooting arm on fire, Horny scored twenty quick points in the first stanza. Matched up against Jeff was a young star named Latrell Sprewell. As the second quarter began, Jeff hauled his battered limb out of bounds to enter the ball. If only a camera could have focused on Sprewell's face as he observed that crooked walk. *Puzzled, discouraged,* and *defeated* don't begin to describe what Sprewell was feeling. If a look could talk, his would have said, "How can someone who moves like that possibly have scored twenty points on me—already?"

Jeff didn't care who got the credit. I watched him win games scoring over thirty-five points. Other times I enjoyed watching him carry us to victory while scoring only a couple. He consistently made the necessary play at the right time with passes, rebounds, or defensive stops. After the game I couldn't see a difference in his mood, whatever his numbers, so long as we had won. Jeff cared only about winning. Off the court, like Adam Keefe, he became a great friend. We could talk hoops, kids, ethics, politics, whatever. Our children went to school and played sports together, so our lives were intertwined off the court as well.

Howard Eisley was another teammate with whom I developed a close friendship. He backed me up at the point though he never seemed like a backup. He was considerably younger than I was but possessed an experienced demeanor that inspired confidence. Our styles were different, but the team kept the same flow with either of us manning the point. The contrast was effective. Howard combined a physical and mental toughness with the quiet strength of a true gentleman. He was a quality person as well as an excellent player. This was a rule and not a bonus with our team. During a long season, it is priceless to have a solid group of people around you. We had acquired just such a battle-tested warrior a few seasons earlier. Antoine Carr, a giant of a man, joined the Jazz relatively late in his career. He came to us labeled as a reserve, but he patrolled the lane with a big bark and a serious bite. He had thoroughly impressed me years before with his performance in the 1984 Olympic Trials in Bloomington. I thought he was the most explosive and powerful talent in the entire tryout. "Big Dog" nicely complemented our younger five-man, Greg Ostertag. Whenever Big Dog entered a game, the fans would go wild. Bounding off the bench, he would throw off his sweats and darn near knock Coach over as he sprinted to the scorer's table. A complete player took the floor to those roars. Opponents couldn't guard him with a small defender because he had the savvy and skill to overpower them. If they tried to use a big man, he would step out and knock down jumpers. Antoine rebounded well and blocked shots with timing and attitude. He was a special and indispensable cog in the Jazz machine.

Three other invaluable contributors were riding on the bus that night. Two of these, Chris Morris and Greg Foster, suffered the indignity of an aborted trade for Roni Seikaly of the Miami Heat during the course of that season. Talented beyond belief, "C-Mo" once led us to victory with a twenty-five point effort as a reserve in a huge playoff game in San Antonio. The amazing part of that performance was that he hadn't been playing significant minutes on a regular basis for about six weeks prior to the outburst. When called on, he was always ready and answered loudly. When Chris wasn't playing, he remained positive and pleasant. The second player in that valuable threesome was Greg Foster—a wily veteran who understood his role and provided consistent and reliable performance in limited minutes. I personally benefitted from the positive input I received from "G-Force." He helped me play better with his enthusiasm. I enjoyed playing with Greg.

Last but not least on that bus sat our twelfth man—Stephen Howard. Stephen was a great teammate in a role that is not easily filled. He did everything Coach asked and did it with zeal and an extraordinarily loud voice. Coach used to ask him, "Did you learn to whisper in a sawmill?" I was certain he had made me better in practice as he had an infuriating knack for stealing my passes. Stephen literally seemed to know where I was going to throw each pass. I was glad he played for us—twelfth men who are real assets to a team are hard to find! After so many years for Karl and me, these men were the best teammates that we could have hoped for.

Late that night, as our chartered aircraft touched down in Salt Lake City, tens of thousands of excited fans lined the streets to congratulate the team. The thrill of victory had nearly subsided as fatigue and the realization of the job in front of us had set upon our bodies and minds. The impromptu parade was still touching and much appreciated.

The next day we departed for Chicago and could see the

NBA's summit for the first time from the windows of the air-plane. We felt confident in any conditions we might encounter and were secure in our abilities. The chance of a lifetime loomed within our reach.

When we arrived at our hotel in Chicago, one thing seemed painfully obvious: it was too crowded at assault camp. The press had taken up residence in hordes. Media from all over the country and the world sought our comments in league-mandated press sessions. Immediately upon our arrival, we were ushered into the pressroom, where we answered and reanswered the same questions posed in a multitude of languages. In the midst of all of this, I was whisked off to an interview with Dan Patrick. I enjoyed the personal exchange and the reprieve from the mob. Dan poked a little good-natured fun at my well-known discomfort with the press. I relaxed and enjoyed the interview and the ribbing.

The truth of the matter was that our team was more than ready to take to the court. We were all growing weary of the hoopla. Answering the repetitive questions only diverted our attention to the things the press thought were important. At that time, in our competitive frame of mind, nearly every question seemed silly. The process became an ever greater challenge to deal with courteously and intelligently.

D-Day finally arrived. It was our first time playing in June. By now we had been through all the battles but the big one, so we weren't struck by the added intensity. The elevated pitch felt normal. As teams move on in the playoffs, every possession begins to feel like the last ticks on the clock of a regular-season game. The focus is keen. Increased adrenaline levels course through veins from the opening tip, and play is more intense than usual. Players live and breathe at a level they couldn't imagine outside of these circumstances.

CHAMPIONSHIP RINGS

When I try to recall the specific details of each game in the 1997 championship series, my recollection often blurs—perhaps as a protective mechanism against reliving the pain of losing. I remember the games were close, with both sides putting forth maximum effort. In that atmosphere, both outstanding plays and excruciating mistakes take on exaggerated proportions. Outcomes that are seemingly set in stone change in the blink of an eye. I clearly remember that game one ended with just such a fickle twist. Things looked bleak. We only had a single point advantage as Michael Jordan stepped to the foul line for two shots with only a handful of ticks remaining on the clock. Inconceivably, he missed both free throws. The reprieve proved to be temporary. The carom from the second miss somehow found the grasp of one of our Chicago hosts. He quickly put it where Michael had intended. They were the deciding points.

The grappling to be king of the mountain lasted six games. Incredibly, the total point differential for the entire series was four. What I remember most is the preparation, camaraderie, and effort that got us there. I'm satisfied that we left no stone unturned and wanted to immediately try again. The team could still taste the air at the summit as we left the windy city. We would return to climb again.

• • •

Minor knee surgery caused me to miss the first eighteen games of the next season. Howard Eisley, along with newcomer Jacque Vaughn, more than handled the point guard duties in my absence. This turned out to be nothing more than a bump in the road for both me and the team. That season our performance mirrored our expectations as we tied Chicago for the best record in the league with sixty-two wins. Karl celebrated the team's success with his first MVP season. It appeared that the pieces for a second summit assault were falling into place.

We marched through the playoffs but not without effort. The Western Conference, never a picnic, presented major challenges with both Houston and San Antonio in our path. We battled through both archrivals only to face the Lakers, who themselves boasted sixty-one wins. It promised to be a whopper of a conference final. This was the Jazz's fifth appearance in seven years in the conference championships, while the Lakers were loaded with the likes of Shaquille O'Neal, Kobe Bryant, and Derek Fisher. Contrary to everyone's expectations, including our own, we dismantled the Lakers in four games.

We were playing our best basketball at the right time. I remember making our way to our locker room in the Forum after the deciding game. The tunnel was lined with Hollywood reporters and probing cameras. I'm sure they scratched their heads at our matter-of-fact demeanor after such a monumental and unexpected accomplishment. Stoic expressions persisted into the locker room. I was reluctant to celebrate in front of the ever-present cameras, hoping instead to soak up the moment only with my team. I wonder sometimes if my mind-set ruined a well-earned bash for the Western Conference champs. I hope not. I like to think the subdued celebration was because each of us knew we had bigger fish to fry.

The pinnacle of our sport awaited us for the second consecutive season. The NBA Championship was again within our sights, only this time we had the home-court advantage nicely tucked into our hip pockets. Peaking at the right time, we were ready. We could only watch as the Bulls battled the Pacers for the right to face us in Salt Lake City. Their series dragged on and on as Reggie Miller and the Pacers proved a stiff challenge for the defending champs. The Bulls finally prevailed in a slugfest, but by the time the Eastern finale ticked to a close and TV executives established a format, ten days would pass since our victory in L.A. The question rumbling throughout the media room became: where does the advantage lie? Is it with the battle-worn, weary Bulls or the well-rested Jazz? The answer would be played out on the floor. During our hiatus we tried to simulate the playoff environment as best we could. The fact is, championship intensity simply cannot be achieved in practice. Nevertheless, we forged ahead with our preparation, focusing on our improvement instead of a game plan for an opponent yet to be determined. When Chicago successfully completed their side of the bracket, we were ready to test our training.

We seemed to shake off any rust from the extended break, wearing down the weary Bulls in game one. But by game two, Chicago recovered their legs to even the series. They accomplished this with a very sick M. J. Despite his illness, Jordan rallied them to the win. I always braced myself for big games from an opponent who announced he was sick or hurt. As I've said before, it's an odd but true phenomenon that ailing players often achieve extraordinary results in their weakened condition. The odd rule seems to be that competitors who try to play while ill usually succeed in a big way. Players who choose to sit it out never know how they would have done.

Chicago took charge of the series by winning the next two games at home to go up 3–1. The first game in Chi-town went down as the most lopsided score in championship history. The Bulls outscored us 96–54. Surprisingly to some, we rebounded to ruin the Windy City party scheduled after game five. We jumped back into contention with that tough road win. Heading home to the Wasatch Mountains, we felt that the tide had turned in our favor.

Game six lived up to our expectations. The contest again came down to a photo finish—the Bulls winning by a nose. I can't recollect all the details of the heartbreaking loss, but I do remember Michael's winning basket as time ticked towards zero. The shot has been replayed on television enough, so I believe my recollection is pretty good. I also recall my failed long shot attempt as the horn sounded. Our season and our dreams of a championship bounded off the rim with that miss.

I had come to believe that I would win an NBA Championship before my time was up, completing a two-sport circle that my grandfather had begun in 1926 by winning an NFL championship with the Frankfort Yellow Jackets. Though I was certain we had all of the tools to make it happen, my fondest visions of standing at the top of that very tall NBA mountain were snatched away twice by a true championship team. This offered little consolation. I tip my hat to Michael, Scottie, Coach Jackson, and the rest of the Chicago Bulls. They earned it. My only solace rested with the fact that in a few months, we would get to try again. "It's not how many times you get knocked down, but how many times you get back up that matters," as my dad would always say. We remained towards the top of the league for the next few years but wouldn't knock again at the championship door. Those two series with the Bulls would be my last chance to cross that threshold.

CHAPTER 17

The Clock Strikes Twelve

In September of 2001, I shook hands with Larry Miller signifying the completion of presumably my last NBA contract negotiation. I wondered if I would play through to its end at age forty-one. I didn't know where this notion came from; I had always liked to finish what I started. I guess I realized that the future wasn't completely within my control with the inevitable intervention of Father Time. Thoughts of the end of the trail began to appear on the horizon. In truth, the process of coming to grips with the reality of retiring had long been underway. Countless scenarios had been bouncing around in my head for years without ever finding their way to the surface.

As an athlete I was no stranger to physical limitations. I was aware of my body and cognizant of the new boundaries that came with each passing year. For me, losing a step hadn't become an issue. I could still run. The one encroaching limitation I noticed was a declining ability to stop abruptly. So, in a sense, I had actually gained a step—on the stopping end. Though the difference felt negligible, the brake pads had begun to show a little wear. Your body knows your limitations before your conscious mind ever considers them. Instinctive movements such as abrupt directional changes and engaging the afterburners begin to require forethought and force of will. Fortunately, wisdom gleaned from experience makes up for most of the physical deficiencies that begin to appear. When I shook Larry's hand, I felt I could still play and compete.

The age an athlete considers retirement is abnormal when compared to the general population. At the age of forty, in the real world, you're practically a whippersnapper, while in professional sports you're Grandpa Moses. At thirty-eight, I couldn't even fathom what retirement meant. It was something that old people did. Dad worked well into his seventies behind the bar at Jack and Dan's, vowing, "They will drag me out of here feet first!" So, getting up and going to work as long as I could stand up was permanently engrained in me from my earliest days.

The thought that I might retire before Dad was out of sync with the normal rhythms of life in our neighborhood. I had no understanding what retirement might mean for me and my family. Just as Dad's job had defined our family activities in many ways, mine blanketed Nada and the kids. The NBA's strange but special life was the only one we knew together. The kids saw David Robinson and Michael Jordan as coworkers at my version of a nine-to-five job. They shot baskets on the Delta Center floor with NBA players as routinely as I entered Dad's tavern as a boy to get a quarter for french fries from the Dairy Freeze across the street. Our lives had revolved around my job for the past nineteen years. Leaving that behind was going to be difficult for all of us.

• • •

In testimony to Larry's sentiments about my ability to play on, I sat generously perched towards the top of the pay scale for point guards when I left his office. As I closed the door behind me, I intended to continue playing the game I loved at a level that satisfied both the team and me. They were going to have to rip the jersey off of my back and drag me out of the gym to get me to stop playing.

I began the first season of that final agreement like any other, playing good games as well as some bad. My workout regimen hadn't diminished; in fact, it had only gotten better with the more efficient program. I felt strong and fast. With borrowed intelligence from biomechanics expert Greg Roskopf and a lot of trial and error, Steve Delong had my program well set. What was slightly different was my mental approach. Gone was the bravado and devil-may-care attitude reserved only for the young. Thoughts that had never entered my mind in my twenties or early thirties began creeping into my head. They weren't haunting or keeping me awake, just present.

Factoring into the retirement equation was a strong sense of loyalty to my teammates and coaches. I didn't want to let them down in any way. Many of these people were dear friends, which only amplified my concerns. These relationships and loyalties provided a driving force that motivated me but also posed a burden that seemed to grow heavier over time. I wrestled with the notion that I might not be able to muster the right stuff to meet my own continuing expectations. I wanted to be the one to recognize when I could no longer cut it and was determined not to let that responsibility fall on Larry or my coaches.

Obviously, I'd been thinking about the various implications of retirement for some time. The road there would not be traveled quickly or easily. I anticipated increased chinks in my armor but didn't foresee the impact of departing friends, nor the resulting change to team chemistry and culture. These considerations would play a significant role in my decision to stop playing.

Jerry Sloan understood the athletic aging process perhaps as well as anyone. He knew the value of older vets—provided they weren't run into the ground. Coach had been implementing a conservation policy with most of the old guard for some time. I wasn't particularly fond of his decision and told him so. The program included limiting playing time where possible and clipping our practice regimens. I lived for the games and still loved to practice. Coach was pretty clear that he had a responsibility to maintain the team at the highest possible level, which included, in his words, "Keeping you guys [Karl, Jeff, and me] around as long as I can." I trusted him completely despite my objections.

I had watched as two exceptional players, Darrell Griffith and Mark Eaton, retired during my first decade with the Jazz. I remember thinking that these guys were too good to be retiring. Watching someone hang up his sneakers while he's still capable of making a significant contribution to the team was an odd phenomenon that I only partially understood as a young player. I had an inkling of what kind of physical pain they endured to get ready to play every day, but I couldn't completely empathize. Naïvely, I thought, *Why would anyone ever retire from this? You get paid to play basketball—what a deal!* Frank Layden used to say, "It beats working."

In later years I watched as two other teammates decided to pull the curtain on their careers. Antoine Carr approached me on a team flight to bounce around the idea. He was down and frustrated with many things that I would find out later weren't unique to him. I wish, to this day, I had had a more seasoned understanding when we spoke at 40,000 feet because I would have urged him to stay or told him truthfully how incredibly crucial he was to our success. At minimum I should have told him how much I appreciated his contributions and asked him to think it over. In my mind-set at the time, it was his decision to make, and I didn't feel as though it was my place to intrude. I reasoned that if he left, we would just have to cinch up our belts a little tighter and get it done.[1]

The retirement of my other departing comrade was less of a surprise. Jeff Hornacek and I had talked a lot about him hanging up the sneakers. At that point I understood his motivation better than I had with Darrell, Mark, or Antoine. I pleaded with Jeff to reconsider, but his mind was set. He was certain of his decision. Although he never spoke of it, my guess is that he finally got tired of dragging his leg around and knocking heads with the ever-bigger two guards being thrown at him. Losing Shandon Anderson to help him carry the load couldn't have helped.[2] Perhaps there were many reasons that we didn't cover in our discussions. The bottom line was that he was not changing his mind.

I didn't understand at the time what Jeff's departure would mean to the team and to me. The Jazz suddenly became young, anchored by a couple of aging veterans with marquee histories. Prior to that, in stark contrast, we had been a veteran team bolstered by a few young players who were on the rise. We had honed a style of play that was crucial to our success. The new mix made that recipe a little more difficult to follow.

Personally, I lost a companion when Jeff left. He was a solid friend on and off the court. We ate many meals together on the road and shared the same important interests such as our kids and basketball. We were both gym rats and students of the game. Talking hoops with Jeff never grew old.

• • •

The team culture, which for years had nicely folded in older and younger players, changed abruptly after Horny retired. In his absence I reached out to some of the newcomers but with little success. The "'90s guys," as we jokingly called them, had new-age distractions and interests. It increasingly seemed to me that electronic gadgets had virtually eliminated the need to get to know teammates. The young players brought their friends and family along on road trips, housed inside tiny electronic devices. These players engaged with them in solitude inside the confines of ear-phoned technology. The trips and bus rides became lonely affairs. Camaraderie gave way to comfortable high-tech isolation.

Twenty-first century technology spread to the elder states-men as well. I recall one occasion in training camp when Jeff and Adam knocked on my door to go get some lunch. When I opened the door, all three of us were talking to someone else on our cell phones. In that instant we all felt the disappointing reality of the moment; we too had fallen victim to the forces of progress. We turned off our phones and went to lunch. As we ate, I was mindful of having joined the new millennium.

I still fondly remember many meals in my early years with such colorful characters as Adrian Dantley, Rich Kelley, and Billy "The Whopper" Paultz. They were older and our meals together didn't lead to bosom buddy relationships, but I loved listening to their stories, hearing their viewpoints on things on and off the court, and absorbing some of the wisdom they had stored up from years of playing in the league.

I didn't fully detect these cultural transitions as they were oc-curring but I began to feel them with greater impact. Things such as team bus rides were at once the same and very different. A few short years before, when we were rolling through the league tally-ing sixty-plus wins, bus rides were focused with a quiet intensity heading to the arena and filled with lively banter returning if we managed to win. Good-natured insults and trash-talking randomly peppered the air around pockets of laughter and rows of quiet conversation. A cultural time gap had begun to appear as a new generation of players filled the seats of the bus and the stalls of the locker room.

The cultural shift was probably accelerated by one of the best tools that had become available to everyone in the league—chartered aircraft. Spacious seating allowed players to sit alone. Although being "free to move about the cabin," as the flight attendants say, many passengers sought electronic solitude. Karl used to tap hard on their headphones and bark, "Don't tune your teammates out. I know what those headphones mean. They mean you don't want to talk to us!" His was a pretty funny approach to the problem. Although the new chartered arrangements were much better in every way imaginable, something was lost. Some of my best friendships in the NBA had been built during side-by-side trips in the cramped commercial airplanes of our past. We couldn't get away from each other back then. I missed the camaraderie of those days but, ironically, wasn't ready to trade the comforts of this new age to go backwards.

The result of these combined circumstances was that I ate more room service in my final season than I had in the prior eighteen combined. The games continued to be fun, but eating alone and clicking the remote in my hotel room felt like a waste and exaggerated what I was missing out on at home—namely the kids and their growing activities. Throughout my career I had dined almost exclusively with teammates with rare exceptions for close friends and relatives. Now my list of dinner partners was shrinking. I chomped on many of my meals alone.

• • •

Karl and I remained close but seldom ate together in later years. Like it or not, my seasons were becoming increasingly solitary. I think my career was older than two of my teammates. In most ways I related better with Coach Sloan and Phil Johnson than I ever could with a teammate half my age. The three of us had worked together for eighteen years. We had shared some incredible times in and out of the trenches. After so many years, it made sense that I would have a deeper and more developed relationship with the coaches and the Jazz ownership than with our new arrivals.

Some of the older veterans who hadn't been around our squad didn't understand the importance of these longtime friendships. They seemed to take offense to any player's connection with the "brass," regardless of their history. The grumbling created an undercurrent I hadn't experienced at any other time of my career.

Behind the scenes, trivial issues I would have never considered for a moment took center stage. Parking spots for friends, seating arrangements, and hospitality-room food became bones of contention. On the court, some new players took issue to weight training before practice and twenty-minute stationary bike rides after games for those who hadn't played at least twenty minutes. The "Tour de France" was intended to keep every man on the roster in great shape. Most of all, some seemed to have a problem with Coach's insistence that Karl and I sit out most of the live practices. Jerry was convinced that this was best for the team. Younger players needed the work, and we needed to avoid excessive pounding. I wanted to practice and told Coach so, but he was the boss, and I trusted his judgment. He knew we would be ready for the games.

Karl confirmed Jerry's wisdom towards the end of a light practice. A spontaneous 1-on-1 tournament from the block cropped up. The younger participants taunted The Mailman with a flurry of verbal attacks. "Come on, old man. Get some of this," they chirped. "You can't hang, old man . . ." The Mailman eventually had heard enough. He pulled himself out of his seat, grunting like a grandpa struggling out of his rocker. Slowly he strode with his best twenty-point limp to take on the young bulls. I watched his eyes light up as the ball was put into play. The youngsters, as well as a few lippy vets, were doomed from the start. He mercilessly pounded each and every challenger into submission. A man against boys; it wasn't a fair fight. The popping off was silenced, for a moment, as he returned to his seat with a wink and a smile, but the stubborn undertow of friction between younger and older players remained.

In a sad irony, our years of collaboration that had brought our team to the highest level of the NBA was now holding us suspect. This is a hard time to look back on and examine because it involves circumstances and conditions that I would rather forget. Harry Truman, recognizing the responsibility of leaders once declared, "The buck stops here." I can see that in this case that resting place should have been with me. I was unable or unwilling at the time to confront or even notice the problem and seek a solution. This wouldn't have happened in prior years. I think I would have noticed and acted to bring these relatively trivial issues into the sunshine where they would have evaporated quickly. Instead, I chose to abstain. I settled on doing crossword puzzles on the plane and eating alone in my room.

Eventually, midway through that last season, I did approach Karl in his room after a game in Philadelphia. Even if I wasn't going to do anything about it, I wanted to know whether or not I was imagining the festering issue. With Karl's insight the picture cleared for both of us. Still, I remained reluctant to engage.

Every year I had seen rifts and fights among players, sometimes even with coaches. Usually issues were resolved with a face-to-face meeting without others present. Man to man, with no turf to defend in front of spectators or other interested parties, all the issues dissolved pretty easily. I suppose I didn't really want to deal with the school-yard nonsense anymore. Was this a function of my age, my mind-set, or both? Whatever the case, my unwillingness to accept responsibility and confront the problems were clear signs that I was inching closer toward retirement.

• • •

Besides departed friends, changing cultures, and dodged responsibilities, fear, strangely enough, crept into my ongoing reflections on retirement. I worried about things that had never before entered my mind. My health, for example, became an ongoing concern. Dr. Buhler had kept me balanced and healthy, but I began to wonder more frequently, *What type of wear and tear could I continue to inflict on my body without long-term consequences?* One serious injury might shelve my hopes and dreams of being able to participate in activities and sports with my children as they grew older.

Just as with Ebenezer Scrooge, the Ghost of Christmas Present offered me a little insight on just how quickly those plans can change for the worse. His warning came versus the Lakers at home when Kobe Bryant drove to the hoop late in the game. I swiped at the ball but somehow my right index finger became scissored between his knees as he accelerated towards the basket. My finger dislocated and popped back, leaving an open flesh smile from one side of the joint to the other. I could see the exposed flexor tendons when our trainer, Gary Briggs, bent it back for observation. They stitched it up and bandaged it so I could play the next night in Seattle, but the knuckle remains permanently damaged. Thankfully, it was only a finger, not a knee or hip. But these are the very things I had begun to worry about.

Strangely, as I aged I also had a fair amount of concern over the possibility of hurting someone else in a freak accident. An injury that occurred in a typically intense battle versus the Sonics makes my point. Gary Payton was hounding me as usual on the wing as I dribbled, trying to initiate offense. In a surprise attack, he suddenly lunged at the ball. Instinctively, I flinched to protect it with my forearm while keeping my dribble alive. My elbow struck him directly on the Adam's apple. He immediately dropped to his knees, momentarily without breath, making horrible gurgling sounds. I was genuinely worried. Gary was a tough guy not prone to crumbling. Luckily, he ended up fine. He understood that it was completely unintentional—just a part of the game. It was becoming more than that for me, however. I found myself wondering if that could have happened when I was a younger player. I would have hated to hurt his or anyone's career by causing a serious injury because of aging reflexes. In truth, my reflexes were just fine, but the fact that I thought about these things *at all* was revealing.

Time had also brought on a greater concern for maintaining my performance level and general reputation. What people thought of me as a player and a person had become extremely important to me. I wanted to pass on a good name and a legacy my children could be proud of. Under the microscope of the public eye, that can be difficult. One questionable outburst in the media or one unfortunate play between the lines of the court could sully a reputation built over years. My heart goes out every time I see a replay of Bill Buckner's error at first base that allowed the New York Mets to win the pennant. I had followed Bill's stellar career since he played for our own Spokane Indians in the minor leagues. He was an outstanding player, yet that one uncharacteristic error is how many people remember him. I still have so much respect for him, but I didn't want to suffer his fate.

Many people had had a stake in my success. Reflecting poorly on any of them was unacceptable. Mostly I didn't want to disappoint Jerry Sloan. He would be in a tough spot when the time came to release me, although he probably would have denied it. He made decisions in the best interests of the team with just one final motivation—winning. His motives remained pure and beyond reproach for that reason. In the end, I knew it would be tough for him to give me my walking papers, though he certainly would if put into a corner. I had no intention of putting him in that position.

• • •

Nada and the children had lived, slept, and eaten around my schedule for my entire career. Nothing could ever match the opportunity we had been given to be a part of the Jazz organization and the NBA life. Still, nothing lasts forever, and I was beginning to sense that the time for moving forward was rapidly approaching. Selfishly, I was growing tired of missing so many family events and activities. I knew I wasn't the Lone Ranger in frequently skipping important milestones in my kids' lives. I suspected every working parent was absent from interesting and valuable chapters in their children's scrapbooks. The tradeoffs for these absences were well worth it. Nada and the kids loved our version of the NBA lifestyle as much as I did. Yet I knew I was becoming less willing to miss one of my kid's great slides into second base or sustained onstage high notes.

Several years before my retirement, at the very dawn of any

thoughts along those lines, a respected opponent offered me a little wisdom. Isiah Thomas, who was coaching Indiana at the time, chased me down in the Jazz parking lot after one of our games. Unprompted, he told me, "Don't let anyone run you out," finishing with this bit of encouragement, "You are playing great. Play as long as you still love it." His comments were helpful and particularly meaningful because of the recurring positive role he had played in my life. Isiah had given me a boost in high school at the National AAU Championships by setting the performance bar higher. He defused the Olympic controversy by calling Dad to make certain we understood his real sentiments. Now he had given an old opponent a shot in the arm. Isiah didn't *have* to make these gestures, but I have always appreciated the fact that he did.

More time passed, and at age forty-one I was ancient for an NBA player, especially a 6'1" version, but young for a retiree in the real world. What would I do once I cut the cord? One of the NBA speakers who visited our team yearly to help us prepare for the future outside of basketball offered this analogy. He held a pencil in his hand and pointed to the very sharp lead end and told us, "Right now you are the tip of this pencil. The moment you retire, you become the bottom." He advised us to plan and prepare for the inevitable. In our case, it wasn't easy to anticipate all the contingencies for a family of eight.

• • •

All of these retirement considerations were tucked neatly away out of mind as the team prepared for what turned out to be my final playoff series. In 2003, we were again pitted against the Sacramento Kings. Ironically, I played my first NBA preseason game against the Kansas City Kings. This Sacramento version was

John drives against the Sacramento Kings' Bobby Jackson
in game two of the playoffs.

young, talented, and on the rise. They had earned the number two seed in the Western Conference that year. We had lost one of our key youngsters, Shandon Anderson, to free agency. Add to this the gradual departures of Antoine, Jeff, Howard Eisley, and Adam Keefe; we clearly weren't the same team that had battled the Bulls in 1998.

We entered the series as a seventh seeded underdog. Our matchup ended without fanfare or surprise. The favored Kings dispatched us in five games. It was the first year the NBA implemented the seven-game, first-round format. We might have had a chance in a five-game series, but as it was, we made a quick and quiet exit.

As the clock was winding down on game five and the series, I sensed that it might be my last time on the floor. Unexpectedly, I received a warm applause from the normally rabid Sacramento fans. The gesture was much appreciated. After the postgame interviews, I received another surprise. I was presented the game ball signed by the entire Kings team. It was an unexpected and classy gesture that I accepted as a great honor. It seemed they knew something that I didn't—something that I wouldn't know for at least the next fourteen hours.

That was the beginning of the events that would lead to my retirement. Because it was such a hard decision—to give up the life I had known—and because I wasn't exactly sure how to go about making the announcement, I got a little ahead of myself and ended up making some mistakes and hurting the feelings of those who cared about me most.

I sat next to Karl on the flight home. We hadn't done that in a long time. It was like the old days. We talked, mostly philosophically, about retirement. It was a "What would we do if . . ." kind of conversation. Without noticing, I think I was starting to let go of the game for the first time. I tried to make Karl aware of my thoughts and feelings. I was beginning to test the idea of hanging up my sneakers with those closest to me. Laying my cards on the table with my oldest and closest teammate was an important responsibility. Unfortunately, it was one that I apparently didn't meet very well. I was probably counting on the notion that Karl could actually read my mind like many people thought. I didn't or couldn't speak the words as directly as he deserved. This was a recurring theme in the hectic hours preceding my announcement.

When our plane landed, absent any parades or celebrations, I tipped the valet like everyone else and then drove home alone. Part of me must have known my path was set; still, I hadn't been able to plainly say so. I talked with Nada and with the kids before they left for school the next morning, but I spoke in generalities, only saying, "You know, I might not play basketball anymore." I knew I had to speak with Mom and Dad, Larry Miller, and Jerry Sloan before I could be sure of anything. Perhaps I was beating around the bush to avoid saying anything I couldn't retract. The fact is, I didn't want to come to a decision until all the ballots were cast and I actually had a plan.

I believed I had sufficiently conveyed to my family my intention of retiring that day. As with Karl, I was again asking for a pretty perceptive leap from the troops. Not until I spoke with Mom and Dad over the phone that morning did I use the words, "I'm thinking about retiring." This time the message was received and understood. Dad's response was simple; he said something to the effect that he didn't disagree and that it was time. Mom was on board as well.

Next, I called Larry Miller and asked if we could get together before the customary year-end meeting at the Delta Center. He welcomed me into his office about thirty minutes later. I told him I had somewhat come to the decision to retire, but I wanted to hear his thoughts first. We talked a long time and covered a lot of territory. In the end, even Larry couldn't find anything I had missed. I wasn't able to actually tender my resignation, but we both knew I wouldn't be coming back.

The final hurdle was meeting with Coach Sloan. As the senior player on the team, I was first to see him and our GM, Kevin

O'Connor, for our year-end debriefing. I trusted Kevin completely, so I spoke freely in his presence. "Coach," I sputtered, "I think I'm done." Kevin immediately excused himself and left the room. The ensuing meeting was short and to the point. Jerry offered his hopes that I would consider sticking around in a variety of capacities, including playing the next season. His comments were personal and heartfelt. I had never questioned his friendship, loyalty, or support. We shared a special relationship that was evident in our discussion. After considering all options and suggestions that Coach made, I remained confident with my decision. Jerry, as I thought he would, fully supported me.

Up until then, everything was private—with the exception of Karl, no media or teammates had been consulted. Since cell phone reception was poor in the bottom of the Delta Center, I snuck back into the equipment room to use T. C.'s landline to telephone Nada. I wanted to confirm with her that I was taking the final step. As luck would have it, she couldn't be reached despite numerous attempts. I felt I needed to finish what I had started—quickly and without ceremony.

• • •

They say that a person gets tunnel vision when under stress. In my case it felt as though I was on a luge course at one hundred miles per hour. From the equipment room, I quickly walked to the locker room to pack up my gear, just like any other year. As I came out, I addressed a small group of media gathered for some final team interviews. To the extent that I could speak, I responded to a simple question about next year's team by blurting out, "I think I'm finished." Even after all of that, I still said, "I *think*!" The follow-up question elicited a tearful response that stuck in my throat. I thanked the reporters, ducked my head, and began the long walk out of the building. Of the other players, only Greg Ostertag was close enough to witness the scene. He followed me out the door and walked beside me down the long hallway of the Delta Center. Greg was a good guy who had grown up in front of me. He helped me a lot in that tough time.

A sense of sad relief came over me as I found safe haven in my car. I had made it through the tough part—or so I thought. I called Nada hoping she would raise my spirits. This time she picked up on the first ring.

"Well, I did it," I said.

"You did what?" she quickly shot back.

"I retired."

Shocked, angry, and upset, my wife let me have it pretty good. I won't share the details except to say that she had no idea I was planning to retire that day nor did the kids. I knew I had talked with them. She also overheard the conversations with Mom and Dad and was aware I had met with Larry—so how could she not know? If she was truly in the dark after all that, then the kids obviously were also.

Smack in the middle of all of the turmoil, my cell phone "clicked in." It was Karl. I never did get to him before my dash out of the Delta Center. He was shocked as well, and his nose was bent a little out of shape. He just asked, "What . . . how . . . why?" without completing the sentences. Karl wasn't mad, but I could hear in his voice that he was a little wounded that he found out from someone else. Explanation eluded me, and I told him so. I added feebly that I thought I told him the night before on the plane and pointed out that Nada was on the other line feeling the same way. I knew I had made a mistake—it was the theme of the day.

Right or wrong, the die had been cast. I needed to reach the kids before they heard the news from someone else. The odds of that happening weren't good with everyone spread out at baseball games, golf courses, and volleyball tournaments. I had put the kids and myself in a tough spot. The whole process was poor seamanship. Such a momentous change in their lives, and they had to hear it in public and on the fly. True to form they handled my blunder with a maturity that made me proud. Michael still gives me the business about how he was "shafted" and scarred for life as a not-too-subtle reminder to do better next time.

• • •

For the remainder of that day, the silent thoughts that had been developing for years finally percolated to the surface and escaped. The small snowball that had started rolling a few years before finally came to rest. My NBA career with the Utah Jazz was over.

Despite the messiness, I maintain that my announcement had to happen the way it did. I couldn't have taken a personal send-off with kind words and gifts. I didn't look at it as a celebration. To me it was a painful, ugly ordeal that I had to endure alone. Making it larger would only have made it more painful. I barely managed my emotions as it was. Including my wife and kids, or anyone else dear to me for that matter, in a public forum would have been impossible for me. I have told Nada since that I am not sure I could have done differently if I had wanted to. Everything came to an unexpected quick boil that day. The momentum had increased in intensity with every step I took until I blurted out my decision with the mistaken notion that I had already covered all of my bases.

The next three days were a mix of relief and sadness. I felt miserable. The hard realization that something I had loved so much was over made for some dark days. Eventually the sun did rise again and a pretty heavy burden was lifted. As cooler heads prevailed, Nada admitted that she noticed a relaxed difference the moment I first walked into the house. It took all of three days for me to feel relief. But it felt good when it came. As I had hoped, I was able to rip the jersey off of my own back but remained grateful to everyone who participated in the process that guided my decision. Though I have some regrets about the disjointed way I made my announcement, I have never looked back or regretted my choice—I had played long enough and managed to depart before the clock struck twelve.

• • •

"Not so-o fast," as Jerry liked to tell us. I wasn't out of the woods yet. When the sun finally peeped through the clouds, Larry called with a proposal to fill the Delta Center for a final celebration with the fans—free of admission.

Within a week or two Larry had put together an amazing gala. Fans, teammates, associates, and friends from every walk of life came to say good-bye. Before the packed house, Hot Rod Hundley emceed one of the most memorable evenings of my life. Dad said a few words, followed by Karl, Jerry, Larry, and a host of others from the community. They even renamed a street in front of the arena after me.

The most striking memory of all, however, was listening to Nada's speech. She had worked long and hard on the preparation. Nada had never spoken in front of crowds of any size, let alone in front of 25,000 Jazz fans. My wife was amazing as she knocked the socks off everyone with her gracious remarks and heartfelt expressions of gratitude. I was very proud of her. As I listened to her poignant expressions of thanks to the many dear people who had assisted us on our wonderful journey, I knew I couldn't possibly match her perfectly delivered remarks. But listening to her also left me totally relaxed. Since she had already said all the important things, I was free to simply say good-bye and thank-you from the bottom of my heart. I was also able to publicly express my appreciation to Houston, Michael, David, Lindsay, Laura, and Samuel for being such good kids. The evening was a present from Larry, an opportunity to say "happy trails" to every-one who had so loyally supported the short-shorted choir boy shown that night on the Jumbotron. It was an evening that I will never forget.

PART IV

Free Time to Water Green Shoots

Just Around the Corner

It was life around the corner, nothing quite too far
To blessings beyond my dreams, where I caught a lucky star.
There, down the block a ways, Dad worked long and hard,
Tended bar and friends for years, a stone's throw from the yard.
Just a "down and out" away was the park across the street;
A playground made in heaven where the fellas could all compete.
Started school down the road; we walked most every day,
Dad had done the same to start to find his way.
I grew and moved along to prep for things in store;
Traveled full around the block to seek manhood, life, and more.
Then college, again in place, actually across the street.
I didn't need to travel in search of challenges to meet.
Still, saddled to the star, I must have traveled north;
Found an Alaskan sweetheart but never sallied forth.
Then we moved along to pursue life's dreams and things
In store for quite a ride, not privy to what it brings.
The star had room for eight, as the years unfolded by
Missed the park across the street, still enjoyed the Utah sky.
Then the sunset on the court, radiant in the twilight
In retrospect sublime, my time to catch a flight.
We loaded up the star, undirected in the dark
It landed square at home, kids competing in the park.
Five are off to school; it's only down the way.
Their dad had done the same; I guess we're going to stay.

—Kerry L. Pickett

CHAPTER 18

The Great Cinnamon Caper

Reporting for Duty

People frequently ask what I do with my free time now that I'm retired. I have to think for a moment because it doesn't seem as though I *have* much free time. My standard response is that I don't know precisely, but I feel busy and productive, and I go to bed each night tired. Ten years have passed in what seems like a bit of a blur since my retirement and the family's return to Spokane. They say time flies when you are having fun; if so, I must be enjoying myself.

In fact, I can't believe it's already Thursday again. It's time for me to drop by Dad's house on Superior Street, like most Thursdays, after I deposit Sam at St. Al's. These *Tuesdays with Morrie* sessions have become a nice ritual even if they are on Thursday. Actually, Mom and I initiated the tradition shortly after my retirement, while Dad was still wearing out the tiles behind the bar. Mom passed away a few years later,[1] and Dad and I have kept up the meetings. Usually it's just the two of us, unless Steve pokes his head in and blocks my car in the driveway just to be ornery! For over four years now, schedules permitting, I have migrated from Dad's to a weekly meeting with Coach Pickett for this book. Beyond these rituals, I have plenty of things to keep me busy in the absence of a *real* job.

I have appointed myself head groundskeeper for nearly an acre of lawn, which includes several gardens, seemingly unlimited trees and hedges, and a respectable Whiffle-ball field that all combine to make up the yard at our new house. My desire to maintain residency in the old neighborhood was overruled by Nada, who held me to my promise of finding more space for our large family. I gave in, but had to be dragged kicking and screaming into a new neighborhood.

I probably take my lawn job a little too seriously. I feel obligated to consult experts then try to meticulously emulate their techniques. The truth is, that's too much information in the hands of an amateur. It's all I can do to complete my weekly chores before the Clean Green truck picks up the tangled, thorny, and leafy evidence of my efforts on Friday mornings. Moonlight mowing by headlights has been required from time to time to meet my deadline!

Winter offers only a slight reprieve from yard duty. Record snowfalls have had me mumbling to myself and Nada. I told her in a snow-induced fit, "I am going to move the whole family to Palm Springs." Then I remembered all of the raking I did and added, " . . . and have every tree in our yard cut down while we are gone." My threats were a ridiculous bluff that nobody took seriously. I'm too much of a "tree hugger," as The Mailman would call me.

In fact, I am hoping to spend a lot more time helping to protect the larger environment. I admire what our friends from the Wasatch Mountains, Doug and Lynne Seus, have been able to accomplish with the help of Bart the Bear. I try to focus on many ecological causes, but our water supply is at the top of my list.

Future wars may be fought over H_2O, replacing oil as the prize of victory. I don't think we should add things to our water by accident with pollution, or on purpose with toxic chemicals such as fluoride. "Leave 'er lie where Jesus flung 'er," my Dad used to say. In other words, keep it natural. I'm convinced no effort or expense should be spared to preserve and protect our *most* valuable resource.

I have many interests, pursuits, and responsibilities in retirement. Some of these I only dabble in while others I pursue with greater passion. At fifty, I maintain my annoying youthful curiosity and still hover over the shoulders of repairmen, *helping* whenever I can. That curiosity keeps my ears and eyes open to opportunities and projects that offer their own rewards.

• • •

As I have mentioned, I am busy. I'm involved in several businesses that require my attention and test my college education, but which don't take up a lot of time on a day-to-day basis. I am not an expert at anything, except for, arguably, some elements of basketball, so I go into almost every new venture as a rookie. It is important that I am the only rookie, so I try to surround myself with real experts. I make a point of choosing projects that are fun and offer more intrinsic value than what shows up on a pro forma statement. Sometimes these ventures make money, sometimes not; but they all make sense to me.

I also have more than a passing personal interest in the study of biomechanics and the body's capacity to heal itself, particularly in the athletic realm. Having experienced such great personal results in my own career, I find myself often consulting, advising, and working with young athletes to help them make good choices regarding their health. I have shared this mission with

Steve Delong for a long time. My initial excitement was sparked, ignited, and then sustained by Dr. Craig Buhler of the Jazz, and later Greg Roskopf, as I experienced and witnessed the extreme benefits of their treatments and philosophies. Steve and I pursue this shared interest through many avenues and reconnect with these mentors whenever we can.

Finally, as you might expect, most of my days are peppered with activities related to basketball and sports in general. My love for this type of work probably helped inspire a project I undertook a couple of years before retirement. As I secretly hoped it would, the completed project has fit my retirement dreams perfectly.

Long before I retired, I purchased a mostly abandoned warehouse in the old neighborhood directly across from Gonzaga's campus. I had passed the building most days in the summertime on the way to the gym without ever taking special notice. Then, an old friend and classmate, Greg Byrd, formally introduced me to the structure. He saw the property as a potentially profitable investment to be bought and sold in short order. Some time later, with the vacant mess grudgingly still in my possession, I bumped into a guy in Salt Lake who changed the way I looked at youth sports and my empty hull of a building.

Scott Cate, a successful entrepreneur in the telephone industry, took me under his wing to illustrate how to help young athletes more nearly reach their potential. He showed me a baseball batting facility he had built for a local public high school. I watched as the players practiced and learned about the kids' willingness to work when tools were provided. I was hooked when I saw how they came to practice voluntarily and worked tirelessly on their skills. They were serious about their efforts and were rewarded with marked improvement. Most of them earned the

John teaching at Basketball Cornerstones Camp, 2001.

opportunity to play high-school baseball, and many continued swinging and throwing in college. I liked how Scott had the kids earn their own stripes.

My experience in those batting cages spawned another look at my old warehouse in Spokane. There was a small section of the building slightly separated that appeared to be suitable for a setup similar to Scott's. He thought the space would make an unbelievable baseball practice facility. His excitement proved contagious and a project was born. I began to see something much different and more important in store for my hulking albatross than a quick sale. I wondered if it might not be the perfect home for an orphaned basketball floor and some players to be named later.

The wooden expanse came with a unique history. Years earlier, the court from the old Salt Palace had come into my possession. Although it was still collecting dust in a storage room in Utah, I was beginning to envision kids in Spokane running up and down the old maple surface that the Jazz had called home.

When Larry Miller built the Delta Center, his custom-made floor proved to be the only flaw in an otherwise masterpiece building achievement. The floor quickly warped and lifted in the corners, actually causing one of our Jazz games to be rescheduled. The manufacturer immediately sent out a new court whose karma was no better than the first. The truck transporting the replacement floor crashed, rendering the relief hardwood useless. Fresh out of alternatives, Larry ordered the Salt Palace surface to be assembled and installed at the Delta Center until another court could be assembled.

Sometime later I happened by the Delta Center as a work crew was finally making the switch to the brand-new floor that fit the name on the building. Without a plan of any kind, I called Larry to ask what he was going to do with the old court. He had planned to trade it back to the company for a discount on the new one. I offered to pay the difference if I could keep it. He agreed and consented to tuck it safely away for me.

With these pieces of a vision twirling in my head, I asked Coach Pickett and Gini to sift through the possibilities and potentially ramrod a project. I think they were as excited as I was. The undertaking proved more ambitious than any of us expected, and we soon realized some expert assistance was needed.

We settled on Garco Construction, a Spokane general contracting company. The firm is owned in partnership by Tim Welsh, who grew up in St. Al's Parish. His construction team had built several buildings and schools in Spokane as well as the city's sports centerpiece, Spokane Veterans Memorial Arena, a 12,000-seat, multi-use. I knew Tim would take great pains to help us turn the empty building into a facility the town and the neighborhood would be proud to have.

The project turned out to be a greater adventure than any

of us had imagined. The ceiling in the old building was too low for competitive play, so we found a roof-raising specialist to lift the entire domed structure eight feet. This was accomplished by using a centrally controlled computer operating scores of hydraulic jacks in perfect sequence. We took special pains to retain the building's existing wooden bow trusses. We steam cleaned them, attended to their structural integrity, and, presto, we were "lacing 'em up" in a gym straight out of the movie *Hoosiers*. The place is genuinely nostalgic despite the modern upgrade. We don't allow advertisements of any kind, in part, to maintain the look and feel of the gyms but also to preserve the building as a place of pure athletics, free of marketing bombardment.

I decided to go out on a limb in naming our new venture. After reviewing many suggestions, I settled on "The Warehouse" for its direct simplicity. If we accomplished what we hoped, no other title would be necessary. In the end, I think we have succeeded. The Warehouse has become a household name around Spokane's athletic community. It's a treat to play and coach on the Salt Palace floor under the bow trusses only blocks from home, Jack and Dan's, and Gonzaga.

The facility gets used by kids and adults alike from the city of Spokane and beyond. The YMCA runs youth leagues and practices for players as young as five years old. The city's AAU, which is run by the Hoopfest Association, fills the place every Saturday, but you don't have to be a "hooper" to get in the door. The building also has six volleyball courts, and indoor soccer leagues fill the whole space many Sundays. Generally there is also a crew hitting or throwing after school in the indoor baseball facility that initiated the project. The city's adults get their blood pumping by engaging in kickboxing, belly dancing, spiking volleyballs, swinging bats, and shooting hoops. The local boys in blue have a noon basketball league, so the place stays pretty safe. We try to remain open to new ways the building can help the community. At various times the structure has been the setting for weddings, dances, and even funeral receptions.

In the summer the courts get no rest. The Gonzaga University men's and women's basketball programs have camps and tournaments throughout the break. Our own tournament director, Jared Tikker, wedges a pretty competitive summer league of about a hundred teams in between camps and vacation activities. The facility also hosts hundreds of squads from the Greater Northwest and Canada in various tournaments throughout the year.

The office section of the building houses Coach Pickett's Warehouse staff and the Spokane Youth Sports Association. The whole operation is a little more complex and detailed than meets the eye but runs smoothly under Gini Pickett's guidance. I'm proud of the fact that the facility has earned a spot in the community, having celebrated our tenth anniversary in 2012.

I spend many hours at The Warehouse, coaching, spectating, and even trying to run up and down the old Jazz court on Sundays. Resurrecting the Sunday League has proved to be an indispensable highlight of my life. I have enjoyed the thrill of playing the game I love with my three oldest boys and my brother's three sons on a regular basis. For a couple of hours, we put away our parent/son/nephew roles and just play basketball. Nobody coaches, teaches, or advises, and there are no spectators. The lessons are self-taught in battle, and I have treasured every minute. I handpick the participants in the Sunday League; in this instance, it is not an open gym. As a result, we have a nice mix of older players with terrific résumés from college and professional ranks as well as young players trying to learn the ropes. The blend is healthy and constructive for all of us. I want to try to stay in shape and maintain enough sharpness and skill to continue playing with Sam when he is old enough to join us in a year or two. Unexpectedly, The Warehouse has become something of a gathering place similar to yesterday's country store. Familiar faces pass through and say hello as they hurriedly slide by other spectators to get to their own court. I see many old friends in a week and enjoy the homespun feel that has developed under the Hoosierlike trusses. Even Coach Linebarger came out of retirement, without his hack paddle, to coach my son David through a successful AAU career. He was the first of many to suffer me as an assistant.

The next was Coach John Lugviel, who "hired" me to help with his girls' Red Robin team when no one else wanted the job. His Red Robin team, which included my oldest daughter, Lindsay, soon established a reputation for excellence. My younger daughter, Laura, continued the tradition. We won the championship four out of six years with three undefeated seasons. The fact that we didn't pass any "eyeball tests" made our run that much more satisfying. I doubt I will ever enjoy a coaching experience more special than the time I spent with these tough and disciplined young ladies. I'm lucky that both of our daughters were part of the program. Lindsay moved on to play five years for the Spokane Sandpipers, Coach Pickett's traveling club basketball team. Laura followed suit and is still playing for the Pipers. For over ten years, Coach's staff has consisted of two old friends—Mark Bowman and John Blake. He insists that the girls refer to them as "Coach" in place of a couple of his own pet monikers—"Iron," and "Shakey." Iron is the same fellow who retrieved me from my hotel room at the AAU National High School Championships following a discouraging lesson at the hands of Isiah Thomas and his Chi-town teammates. Shakey was one of the original park quarterbacks—the kid fresh out of Vietnam.

I want my children to be around men such as these. They demand personal responsibility from the girls. Playing time is earned, not given. The "Pipers" must be on time and ready to go. They are required to call Coach Pickett *themselves* with any problems or conflicts. People willing to take the yoke of responsibility to help successfully raise our children are uncommon. I'm thankful that these coaches insist on things I deem important but don't or can't always enforce.

I'm convinced that my daughters, along with these young women, will be better prepared for life as a result of falling under this kind of leadership. The athletic experience is much shallower when it is set up only to artificially prop up self-esteem. Competitive sports are supposed to be hard, and at times painful, as well as joyous, fun, challenging, and educational—just like life. Good teachers like Pickett, Shakey, and Iron understand that you can balance discipline with caring.

I try to follow the Sandpipers' philosophy in my only head-coaching capacity. I took the plunge as a "skipper" for the first time three years ago for the Griffins, the third-grade team my youngest son, Samuel, played on.[2] We borrowed the name from Westminster College in Salt Lake City where our second son, Michael, played. Oddly, it was also the practice site for the Jazz in my early years with the team. The kids liked their unique name because the fearsome mythical beast guards treasure! As we begin our 2012 season as sixth graders, I remind myself how crucial it is that I don't spoil our father/son relationship because of our coach/player roles. It is really easy to overcoach your own children because you see, in magnified form, every misstep they take. I tell all my children that it is far more important to me what kind of person they are than what type of player they are, and I mean it.

The same holds true for all the boys and girls that I coach, related to me or not.

Reminiscences

Since our return to Spokane, we have had our normal ups and downs, but the family has been mostly healthy and happy. The Lilac City has been a good place to call home, though we still think of Salt Lake as a second home. Nearly twenty years, and counting, of memories there will warm us long into the future.

As the fall of 2012 approaches, the kids are nearly grown, except for Samuel. Houston and Michael have both graduated from college. Houston played five years for the University of Montana Grizzlies football team and is pursuing his inventive interests in the computer world with his old buddy from Salt Lake, Luke Hristou. Michael finished his basketball career at Westminster with some pretty impressive credentials and is starting his second season of professional basketball in Karlsruhe, Germany. David will be a red-shirt junior for the Bulldogs and is enjoying the team's hard-earned success, as well as his own. He earned a full-ride scholarship from Gonzaga University following his first full season. All three boys had to take the hard road. They all walked on and had to "grind it out" in order to play.

Lindsay's off to play basketball for the Montana State Bobcats in Bozeman on a basketball scholarship. The "Cat/Griz" game, already a heated in-state rivalry, will have even greater meaning in our house. Laura hopes to help Gonzaga Prep to new heights in soccer and basketball as she begins her sophomore year. The girls played together last season for Gonzaga Prep, where I am an assistant coach. We went on to finish fifth at state, the highest in school history. Having both girls playing together as significant contributors on the team was special for them and for me.

*Stockton family Christmas card. Left to right: Houston,
Michael, Lindsay, Samuel, Laura, and David.*

Samuel is growing up fast. He has been dragged from birth to
endless sporting events of all kinds at all levels. Remarkably, he's
turning out to be a very happy kid who participates in everything
from choir to sports. He is almost always smiling and in constant
motion. Sam was a little tardy for most of our NBA life, but has
been brought up to speed through hanging around his brothers
and sisters. At age eleven, he holds his own in a household full of
older siblings.

• • •

Time has flown so quickly that as I look back on the kids'
childhoods, it seems only yesterday that they were continually
involved in some mischief that exceeded what we thought of
as their limits. Lindsay takes the cake, almost literally, in that
department. When Lindsay was only about a year and a half
old, Nada and I thought she was tucked safely in her crib one

morning when we were awakened by the sound of cupboards opening and closing downstairs in the kitchen. Expecting to find the boys foraging for breakfast, we were surprised by an equally shocked Lindsay, barely clad in a half-attached diaper, standing on top of the counter. Our first thought, *How did she get up there?* was quickly trumped when we saw what she had accomplished. After scaling the drawers, she had scraped all the frosting off a full batch of homemade cinnamon rolls Nada had baked the night before. Next she climbed another cupboard to retrieve a cinnamon shaker and cleverly sprinkled its contents over the vandalized rolls before carefully replacing the plastic wrap. She had covered her tracks with the skill of a career burglar and almost got away with the heist. Fortunately, Lindsay has since channeled her energy into more constructive activities such as school and sports.

In stark contrast, Laura displayed almost no early signs of mischief, or she never got caught. She seemed content following Lindsay around—adoringly. It wasn't until her first try at soccer that she finally showed her hand. She was a late season fill-in and apparently knew what to do. To everyone's surprise, she scored goals by the handful and was all over the field. After the game I told her, "Nice job. You didn't even get tired!" She countered, "Oh, yes I did. I just wanted to win so bad I kept running!" To hear one of our kids say that made me think I had died and gone to heaven. Laura took her turn at being my favorite that day!

Occasionally, we still get the whole clan up to the lake for adventures and campfire stories. With the kids scattered as they are, it's increasingly hard to get everyone together. When we manage the feat, they are the best of times. We still insist on making quiet, unrushed time each summer as a sanity check, if nothing else. There's no better place to feel at peace than surrounded by nature's beauty.

ASSISTED

The water sport competition has stiffened mightily as the boys have grown older. Just to stay close, I had to adjust my stubborn resistance to change. After twenty years I broke down and switched to a state-of-the-art ski that was given to me by Larry Miller as a retirement gift. Upon presentation, he informed me that the ski would "cut on a dime and give you nine cents change." The switch helped me dramatically, but the boys like it too. I have no technology to lean on when we drive in for Sunday hoops. Even as they blow past me at my own game, I have to smile at their progress and our shared experience on the old Jazz floor.

I enjoy spending time around our children, who aren't kids anymore, and their friends. Their enthusiasm and endless energy make for some interesting, uplifting, and memorable times. Their optimistic outlook is refreshing in a complicated and challenging world. Given what I have observed in my kids and their friends, my take on the future is that we will be in very capable hands.

The past ten years have been good to me and the family. We've had a labor of love traveling far and wide to watch all of the kids in their various sports. As great as watching the games has been, the real pleasure is in visiting them as adults in their own environments. I'm also enjoying the opportunity to reconnect with some of the heroes of my youth while making new friends and maintaining old ones. I get to be around my children and enjoy the roller-coaster ride that comes with parenting. Basketball provides me the opportunity to be an active participant in their daily lives. The glare of the spotlight has dimmed significantly, and I think that has been healthy for everyone.

The Seeds between the Lines

We happened upon this place without intention or design.
Along a crowded avenue in a building unadorned,
Tucked beside the walls, lay a vacant maple tract.
Unpossessed of Sooners, we chanced to try the piece.
We claimed at first but the squatter's right-of-way and began to blade
    the hardened ground.
Here, easily, but not with any ease, we stayed and turned the patch.
Now, free and clear, by equity we held.
Our time together grew across the years; we flourished outside the tiny
    plat,
Though our spirits were unconstrained by boundaries beyond the
    horizon in the space between the lines.
We harnessed mysteries along the road and laughed with our shoulders
    upon the wheel;
Took pause amid reflections of a leather drawn plow;
Then freely chose the yoke to furrow the uncommon ground.
Unfettered we came upon ourselves yet knew the others' rows.
We reaped abundantly of what we sowed and were gifted even still.
This season next the plot will fallow lie for another's spring to come,
But the yields from the varnished earth redound to tillings hence
To hoe straight tomorrow's rows of the seeds between the lines.

—Kerry L. Pickett

EPILOGUE

My daughter Lindsay spotted me writing a while back and asked, "Why are you doing a book?" As I began to answer, thoughts that I hadn't completely unearthed prior to that moment spilled out. I began by letting her know why I *wasn't* doing the project. From the outset I didn't want the book to be a sales-driven tell-all. Respecting the most personal parts of my own life and the relationships closest to my heart—those of my family—was a line I had drawn from the beginning. The privacy of others had to be respected. This book is, after all, to recognize and thank the people who have had a significant impact on my life. I also wanted to fill in some blanks on the important decisions I had made along my unusual road. Writing provided a medium where I could sift through, recollect, examine, carefully connect, and sort out the events and decisions that had forged the path that became my life. I continued by telling her that I wanted to pass on some history to my children with messages and lessons I had learned along the way. Conversations, no matter how focused, couldn't fully paint the picture I was after. So, I began writing the book.

EPILOGUE

As I spoke, other motivations surfaced, some for the first time. Writing down my memories and describing my current daily routines made me realize I wasn't completely satisfied with where things were headed in my life. Though I loved going to games, working in my yard, and pursuing whatever other projects I might be involved in, I discovered that these things alone weren't overly challenging. These activities kept me squarely in my comfort zone. I needed a push toward something that would stretch me a little.

I thought out loud, to myself as much as Lindsay, about how the spotlight had found me despite my prolonged resistance and how notoriety had ridden piggyback on my desire to be a good basketball player. Maybe there was a message there that I was missing. Perhaps it was time to become more comfortable with the remnants of the celebrity status I had sought so hard to avoid. Like it or not, I found myself with a voice that rang slightly louder than most—an odd quirk of fame. Maybe I should be speaking up now and again in hopes of having some positive impact in one or another arena.

I knew that writing the book wouldn't complete my private pursuit of meeting greater challenges and speaking out on issues and causes that I think are important—it is only a modest beginning. So the project was more than just a time-filler. Describing my life turned out to be challenging, fun, fulfilling, and more than a little educational. My walk down memory lane uncovered a great range of emotions. I hope that the words I have chosen reach people in a positive way.

• • •

I always felt that if I ever wrote a book it would be called *Balance and Vision*. I became familiar with these terms in a basketball context in my early years with Coach Pickett and have adopted them as a foundation for young players trying to learn the game. I like the message because it applies equally to life. In fact, every lesson I ever learned on the court seemed to find its way into my life. The game is wonderfully self-policing and remarkably just in returning rewards or frustrations.

At my basketball camps our coaches put a ball in the kids' hands and teach that they are much more likely to succeed if they maintain balance and vision. We insist that they remain stable, either in a stance or while in motion. In the same breath, we preach, "Keep your eyes up, and be alert." On the court these youngsters quickly learn the merits of these foundational tools. The greater lessons outside the lines seem to come more gradually for all of us—but come they do. If you don't maintain balance, you're going to fall and it's going to hurt. And if you don't see what's in front of you, you'll crash into obstacles and miss opportunities. I've seen enough to know that silly fouls, missed shots, and lost games pale in comparison to real heartache or injury. The lessons basketball teaches us are definitely less telling and far less consequential than the mistakes we might make on life's road. In the end, my dad's philosophy on life remains key: "It's not how many times you get knocked down, but how many times you get back up that matters." Believing that and by continuing to try, I just might succeed. And if my experiences inspire or encourage you to never give up, then writing this book will have been worth it.

NOTES

PART I
Connections

Kerry L. Pickett, "Connections," in "Reach for the Sky: A Poetic Look at Life Metaphors in Sport and Vice Versa" (unpublished work, 2012).

CHAPTER 1
Thoughts from behind a Podium

1. Henry David Thoreau, in *The Treasure Chest: A Heritage Album Containing 1064 Familiar and Inspirational Quotations, Poems, Sentiments and Prayers from Great Minds of 2500 Years,* ed. Charles L. Wallis (New York: Harper and Row Publishers Inc., 1965), vi.

2. C. Vivian Stringer, *Standing Tall: A Memoir of Tragedy and Triumph* (New York: Crown Publishing Group, 2008).

3. Throughout my career I was uncomfortable with obsessive fans and collectors requesting autographs around every corner. I never felt an obligation to provide wares for someone to sell, and I am wary of stalkers who appear at odd locations who just happen to have my poster tucked up their sleeve. An autograph should and can be a win/win situation. I'm sometimes a little embarrassed by requests; for instance, when children approach with a torn piece of paper from their mom's purse, excited to say hello—but that's how it should be. It's hard not to feel good about those kinds of exchanges.

NOTES

Chapter 2
A Thousand Feet Deep

1. The southeastern part of Washington State and a small slice of the northern Idaho Panhandle make up the two million acre area known as the Palouse. Because this area enjoys long, sunny summers and is semi-arid, small grains, peas, lentils, and wheat thrive. See Mike Hall, Douglas L. Young, and David J. Walker, "Agriculture in the Palouse: A Portrait of Diversity," 2–3; available at http://www.cals.uidaho.edu /edComm/pdf/BUL/BUL0794.pdf.
2. Our family farm has had spectacular success for generations in the Palouse, consistently yielding over a hundred bushels of wheat an acre.
3. Howard Lee Barnes, *A Documentary Scrap Book of Football in Frankford* (Philadelphia: Historical Society of Frankford, 1985), 137–38, 141, 146.
4. See ibid. and John J. Fenton, "Frankford Yellow Jackets: National Football League Champions, 1926"; *Ghosts of the Gridiron* (website); available at http://home.comcast.net/~ghostsofthegridiron /Yellowjackets.htm.

Chapter 3
Family

1. After signing the Declaration of Independence, Stockton was betrayed as his location was revealed to Loyalists. He was dragged out of bed during the night and taken prisoner. First in Perth Amboy, New Jersey, and then in New York City, Stockton suffered immensely in brutal and horrific prison conditions. Here the story begins to vary somewhat. There are accounts that Stockton was released, thanks to the negotiations of George Washington, through a prisoner exchange, or that he was given parole by General Howe based on the fact that he would no longer help the war effort. There is also evidence that he "signed Howe's declaration," which offered "pardons to rebels who would swear allegiance to the king and cease their war efforts." It's possible that this evidence came from an enemy's letter, however, because General Howe wrote to the British Parliament and stated that "at no time had a leading rebel sought pardon." After his release, Stockton eventually swore allegiance to the United States of America. However it actually played out, it is safe to

say that his bravery played a huge role in the American cause. Denise Kiernan and Joseph D'Agnese, *Signing Their Lives Away: The Fame and Misfortune of the Men Who Signed the Declaration of Independence* (Philadelphia, PA: Quirk Books, 2009), 93–96; John C. Glynn, Jr. and Kathryn Glynn, "Richard Stockton," *Descendants of the Signers of the Declaration of Independence* (website); available at http://www .dsdi1776.com/Signers/Richard%20Stockton.html; and Robert G. Ferris and Richard E. Morris, *The Signers of the Declaration of Independence* (Flagstaff, AZ: Interpretive Publications, Inc., 1982), 133–35.

2. Originally named the Tacoma Narrows Bridge, "Galloping Gertie" was the third longest bridge in the world when it was opened on July 1 of 1940. However, it was not until November 7, 1940, that it got its nickname. The bridge had only been finished for four months when a windstorm took the bridge and made it look like a piece of ribbon flapping in the breeze before it collapsed into the Puget Sound. Known as "the most dramatic failure in bridge engineering history," this incident has greatly affected the way engineers construct bridges today and is the reason why we have safer bridges. See Washington State Department of Transportation, "More Than a Bridge"; available at http://www.wsdot .wa.gov/TNBhistory/default.htm.

PART II
A Sentimental Journey

Kerry L. Pickett, "Endeavor," in "Reach for the Sky: A Poetic Look at Life Metaphors in Sport and Vice Versa" (unpublished work, 2012).

CHAPTER 6
The Life and Times of a Bullpup

1. National Park Service, "Antietam"; available at http://www.nps.gov/anti /historyculture/casualties.htm.

CHAPTER 7
A Walk across Hamilton

1. Sadly, Coach Fitzgerald unexpectedly died of a heart attack on January 19, 2010, before this work was completed. See Gonzaga University, "Former Coach, AD Dan Fitzgerald Passes Away"; available at http://

NOTES

www.gozags.com/ViewArticle.dbml?DB_LANG=C&DB_OEM
_ID=26400&ATCLID=205172590&SPID=90846&SPSID=627537;
accessed 23 March 2013.

2. Nada still brags to the kids that she is the only one in the family to letter in two collegiate sports. I suspected at the time that she and her identical sidekick ran cross-country more for the free shoes than the conditioning.

3. H. W. Brands, *Traitor to His Class: The Privileged Life and Radical Presidency of Franklin Delano Roosevelt* (New York: Doubleday, 2008), 823.

4. Malcolm Gladwell suggests 10,000 hours of intense and focused practice as the threshold of greatness. Gladwell quotes neurologist Daniel Levitin in his seminal work *Outliers: The Story of Success*: "The emerging picture from such studies is that ten thousand hours of practice is required to achieve the level of mastery associated with being a world-class expert— in anything. In study after study, of composers, basketball players, fiction writers, ice skaters, concert pianists, chess players, master criminals, and what have you, this number comes up again and again. . . . It seems that it takes the brain this long to assimilate all that it needs to know to achieve true mastery." Malcolm Gladwell, *Outliers: The Story of Success* (New York: Little, Brown and Company, 2008), 39–40.

5. Leon made the team, had a successful career in the NBA, and remains a quality league referee in the NBA. See NBRA, "Leon Wood," *The National Basketball Referees Association* (website); available at http://www.nbra.net/Default.aspx?tabid=130; accessed 23 March 2013.

6. In the book *Mr. Red Sox: The Johnny Pesky Story*, Pesky describes a double play that could have only happened in Slabtown, a rough and tumble section of Portland known at the time, at least by the Red Sox, as a productive and young talent pool. The city itself had a large first- and second-generation Slavic-American population. Among these were the three pivots in the one-of-a-kind twin killing that Leovich recounts, "'We made a double play, and the play went from Leovich to Paveskovich to Stepovich.'" The playful irony of this Slavic preponderance was captured by Pesky in recalling, "They were all 'viches'—sons of viches, they used to say." Bill Nowlin, *Mr. Red Sox: The Johnny Pesky Story* (Cambridge, MA: Rounder Books, 2004), 7, 8, 22–23.

NOTES

Part III
Perspectives of a Professional

Kerry L. Pickett, "Perspective: The Flight of a Sandpiper," "Reach for the Sky: A Poetic Look at Life Metaphors in Sport and Vice Versa" (unpublished work, 2012).

Chapter 8
Guardian Angels

1. I was told by Coach Ramsay after the fact that the Blazers intended to select me with their nineteenth first-round pick but didn't want to show their hand, fearing that another team would nab me. Portland would have been a nice fit. The Trail Blazers already had a remarkable second-year player in Clyde Drexler, who was a year younger than me. They had the number two draft choice and selected (instead of Michael Jordan) Sam Bowie, a very skilled, promising big man. The Trail Blazers also drafted my running mate in Chicago, Jerome Kersey, later in the second round. I suspect their whole team would have been fun to play with, and I did like Portland.

2. Jim was a low-profile player representative with limited experience at the NBA level. Fitz trusted him and thought he would be perfect to find me a European team and a solid contract. To everyone's surprise, I ended up as the same small fish in the much larger NBA pond.

Chapter 9
A Foot in the Door

1. Goodreads, "St. Ignatius of Loyola Quotes," *Goodreads* (website); available at http://www.goodreads.com/author/quotes/336357.St_Ignatius _of_Loyola; accessed 26 March 2013.

2. After that game we would always wear our base purple except on special occasions like St. Patrick's Day. Our uniforms were unique and not necessarily liked by some of the more fashion-conscious players. Our socks had three different stripes of varied width; gold, green, and purple rings, which just happened to represent the colors of the Catholic Diocese of New Orleans, the birthplace of the Jazz. Our warm-ups were long-sleeved sand-knit that looked and felt like wool pajamas. In fact, some of the players referred to them as "Garanimals," after the well-advertised

children's sleepwear. I just wore what they gave me and volunteered no opinion.

3. Highlighting this tragedy of addiction is a story about the same friend and his perhaps tenuous grip on reality. We found ourselves laughing uneasily at practice one day when kids from the Special Olympics program had joined us. We began scrimmaging playfully to put on a show for the kids. He proceeded to post up his man aggressively and score like it was the playoffs, clearly out of place. Each time, one of us would grab him and say, "What are you doing? Take it easy!" His response, "Hey, thirty is thirty!" meaning he didn't care who he scored on, it still counted. Half funny, half unnerving, I was never sure if he was totally serious or not.

CHAPTER 11
Fatherhood

1. Rabindranath Tagore, in *The Treasure Chest: A Heritage Album Containing 1064 Familiar and Inspirational Quotations, Poems, Sentiments and Prayers from Great Minds of 2500 Years*, ed. Charles L. Wallis (New York: Harper and Row Publishers Inc., 1965), v.

CHAPTER 12
A Gilded Opportunity

1. Larry H. Miller, *Driven* (Salt Lake City: Shadow Mountain, 2010), 116–17.

2. Ibid., 115–37.

3. Incidentally, that game featured two novelties. Manute Bol and Muggsy Bogues both played for Washington at the time. Muggsy, a rookie, was unique in that he only measured 5'3". At the opposite end of the spectrum, Manute, in his third year, stretched the tape to a full 7'7". Manute had the most amazing dunk in that game. Facing away from the basket, his feet on the dotted line, the lower half of the free-throw circle, he fell backwards. Twisting without jumping, he reached out two-handed and soundly jammed the ball into the hoop. The dunk was a double-take moment that took my mind off of the hamstring.

4. Playing basketball was a gift I never wanted to take for granted. Few people get the opportunity to play even once against the type of talent

I enjoyed facing and working with daily. I wanted to take advantage of every moment.

5. On February 10, 2011, Coach Sloan resigned from the Utah Jazz helm after twenty-three seasons and 1,127 wins. He was the "longest-tenured coach in the four major professional sports." Ty Corbin was named the head coach and continues to hold that position to this date. ESPN, "Utah Jazz coach Jerry Sloan Resigns"; see *ESPN NBA* (website); available at http://sports.espn.go.com/nba/news/story?id=6109031; accessed 23 March 2013.

6. Phil retired alongside Coach Sloan in 2011. Phil's remark about his decision to retire with Coach was simple: "I came with him and I'll leave with him." Ibid.

7. Alfred Lansing, *Endurance: Shackleton's Incredible Voyage* (New York: Carroll & Graf, 1986).

8. Stephen E. Ambrose, *Undaunted Courage* (New York: Simon & Schuster, 1996).

9. David McCullough, *Truman* (New York: Simon & Schuster, 1992).

10. David M. Kennedy, *Freedom from Fear* (New York: Oxford University Press, 1999).

11. "Working cooperatively with landowners, local communities, and state and federal agencies, Vital Ground addresses the issue of habitat fragmentation head-on by permanently protecting crucial lands for the benefit of grizzly bears and other wide-ranging wildlife. Vital Ground places special emphasis on protecting specific key landscapes. . . . To date, Vital Ground has helped protect and enhance nearly 600,000 acres of crucial wildlife habitat in Montana, Idaho, Wyoming, Alaska, and British Columbia. The organization's dedication to conserving grizzly bear range goes beyond saving a single species. When there is enough 'vital ground' to sustain an umbrella species like the grizzly, a multitude of other animals, plants, and fragile ecosystems benefit as well." The Vital Ground Foundation, "What We Do," *Vital Ground* (website); available at http://www.vitalground.org/What_We_Do; accessed 26 March 2013.

NOTES

CHAPTER 13
The Olympics, 1992

1. Jeff Fenech, "Olympic Quotes," *About.com* (website); available at http://
quotations.about.com/od/sportsquotes/a/olympics2.htm; accessed 26
March 2013.

2. One particular call I received involved an incident with Dennis
Rodman. The league called to confirm that Dennis had head-butted me
in a game. I told them that I didn't get head-butted. They argued with
me based on the tape. Finally, I said, "Do what you want, but I didn't
get hit." I don't know what they decided. I do know that many players
and teams send such matters to the office for discipline. The Jazz never
sent a tape or complained, to my knowledge. It wasn't Jerry's MO.

3. At the time technical fouls cost about $250 each. Later in my career
the fine would increase to $500 for the first offense and $1000, plus an
ejection, for the second technical in any game.

4. "Based in Colorado Springs, CO, USA Basketball is a nonprofit organization and the national governing body for men's and women's basketball in the United States. As the recognized governing body for basketball in the United States by the International Basketball Federation
(FIBA) and the United States Olympic Committee (USOC), USA
Basketball is responsible for the selection, training, and fielding of USA
teams that compete in FIBA sponsored international basketball competitions, as well as for some national competitions." USA Basketball,
"Inside USA Basketball," *The Official Site of USA Basketball* (website);
available at http://www.usabasketball.com/about/inside.html; accessed
23 March 2013.

5. USA Basketball, "Games of the XXth Olympiad—1972"; available at
http://www.usabasketball.com/mens/national/moly_1972.html; accessed 23 March 2013.

6. The young group lost to the Russians by a score of 82–76 in the semifinal
round. See USA Basketball, "Games of the XXIVth Olympiad—1988";
available at http://www.usabasketball.com/mens/national/moly_1988
.html; accessed 23 March 2013.

7. Cara is the daughter of our close friends Sonny and Kathy from Salt
Lake. She had come along to help us with the kids and enjoy the

Olympics. For a young person, she had proven herself extremely capable and good with the children. At times these tight quarters made her feel more like a babysitter than the friend she had become, especially when one of the boys wet their shared bed. Water runs to the lowest point, so she took the brunt. She toughed out the soggy environment like a Navy SEAL and enjoyed most of her experience, I think.

8. Karl had selected #11 as his Olympic jersey number for just this purpose. In the Olympics, only numbers one through fifteen can be used. As a result, he and most of the rest of the team had to settle for alternate numbers, but I was able to wear my customary #12. Both Karl and Magic wore #32 in the NBA, so Karl would probably have had to defer for seniority reasons anyway.

Chapter 14
The Olympics, 1996

1. Pierre de Coubertin, "Olympic Quotes," *About.com* (website); available at http://quotations.about.com/od/sportsquotes/a/olympics2.htm; accessed 26 March 2013.

2. Lenny Wilkens was inducted to the Naismith Hall of Fame as a player in 1989, as a coach in 1998, and as a team member of the 1992 US Olympic Team in 2010. When he was inducted as a coach, the only other person to be inducted as both a player and a coach was John Wooden. See Basketball Hall of Fame, "Hall of Famers," *Naismith Memorial Basketball Hall of Fame* (website); available at http://www.hoophall.com/hall-of-famers-index/; accessed 23 March 2013.

Chapter 15
Walking with an Unfamiliar Shadow

1. Spokane Hoopfest, "Spokane Hoopfest Association a History: 1990–Present"; available at http://www.spokanehoopfest.net/Organization/History.htm; accessed 26 March 2013.

2. For a detailed account of the murders, see Richard E. Turley, Jr., *Victims: The LDS Church and the Mark Hofmann Case* (Urbana and Chicago: University of Illinois Press, 1992); available at http://books.google.com/books?id=IqrDDrWR_X4C&pg=PA101#v=onepage&q&f=false; accessed 26 March 2013.

NOTES

1. One illustration close to home still raises my eyebrows. Prior to the start of the lockout season immediately following our second trip to the finals with the Bulls, we met with the officials to discuss the new rules and interpretations. The emphasis that season was illegal screens. As usual, they used game video to illustrate what wouldn't be permitted under the new rule. Jeff Hornacek and I were the stars, shown terrorizing the league with our back-crushing screens time and time again. The irony wasn't lost on me or my teammates. The TV ratings for the two championships we had just completed had been through the roof. The referees in those games had found our play completely within the boundaries of the rules, and the viewers enjoyed it. The question that remained for me was, "How were our screens hurting the NBA?" If the screens made it more challenging for high-priced stars to defend a well-executed offense, it's curious that the league would choose to eliminate them or hinder their effectiveness.

2. Thurl eventually rejoined the team several years later. He has remained a beloved member of the Jazz community and a close friend.

3. "In 1966, the league adopted a coin flip between the last-place finishers in each of its two divisions to determine which team would open the draft, a system that remained in place until the first lottery in 1985." See NBA Media Ventures, LLC, "Evolution of the Draft and Lottery," *NBA .com* (website); available at http://www.nba.com/history/draft_evolution .html; accessed 23 March 2013.

4. See "2011–2012 Utah Jazz Media Guide," *Official Site of the Utah Jazz* (website); available at http://www.nba.com/jazz/media/UtahJazz _MediaGuide11–12_v1.0.pdf; accessed 23 March 2013.

CHAPTER 17
The Clock Strikes Twelve

1. Antoine didn't actually retire. He had two minor stints with the Rockets and Grizzlies to close out his NBA career, but his sentiments on this, I think, led him and the Jazz to part ways after this season.

2. In a strange contract negotiation, Shandon unexpectedly signed for a lot

less money with the Houston Rockets and chose to move on. Shandon was a terrific young player who backed up Jeff, who was logging most of the minutes at that time.

PART IV
Free Time to Water Green Shoots

Kerry L. Pickett, "Just Around the Corner," poem presented to John and Nada Stockton on the occasion of his NBA retirement, 2004.

CHAPTER 18
The Great Cinnamon Caper

1. Both Nada and I lost our mothers (Matilda and Clemy, respectively) shortly after moving back to Spokane. Having the chance to be around our moms in their final days was a blessing. We talked about life, death, and things we might have been uncomfortable discussing during better times. We have treasured those moments and those talks.
2. A griffin is a legendary creature with the body of a lion and the head and wings of an eagle. As the lion was traditionally considered the king of beasts and the eagle master of the skies, the griffin was thought to be an especially powerful and majestic creature.

EPILOGUE

Kerry L. Pickett, "The Seeds between the Lines," "Reach for the Sky: A Poetic Look at Life Metaphors in Sport and Vice Versa" (unpublished work, 2012).

INDEX

Italic page numbers denote photographs.

INDEX

INDEX

INDEX

INDEX

INDEX

ABOUT THE AUTHORS

 John Stockton became a member of the NBA Hall of Fame in 2009. He and his wife, Nada, live in Spokane, Washington. They have six children: Houston, Michael, David, Lindsay, Laura, and Samuel.

 Kerry L. "Coach" Pickett met John in 1973 when he started coaching his sixth-grade basketball team. He earned a JD from Gonzaga Law School and practiced law with his wife, Gini, for more than ten years, after which he began directing the basketball camps that John established. Since 2002, he has been the director of The Warehouse athletic facility in Spokane, Washington.